HORACE

SELECTED ODES AND SATIRE 1.9

2ND EDITION

LATIN TEXT
NOTES
VOCABULARY

RONNIE ANCONA

Bolchazy-Carducci Publishers, Inc.
Wauconda, Illinois USA

General Editor
Laurie Haight Keenan

Contributing Editor
Allan Kershaw

Typography, Page and Cover Design
Adam Phillip Velez

Cover Illustration
Lyre Graphic adapted from *Costumes of the Greeks and Romans*
by Thomas Hope

Horace: Selected Odes and Satire 1.9
2nd Edition

by Ronnie Ancona

Bolchazy-Carducci Publishers, Inc.
1000 Brown Street
Wauconda, IL 60084 USA
www.bolchazy.com

Printed in the United States of America
2006
by United Graphics

ISBN-10: 0-86516-608-0
ISBN-13: 978-0-86516-608-0

Library of Congress Cataloging-in-Publication Data

Horace.
 [Selections. 2005]
 Horace : selected odes and Satire 1.9. / [edited and annotated by] Ronnie Ancona.-- 2nd ed.
  p. cm.
 Latin text; English notes and vocabulary.
 The Latin text used is from: Q. Horati Flacci Opera / edidit Stephanus Borzsák. Leipzig :
Teubner, 1984.
 Includes bibliographical references.
 ISBN-13: 978-0-86516-608-0 (pbk. : alk. paper)
 ISBN-10: 0-86516-608-0 (pbk. : alk. paper)
 1. Latin language--Readers. 2. Verse satire, Latin--Problems, exercises, etc. 3. Rome--In
literature--Problems, exercises, etc. 4. Odes--Problems, exercises, etc. I. Ancona, Ronnie, 1951-
II. Title.

PA6393.A3A53 2005
478.6'421--dc22

2005009291

IN MEMORIAM

Victor Ancona
1912–1998

CONTENTS

PREFACE TO SECOND EDITION

This second edition has a different "look" from the first. The format is patterned on that of my more recent book, *Writing Passion: A Catullus Reader*, also published by Bolchazy-Carducci. Experience has shown that the eye finds it easier to see all notes and vocabulary at the bottom of the same page. In addition, all pages now have numbers, including those, e.g., where poems begin. This makes reference easier for teachers and students alike. I have updated the bibliography and have added Latin examples, where useful, to the section on Metrical Terms, Tropes or Figures of Thought, and Rhetorical Figures or Figures of Speech. A few errors or places that needed clarification, noticed by me or pointed out by reviewers or users of the text, have been corrected or changed. The one surprise since the book was first published is that some have found it useful even for advanced level college classes, despite the fact that it was targeted for the intermediate college and advanced high school level. It would seem that a wider audience than one might suspect may benefit from extensive commentary. To that potentially new audience and also to the original targeted audience, a reminder that looking at "just the Latin" is always possible, despite the book's heavy annotation, by turning to the unannotated versions of the poems at the back of the book. Finally, my thanks to all who shared with me comments on the first edition. It is with you in mind that this second edition has been produced.

May, 2005

PREFACE

Writing this book has been a joy and a challenge because it has given me the opportunity to attempt to make Horace, the Latin author about whom I have thought and written the most, accessible and exciting for students of Latin. I would like to thank Bolchazy-Carducci Publishers for providing me with the chance to look at Horace anew in order to articulate the ways in which I think the study of Horace can be enhanced.

The book is intended for use by students at the intermediate college level or the advanced high school level. The selections from Horace (twenty odes and one satire) are the required readings in Horace for the new Advanced Placement* Latin Literature Examination given by the Educational Testing Service. I have limited the scope of the book to the poems on the AP* syllabus in order to create a sense of coherence out of that particular curriculum. Of course, teachers at either the college or secondary level are encouraged to bring more poems into their courses, if appropriate.

The book includes an introduction to Horace's life and writings, a select bibliography, the Latin text of the poems, a short introduction to each poem (meant to be suggestive rather than constricting), and a line-by-line commentary located on the same pages with the Latin text, including vocabulary and notes of a grammatical, historical, metrical, or literary nature. Appendices include maps, discussion of the meters of the poems, definitions of metrical terms, explanations of particular tropes or figures of thought and rhetorical figures or figures of speech with examples from the poems of the book, and the Latin text of the poems without notes and vocabulary (for seeing and reading the poems without interruption). Although it does not include every single Latin word in the poems, the line-by-line vocabulary given with the text of each poem is quite extensive. I have provided such extensive vocabulary help in order to give the student extra time for his or her thinking about the material that otherwise might be spent looking up words. The vocabulary at the end of the book includes all of the words in the poems, so that the student who forgets even a basic Latin word may quickly look it up in the back of the book. Both in the general vocabulary

---

* AP is a registered trademark of the College Entrance Examination Board, which was not involved in the production of, and does not endorse, this product.

and in the line-by-line vocabulary I typically give the major meanings of a Latin word rather than one particular meaning that might work best for purposes of translation in a particular context. The reason for this is to preserve for the student the multiplicity of meanings many Latin words have in Horace and to allow him or her to see how Horace repeats vocabulary from poem to poem with the result that individual words resonate with their multiple meanings in different contexts. If I had chosen one English word to define a particular Latin word in a given context, I think I would have deprived the student of access to a central feature of Horace's style. In addition, the approach followed here helps students to increase their real Latin vocabulary, rather than merely to memorize a particular meaning of a word for translation of a particular poem. I also avoid translating difficult passages in the notes. I prefer to give help and then to let the student figure things out independently. When giving grammatical explanations I use standard grammatical terminology, rather than terminology geared to a specific Latin grammar. *OLD* refers to the *Oxford Latin Dictionary*. Other abbreviations should not cause difficulty.

The Latin text is used with permission, from *Horatius, Opera* ed. Borzsák © 1984 B. G. Teubner, Leipzig. The only place I have deviated from Borzsák is at Ode 1.25.11, where I add a hyphen. This text was chosen because it is considered one of the best currently available for Horace. Since many students using this book will be taking the Advanced Placement* Examination, which does not supply long marks or macrons over vowels, I, too, have not included them in the text of the poems and in the line-by-line vocabulary and commentary. However, since many students at this stage will not know all of the vowel quantities, I have marked in the Vocabulary at the end of the book the length of long vowels in metrically indeterminate positions, the long vowels normally marked in the *OLD*. Therefore, the student will be able to find all necessary long marks within the book, except those contained in inflectional endings. These may be found in a Latin grammar or in the student's elementary Latin text. It is my hope that the student who looks at the text without long marks will start trying to scan the poem to determine, for example, whether a final "a" is ablative singular or nominative singular of the first declension. In this way he or she will learn quickly that knowledge of the meter can be a source of necessary grammatical information.

---

* AP is a registered trademark of the College Entrance Examination Board, which was not involved in the production of, and does not endorse, this product.

In writing this text I have consulted a wide range of material on Horace. The bibliography on Horace is vast and there is no way I could have consulted everything relevant. However I have tried to create a text for students that is informed by some of the latest research in Horatian scholarship. I think it is important for students to know that classics scholars are still discussing and arguing about Horace's poems. Therefore, I have included a bibliography that is quite extensive for a student text in order to familiarize the student with some of the sources for this scholarship. Just browsing through the titles of articles can be interesting, for it shows what kinds of issues scholars have chosen to address. The student using the bibliography may find it most helpful to consult recent sources first, for these will include references to relevant earlier works that are still being cited. The student should not feel that it is necessary to use the bibliography, unless required to do so by his or her teacher. However, regardless of particular class requirements, I think I owe students embarking upon serious study of Horace at any level access to information about the research that has been done. I would like to mention here, by author, the commentaries that I consulted most frequently as I wrote the line-by-line notes for each of the poems: Aronson, Aronson and Boughner, Bennett, Garrison, Morris, Nisbet and Hubbard, Palmer, and Quinn (full citations available in the Bibliography). These gave me a continuing sense of what others thought or did not think worthy of comment as well as a scholarly context in which to situate my own remarks.

This book has been in the thinking stage for many years, although the writing of it took place primarily over the last year and a half. I have many people to thank for giving me the professional opportunities that have allowed me to think about the teaching of Horace. For inviting me to be a Faculty Consultant for the Advanced Placement* Latin Examination over several years: Sheila Dickison, Judith de Luce, and Peter Howard; for sharing their collective Horatian wisdom: the AP* Latin Faculty Consultants of summer 1997, and again, Peter Howard for creating a time for me to talk with them. Sheila Dickison, for suggesting me as a speaker for a joint American Classical League–American Philological Association panel in 1995 devoted to New Approaches to Teaching the Odes of Horace, and my Horace students at The Bush School, Carleton College, and Hunter College and The Graduate School of the City University of New York, for asking tough questions.

Finally, there are several people I want to acknowledge for special assistance. For willingness to help in any way she could, my student and research assistant at Hunter, Georgia Tsouvala Yoranidis. For

---

* AP is a registered trademark of the College Entrance Examination Board, which was not involved in the production of, and does not endorse, this product.

believing in this project, Lou Bolchazy, Publisher, and Laurie Haight, Editor, Bolchazy-Carducci Publishers. In particular, Laurie's encouragement, wit, intelligence, gentle prodding, and availability helped this book to its completion more than she can know. For helpful suggestions and careful reading, the two anonymous readers for Bolchazy-Carducci. For feedback on an issue I was pondering, William Anderson. For computer help, Steve Cole. And for patiently stepping over the piles of Horace books that adorned the floor of our home for many months, Steve, again, and David Ancona-Cole.

December, 1998

involving public finances and the public records. The job only inter-
mittently required a great deal of work, yet always brought in a salary,
providing an excellent situation for the poet.

By the early thirties BCE Horace must have started sharing his writing with others. He became friends with the poets Vergil and Varius
(see Satire 1.9 below), who in turn introduced him to Gaius Cilnius
Maecenas. Nine months after the introduction, Maecenas invited
Horace to become part of his group of friends, which included several
famous poets. Maecenas was a very wealthy equestrian, originally
from Etruria, who served as an important adviser to Octavian (later
Augustus) until the late twenties BCE. Thus, through Maecenas Horace
became connected with the ultimate leader of the Roman state. That
connection was to last for the rest of his life. While Horace's relationship
with Maecenas has often been characterized as that between "client"
and "patron," the terms "friend" and "supporter" may describe more
accurately Maecenas' role with respect to Horace, for their relationship
seems to have been based not on financial dependence, but rather on
mutual respect and friendship in addition to artistic support. While
Maecenas did give Horace gifts, as friends often do, there is no specific
evidence, for example, that Horace needed Maecenas for his livelihood
or that Horace's Sabine farm, the country home that he valued greatly,
was necessarily a gift from Maecenas. Maecenas' significance to Horace,
however, is indisputable, and one sign of this is the fact that the first
poem of Horace's initial lyric collection (*Odes*, Books 1–3) is addressed
to Maecenas as are the beginning poems of the *Epodes, Satires* Book 1,
and *Epistles* Book 1.

Little is known of Horace's later life. While he accepted Augustus'
commission to write the **carmen saeculare**, mentioned above, he gra-
ciously turned down a request by Augustus to serve as his personal
secretary. Horace died on November 27, 8 BCE, shortly after the death
of Maecenas.

Horace's Writings

Horace wrote poetry over a period of about thirty years. His first publication in 35 BCE, at the age of thirty, was Book 1 of the *Satires* or *Sermones*
("conversations"), followed five years later by Book 2. Horace's *Satires*
(eighteen poems) follow in the tradition of Lucilius (second century
BCE), whom Horace calls the founder of Latin satire, or *satura*, a genre
considered original to the Romans. Latin satire is verse in a conversational style on a variety of topics written from an individual point of
view. Latin satirists who followed Horace are Persius (first century CE)
and Juvenal (first to second centuries CE). While showing admiration
for Lucilius, Horace attempted to write verse that was more polished.

Horace's satires, composed in dactylic hexameter, touch on a variety of literary, social, and ethical topics and include attacks on various human faults. Satire 1.9, selected for this book, is a witty narrative that deftly combines a critique of a pushy social climber with discourse on literary values. While its fast-paced, colloquial style is quite different from that of the *Odes*, its literary sensibility and its carefully polished Latin show a continuity with Horace's later writing in the *Odes*.

The *Epodes*, or *Iambi* as they are sometimes called, written early in Horace's career like the *Satires*, consist of seventeen dactylic or iambic poems that primarily utilize epodic couplets, that is, one line of a particular metrical structure and length, followed by a line of a different length and sometimes a different metrical structure. These poems are written in the tradition of the early Greek poet, Archilochus of Paros, who wrote poems of attack and blame. According to Horace, his meters and spirit come from Archilochus, but the subject matter and words do not. The *Epodes* include several poems with political themes as well as a number on erotic topics. Stylistically, they stand, in a sense, midway between the "talk"of the *Satires* and the "song" of lyric. While technically the *Epodes* can be called "lyric," this term is typically used to refer exclusively to Horace's *Odes*.

In 23 BCE Horace published Books 1 through 3 of his collection of lyric poetry, the *Odes* or *Carmina*. (These terms come from the Greek for "song" and the Latin for "song" or "poem.") He returned to lyric ten years later and published Book 4 of the *Odes,* which includes much that is in praise of Augustus. Scholars differ as to how this later book of lyrics does or does not allow Horace to retain some kind of independence from the Augustan regime.

Lyric poetry originally signified poetry written to the accompaniment of the lyre. While Horace makes allusion to the musical quality of his lyrics, scholars generally agree that his lyric poems were spoken and not sung. More specifically, lyric poetry meant poetry written in the meters used by the Greek lyric poets: Alcaeus, Sappho, Anacreon, Alcman, Stesichorus, Ibycus, Simonides, Pindar, and Bacchylides. While Catullus, writing a generation earlier than Horace, wrote some poems in the lyric meters used by the Greek lyric poets (for example, Poem 51, his translation and adaptation of a poem by Sappho), Horace took great pride in being the first to do so on a large scale. The Greek lyric poets to whom Horace especially looked for inspiration were Sappho and Alcaeus, who lived and wrote on the island of Lesbos, in Aeolia, the Greek area of Asia Minor, at the close of the seventh century BCE. When expressing both his hopes for his lyric collection in Ode 1.1 and his pride in his lyric achievement in Ode 3.30 Horace alludes to Sappho and Alcaeus through the phrases **Lesboum...barbiton** ("Lesbian lyre") and **Aeolium carmen** ("Aeolic song"). Horace, like his predecessor Catullus, was also influenced by the Alexandrian aesthetics of Callimachus (third century BCE), the Hellenistic Greek poet who described his Muse as "slender," a term that Horace uses for his own Muse as well. These literary aesthetics placed a high value on the small, learned, carefully wrought poem.

The odes range widely in subject matter—from politics to love to literature and beyond. The personal is often mixed with the public. What Horace says is beyond the scope of lyric is frequently incorporated into his poems under the guise of refusal. That is, in the very refusal to write a certain kind of poem Horace addresses topics supposedly at odds with lyric. While Horace was self-consciously writing in a long literary tradition that included much Greek influence, his poems are very contemporary. In addition to the Roman political world that pervades the *Odes*, the social environment Horace inhabited is also evident. For example, while moral and legal codes made illegal and theoretically unacceptable sexual relations between a Roman citizen woman and a man not her husband, Horace's world included many non-citizens, freedwomen, and slaves with whom such relations would have been tolerated. Therefore, the social relations of such poems as Odes 1.23 and 1.25 should not be seen as alien to Horace's Roman world.

The 103 poems of the *Odes* (88 in Books 1–3 and 15 in Book 4) are pieces that form a collection. They can be read selectively, as they will be by users of this text. However, even in the reading of just twenty odes I think it will become clear that the individual pieces relate to each other in countless ways, at the level of vocabulary, theme, and meter. Part of getting to know Horace as a lyric poet involves recognition of these many connections.

In some ways Horace's lyrics may seem to the student quite different from Latin read before, for Horace's exploitation of the possibilities of the Latin language is extraordinary. Word order, which in Latin is already quite flexible, is with Horace even more so. Words that agree with each other may be separated widely, creating a kind of framing or phrasing effect, while words right next to each may not agree with each other grammatically, but may affect each other in terms of sense. The best readers of Horace will be open to the aural and visual effects of his language. At times the lyrics are brief and elliptical. Often they end up at a different place from where they began. The German philosopher and classicist, Friedrich Nietzsche, described the effectiveness of Horace's lyrics as a "... mosaic of words, in which every unit spreads its power to the left and to the right over the whole, by its sound, by its place in the sentence, and by its meaning..." (*The Complete Works of Friedrich Nietzsche*, vol. 16, *The Twilight of the Idols*, Oscar Levy, ed.,

Anthony Ludovici, trans., London and New York, 1927: 113). While students may want to and may be asked to "translate" Horace's lyrics (a requirement of the AP Examination), they should be aware of the extent to which translation will shut down possibilities of meaning in this author. For example, it is usually impossible to "translate" into English Horace's careful placement of words. In addition, while translating requires picking the best English meaning for a particular Latin word in a given context, that very process of "selection" limits to one the multiple senses which that word may have in Latin and which may be operating in a particular poem. The student will quickly find out that "translating" and "understanding" Horace's lyrics may overlap but are not identical, for "understanding" involves grasping the concept that turning Horace into English necessarily entails the loss of so much that is essentially Horatian.

While Horace utilized lyric meter in the **carmen saeculare**, or centennial hymn of 17 BCE, he returned to the meter used in the *Satires*, dactylic hexameter, for the writing of the *Epistles*. These verse essays (Book 1 contains twenty, Book 2 contains three), written in the form of letters, address a variety of topics, many of a literary or philosophical nature. Epistle 2.3, also called the Ars Poetica, includes comments on the problems of literary composition.

BIBLIOGRAPHY

This is a select bibliography of works in English. An attempt has been made to include much that has been written on Horace recently. While articles on individual poems have been listed at the end of the bibliography, the student will find it valuable to consult any pages relevant to a given poem in the book-length works as well.

Commentaries:

Aronson, A. and Robert Boughner. *Catullus and Horace: Selections from Their Lyric Poetry*. White Plains, N.Y., 1988.

Aronson, Andrew. *Catullus and Horace: A Selection with Facing Vocabularies and Notes*. Amherst. Mass., 1989–90.

Bennett, Charles E. *Horace: Odes and Epodes*. 1901. Reprinted, New Rochelle, N.Y., 1981.

Brown, P. Michael. *Horace Satires I*. With Introduction, Text, Translation and Commentary. Warminster, England, 1993. Reprinted 1995.

Garrison, Daniel H. *Horace: Epodes and Odes*. Norman, Okla. and London, 1991.

Holder, Alfred, ed. *Pomponi Porfyrionis Commentum in Horatium Flaccum*. 1894. Reprinted, New York, 1979. (ancient commentary on Horace, in Latin)

Hornsby, Roger A. *Reading Latin Poetry*. Norman, Okla., 1967.

Mankin, David. *Horace: Epodes*. Cambridge, 1995.

McKay, A. G. and D. M. Shepherd. *Roman Lyric Poetry*. London, 1969.

Morris, Edward P. *Horace: Satires and Epistles*. 1939. Reprinted, Norman, Okla., 1968.

Nisbet, R. G. M., and Margaret Hubbard. *A Commentary on Horace: Odes Book 1*. Oxford, 1970.

Nisbet, R. G. M., and Margaret Hubbard. *A Commentary on Horace: Odes Book 2*. Oxford, 1978.

Nisbet, R. G. M. and Niall Rudd. *A Commentary on Horace Odes Book III*. Oxford, 2004.

Page, T. E. *Q. Horati Flacci: Opera*. London, 1896.

Quinn, Kenneth. *Horace: The Odes*. London, 1980. Reprinted, Bristol, 1997.

Shorey, Paul, and Gordon J. Laing. *Horace: Odes and Epodes*. 1910. Reprinted, Pittsburgh, 1960.

Smith, Clement L. *The Odes and Epodes of Horace*. New York, 1894, 1903.

Thomas, Richard. *Horace Odes 4 and Carmen Saeculare*. Cambridge, forthcoming.

Watson, Lindsay. *A Commentary on Horace's Epodes*. Oxford, 2003.

West, David. *Horace Odes I Carpe Diem: Text, Translation, and Commentary*. Oxford, 1995.

West, David. *Horace Odes II Vatis Amici: Text, Translation, and Commentary*. Oxford, 1998.

West, David. *Horace Odes III Dulce Periculum: Text, Translation, and Commentary*. Oxford, 2002.

Wickham, Edward C. *Q. Horati Flacci Opera*. Oxford, 1912.

Williams, Gordon. *The Third Book of Horace's Odes*. Oxford, 1969.

General Works:

Ancona, Ronnie. *Time and the Erotic in Horace's Odes*. Durham, N. C., 1994.

Anderson, William S., ed. *Why Horace? A Collection of Interpretations*. Wauconda, Ill., 1999. (contributions by Pomeroy, Vessey, Rudd, Anderson, Segal, Davis, Ancona, Akbar Khan, Johnson, Fitzgerald, Woodman, Moles, Reagan, Witke, Putnam, Fredricksmeyer).

Anderson, William S. *Essays on Roman Satire*. Princeton, 1982.

Armstrong, David. *Horace*. New Haven and London, 1989.

Armstrong, David, ed. *Arion: Horace Issue* 9, 2 and 3. Austin, 1970.

Babcock, Charles. "*Carmina operosa*: Critical Approaches to the 'Odes' of Horace, 1945–75." *Aufstieg und Niedergang der Römischen Welt* 2.31.3. Berlin, 1981: 1560–1611.

Batinski, Emily. "Horace's Rehabilitation of Bacchus." *Classical World* 84 (1990–1991): 361–78.

Bowditch, Phebe Lowell. *Horace and the Gift Economy of Patronage*. Berkeley, 2001.

Boyle, A. J. "The Edict of Venus: An Interpretive Essay on Horace's Amatory Odes." *Ramus* 2 (1973): 163–88.

Campbell, A. Y. *Horace: A New Interpretation*. London, 1924.

Coffey, Michael. *Roman Satire*. London and New York, 1976.

Coffta, David J. *The Influence of Callimachean Aesthetics on the Satires and Odes of Horace*. Lewiston, N.Y., 2001.

Collinge, N. E. *The Structure of Horace's Odes*. London, 1961.

Commager, Steele. *The Odes of Horace: A Critical Study*. New Haven and London, 1962. Reprinted, with forward by D. Armstrong, Norman, Okla. 1995.

Connor, Peter. *Horace's Lyric Poetry: The Force of Humour*. Berwick, Victoria, Australia, 1987.

Davis, Gregson. *Polyhymnia: The Rhetoric of Horatian Lyric Discourse*. Berkeley, 1991.

Dettmer, Helena. *Horace: A Study in Structure*. Hildesheim, 1983.

Fantham, Elaine. *Roman Literary Culture: From Cicero to Apuleius*. Baltimore, 1996.

Fraenkel, Eduard. *Horace*. Oxford, 1957.

Freudenburg, Kirk. *The Walking Muse: Horace on the Theory of Satire*. Princeton, 1993.

Galinsky, Karl. *Augustan Culture*. Princeton, 1996.

Gold, Barbara, ed. *Literary and Artistic Patronage in Ancient Rome*. Austin, Tex., 1982.

Griffin, Jasper. *Latin Poets and Roman Life*. Chapel Hill, N.C., 1986.

Gurval, Robert Alan. *Actium and Augustus: The Politics and Emotions of Civil War*. Ann Arbor, Mich., 1995.

Habinek, Thomas, and Alessandro Schiesaro, eds. *The Roman Cultural Revolution*. Cambridge, 1997.

Habinek, Thomas N. *The Politics of Latin Literature: Writing, Identity, and Empire in Ancient Rome*. Princeton, 1998.

Harrison, S. J., ed. *Homage to Horace: A Bimillenary Celebration*. Oxford, 1995. (contributions by Harrison, Syndikus, Tarrant, Putnam, Cairns, West, Harrison, Du Quesnay, Watson, Muecke, Hubbard, Jocelyn, Fowler, Brink, Mayer, Williams, La Penna, McGann).

Hutchinson, Gregory. "The Publication and Individuality of Horace's "Odes" Books 1–3." *Classical Quarterly* N.S. 52 (2002): 517–37.

Johnson, Timothy. *Symposion of Praise: Horace Returns to Lyric in Odes IV.* Madison, Wisc., 2004.

Johnson, W. R. *Horace and the Dialectic of Freedom: Readings in Epistles 1.* Ithaca, N.Y., 1993.

Johnson, W. Ralph. *The Idea of Lyric: Lyric Modes in Ancient and Modern Poetry.* Berkeley, 1982.

Kiernan, Victor. *Horace: Poetics and Politics.* New York, 1999.

Konstan, David, ed. *Horace: 2000 Years. Arethusa* 28.2 and 3, Baltimore, 1995. (contributions by Konstan, Anderson, Dunn, Jaeger, Putnam, Oliensis, Santirocco, Dyson and Prior, Frischer, Roberts, Kilpatrick, Schiesaro)

Kresic, Stephanus, ed. *Contemporary Literary Hermeneutics and Interpretation of Classical Texts.* Ottawa, 1981. (includes articles on Ode 1.9 by Murray, Palmer, Segal)

Leach, Eleanor Winsor. "Horace's Sabine Topography in Lyric and Hexameter Verse." *American Journal of Philology* 114 (1993): 271–302.

Lee, M. Owen. *Word, Sound, and Image in the Odes of Horace.* Ann Arbor, 1969.

Levi, Peter. *Horace, A Life.* London, 1997.

Lindsay, Hugh. "Suetonius on the Character of Horace." *Journal of the Australasian Universities Language and Literature Association* 83 (1995): 69–82.

Lowrie, Michèle. *Horace's Narrative Odes.* Oxford, 1997.

Lyne, R. O. A. M. *Horace: Behind the Public Poetry.* New Haven and London, 1995.

Lyne, R. O. A. M. *The Latin Love Poets: From Catullus to Horace.* Oxford, 1980.

Martindale, Charles, and David Hopkins, eds. *Horace Made New: Horatian Influences on British Writing from the Renaissance to the Twentieth Century.* Cambridge, 1993.

McNeill, Randall. *Horace: Image, Identity, and Audience.* Baltimore, 2001.

Miller, Paul Allen. *Lyric Texts and Lyric Consciousness: The birth of a genre from archaic Greece to Augustan Rome.* London and New York, 1994.

Minadeo, Richard. *The Golden Plectrum: Sexual Symbolism in Horace's Odes.* Amsterdam, 1982.

Nisbet, R. G. M. "The Word Order of Horace's 'Odes'." In *Aspects of the Language of Latin Poetry*, edited by J. N. Adams and R. G. Mayer, 135–54. Oxford, 1999.

Oliensis, Ellen. *Horace and the Rhetoric of Authority*. Cambridge, 1998.

Palmer, Arthur. *The Satires of Horace*. London and New York, 1964.

Porter, David H. *Horace's Poetic Journey: A Reading of Odes 1–3*. Princeton, 1987.

Putnam, Michael C. J. *Artifices of Eternity: Horace's Fourth Book of Odes*. Ithaca and London, 1986.

Putnam, Michael C. J. *Essays on Latin Lyric, Elegy, and Epic*. Princeton, 1982.

Putnam, Michael C. J. *Horace's Carmen Saeculare: Ritual Magic and the Poet's Art*. New Haven, 2000.

Putnam, Michael C. J. *Poetic Interplay: Catullus and Horace*. Princeton, forthcoming.

Raaflaub, Kurt A., and Mark Toher, eds. *Between Republic and Empire: Interpretations of Augustus and His Principate*. Berkeley, 1990.

Reckford, Kenneth. *Horace*. New York, 1969.

Reckford, Kenneth. "Some Studies in Horace's Odes on Love." *Classical Journal* 55 (1959): 25–33.

Romano Forteza, Alba. "Gender-Orientated Discourse in Horace." *Cuadernos de Filología Clásica. Estudios Latinos* 6 (1994): 91–102.

Rudd, Niall, ed. *Horace 2000: A Celebration*. Ann Arbor, 1993. (contributions by Huxley, Griffin, Seager, Feeney, Rudd, Murray, Arkins, Hardie).

Rudd, Niall. *The Satires of Horace*. Berkeley and Los Angeles, 1966.

Santirocco, Matthew, ed. *Recovering Horace*. *Classical World* 87.5. Pittsburgh, Penn., 1994.

Santirocco, Matthew. *Unity and Design in Horace's Odes*. Chapel Hill, N.C. and London, 1986.

Shackleton Bailey, D. R. *Profile of Horace*. Cambridge, Mass., 1982.

Simpson, Christopher. "'Exegi Monumentum': Building Imagery and metaphor in Horace, 'Odes' 1–3." *Latomus* 61 (2002): 57–66.

Sutherland, Elizabeth H. *Horace's Well-Trained Reader: Toward a Methodology of Audience Participation in the Odes*. Frankfurt-am-Main, 2002.

Treggiari, Susan. *Roman Social History*. London, 2002.

West, David. *Reading Horace*. Edinburgh, 1967.

Wilkinson, L. P. *Horace and His Lyric Poetry*. Cambridge, 1945. Second edition, 1951.

Williams, Gordon. *The Nature of Roman Poetry*. Oxford, 1983.

Witke, Charles. *Horace's Roman Odes*. Leiden, 1983.

Woodman, Tony, and Denis Feeney, eds. *Traditions and Contexts in the Poetry of Horace*. Cambridge, 2002. (contributions by Bradshaw, Du Quesnay, Zetzel, Woodman, Griffiths, Nisbet, Oliensis, Barchiesi, Freudenburg, Moles, Lowrie, Feeney)

Translations:

Alexander, Sidney. *The Complete Odes and Satires of Horace*. Princeton, 1999.

Carne-Ross, D. S., and Kenneth Haynes, eds. *Horace in English*. London, 1996. (contains a wide variety of translations from the past and present)

Clancy, Joseph P. *The Odes and Epodes of Horace*. Chicago, 1960.

Ferry, David. *The Odes of Horace*. New York, 1997.

Lee, Guy. *Horace Odes and Carmen Saeculare*. Leeds, 1998.

McClatchy, J. D. *Horace: The Odes, New Translations by Contemporary Poets*. Princeton, 2002.

Mulroy, David. *Horace's Odes and Epodes*. Ann Arbor, Mich., 1994.

Passage, Charles. *The Complete Works of Horace*. New York, 1983.

Raffel, Burton. *The Essential Horace*. San Francisco, 1983.

Rudd, Niall. *Horace: Odes and Epodes*. Cambridge, Mass., 2004.

Rudd, Niall. *Horace: Satires and Epistles, Persius: Satires*. London, 1979. Reprinted, London, 1981.

Storrs, Ronald, ed. *Ad Pyrrham: A Polyglot Collection of Translations of Horace's Ode to Pyrrha (Book 1, Ode 5)*. London, 1959.

West, David. *The Complete Odes and Epodes*. Oxford, 1997.

Recordings:

Sonkowsky, Robert P. *The Living Voice of Latin Literature: Selections from Catullus and Horace*. Booklet and two cassettes. Guilford, Conn., 1984. Distributed by Bolchazy-Carducci Publishers, Wauconda, Ill.

References Works:

Bo, Domenicus. *Lexicon Horatianum.* (2 volumes) Hildesheim, 1965.

Halporn, James W., Martin Ostwald, and Thomas G. Rosenmeyer. *The Meters of Greek and Latin Poetry.* Revised edition, Indianapolis, 1994.

Iso Echegoyen, José-Javier. *Concordantia Horatiana: A Concordance to Horace.* Hildesheim, 1990.

Workbooks:

Ancona, Ronnie, and David Murphy. *A Workbook for Horace.* Wauconda, Ill., 2005.

Works on Individual Poems or Groups of Poems:

Satire 1.9

Anderson, William S. "Horace, The Unwilling Warrior: *Satire* I,9." *American Journal of Philology* 77 (1956): 148–66. Reprinted in Anderson, William. *Essays on Roman Satire.* Princeton, 1982.

Brucia, Margaret A., and Madeleine Henry. *Satire 1.9: The Boor.* Wauconda, Ill., 1998.

Courtney, E. "Horace and the Pest." *Classical Journal* 90 (1994): 1–8.

Feldman, Louis. "The Enigma of Horace's Thirtieth Sabbath." *Scripta Classica Israelica* 10 (1989–90): 87–112.

Harrison, S. J. "Fuscus the Stoic: Horace Odes 1.22 and Epistles 1.10." *Classical Quarterly* 42 (1992) 543–47.

Henderson, J. "Be Alert (Your Country Needs Lerts): Horace, *Satires* 1.9." *Proceedings of the Cambridge Philological Society* 39 (1993): 67–93.

Mazurek, Tadeusz, "Self-Parody and the Law in Horace's *Satires* 1.9," *Classical Journal* 93 (1997): 1–17.

Rudd, Niall. "Horace's Encounter with the Bore." *Phoenix* 15 (1961): 90–96.

Zetzel, J. E. G. "Horace's *Liber Sermonum*: The Structure of Ambiguity." *Arethusa* 13 (1980): 59–77.

ODE 1.1

Dunn, Francis. "Horace's Sacred Spring (Odes I,1)." *Latomus* 48 (1989): 97–109.

Gold, Barbara. "Openings in Horace's *Satires* and *Odes*: Poet, Patron, and Audience." *Yale Classical Studies* 29 (1992): 161–85.

Mader, G. "Poetry and Politics in Horace's First Roman Ode: a Reconstruction." *Acta Classica* 30 (1987): 11–30.

Musurillo, H. "The Poet's Apotheosis: Horace, *Odes* 1.1." *Transactions and Proceedings of the American Philological Association* 93 (1962): 230–39.

Pomeroy, Arthur J. "A Man at a Spring: Horace, Odes 1.1." *Ramus* 9 (1980): 34–50.

Shey, H. J. "The Poet's Progress: Horace Odes I.1." *Arethusa* 4 (1971): 185–96.

ODE 1.5

Brown, J. C. "The Verbal Art of Horace's *Ode to Pyrrha*." *Transactions and Proceedings of the American Philological Association* 111 (1981): 17–22.

Coffta, David J. "Programme and Persona in Horace, Odes 1.5." *Eranos* 96 (1998): 26–31.

Fredricksmeyer, Ernst A. "Horace's Ode to Pyrrha (*Carm.* 1.5)." *Classical Philology* 60 (1965): 180–5.

Gold, Barbara. "Mitte sectari, rosa quo locorum sera moretur: Time and Nature in Horace's Odes." *Classical Philology* 88 (1993): 16–31.

Hoppin, Meredith Clarke. "New Perspectives on Horace, *Odes* 1.5." *American Journal of Philology* 105 (1984): 54–68.

Nielsen, Rosemary, and Robert Solomon. "Rescuing Horace, Pyrrha and Aphra Behn: a Directive." *Ramus* 22 (1993): 60–77.

Putnam, Michael C. J. "Horace *Carm.* 1.5: Love and Death." *Classical Philology* 65 (1970): 251–54. Reprinted in Michael C. J. Putnam, *Essays on Latin Lyric, Elegy, and Epic* (Princeton, 1982).

Quinn, Kenneth. "Horace as a Love Poet: A reading of *Odes* 1.5." *Arion* 2.3 (1963): 59–77.

Sutherland, Elizabeth. "Audience Manipulation and Emotional Experience in Horace's 'Pyrrha Ode'." *American Journal of Philology* 116 (1995): 441–52.

Vessey, D. W. T. "Pyrrha's Grotto and the Farewell to Love: A Study of Horace Odes 1.5." *American Journal of Philology* 105 (1984): 457–69.

ODE 1.9

Anderson, William S. "Horace's Different Recommenders of Carpe Diem in C. 1.4, 7, 9, 11." *Classical Journal* 88 (1993): 115–22.

Cameron, H. D. "Horace's Soracte Ode: (*Carm.* 1.9)." *Arethusa* 22 (1989): 147–59.

Clay, Jenny Strauss. "Ode 1.9: Horace's September Song." *Classical World* 83 (1989): 102–05.

Connor, W. R. "Soracte Encore." *Ramus* 1 (1972): 102–12.

Edmunds, Lowell. *From a Sabine Jar: Reading Horace Odes 1.9.* Chapel Hill, N.C., 1992.

Moritz, L. A. "Snow and Spring: Horace's Soracte Ode Again." *Greece and Rome* n.s. 23.2 (1976): 169–76.

Nielsen, R. M., and R. H. Solomon. "Horace's Soracte: Theory and the Matière Vivante of Classics." *Canadian Review of Comparative Literature* 21 (1994) : 627–641.

Nielsen, R. M. and R. H. Solomon. "Soracte and Sacred Space: Centuries of *carpe diem*." *Latomus* 47 (1988): 821–29.

Springer, Carl P. E. "Horace's Soracte Ode: Location, Dislocation, and the Reader." *Classical World* 82 (1988): 1–9.

Striar, Brian. "Soracte Reconsidered: The Burden of Youth and the Relief of Age in Horace *Odes* I.9." In *Collection Latomus: Studies in Latin Literature and Roman History* 5, edited by C. Deroux, 203–15. Brussels, 1989.

Vessey, D. W. T. "From Mountain to Lovers' Tryst: Horace's Soracte Ode." *Journal of Roman Studies* 75 (1985): 26–38.

ODE 1.11

Anderson, William S. (see under Ode 1.9).

Arkins, Brian. "Horace, *Odes* 1.11." *Collection Latomus: Studies in Latin Literature and Roman History* 1, edited by C. Deroux, Brussels, 1979: 257–65.

Ode 1.13

Keyser, Paul. "Horace Odes 1.13, 3–8, 14–16: Humoural and Aetherial Love." *Philologus* 133 (1989): 75–81.

Owens, William. "Double Jealousy: an Interpretation of Horace, Odes 1.13." *Collection Latomus: Studies in Latin Literature and Roman History* 6, edited by C. Deroux, Brussels, 1992: 237–44.

Segal, Charles. "*Felices Ter et Amplius*: Horace, *Odes*, I.13." *Latomus* 32 (1973): 39–46.

Ode 1.22

Ancona, Ronnie. "The Untouched Self: Sapphic and Catullan Muses in Horace *Odes* 1.22." In *Cultivating the Muse: Struggles for Power and Inspiration in Classical Literature*, edited by E. Spentzou and D. Fowler, 161–86. Oxford, 2002.

Davis, Gregson. "*Carmina/Iambi*: The Literary-Generic Dimension of Horace's *Integer Vitae (C. I,22)*." *Quaderni Urbinati di Cultura Classica*, n.s., 27, no. 3 (1987): 67–78.

Harrison, S. J. (see under Satire 1.9).

Hendrickson, G. L. "'Integer Vitae'." *Classical Journal* 5 (1910): 250–58.

Hubbard, Thomas. "Horace and Catullus: The Case of the Suppressed Precursor in Odes 1.22 and 1.32." *Classical World* 94 (2000–01): 25–38.

McCormick, Jane. "Horace's *Integer Vitae*." *Classical World* 67 (1973): 28–33.

Olstein, Katherine. "Horace's Integrity and the Geography of Carm. I.22." *Grazer Beiträge* 11 (1984): 113–20.

Ullman, B. L. "Horace and the Philologians." *Classical Journal* 31 (1935–36): 403–17.

Zumwalt, N. K. "Horace, C. 1.22: Poetic and Political Integrity." *Transactions and Proceedings of the American Philological Association* 105 (1975): 417–431.

Ode 1.23

Ancona, Ronnie. "The Subterfuge of Reason: Horace, *Odes* 1.23 and the Construction of Male Desire." *Helios* 16 (1989): 49–57.

Bannon, Cynthia. "Erotic Brambles and the Text of Horace Carmen 1.23.5–6." *Classical Philology* 88 (1993): 220–22.

Estevez, Victor. "Chloe and the Fawn: The Structure of *Odes* 1.23." *Helios* 7.1 (1979–80): 35–44.

Fredricksmeyer, Ernst, "Horace's Chloe (*Odes* 1.23): Inamorata or Victim?" *Classical Journal* 89 (1994): 251–59.

Lee, M. Owen. "Horace *Carm.* 1.23: Simile and Metaphor." *Classical Philology* 60 (1965): 185–86.

Nielsen, Rosemary. "Horace Odes 1.23: Innocence." *Arion* 9 (1970): 373–78.

Ronnick, Michele. "Green Lizards in Horace: *lacertae virides* in Odes 1.23." *Phoenix* 47 (1993): 155–57.

Watson, Lindsay. "Horace Odes 1.23 and 1.25." *Journal of the Australasian Universities Language and Literature Association* 82 (1994): 67–84.

Ode 1.24

Akbar Khan, H. "Horace's Ode to Virgil on the Death of Quintilius: 1.24." *Latomus* 26 (1967): 107–17.

Pascal, C. B. "Horatian Chiaroscuro (*Carm.* I,24)." *Hommages à M. Renard 1. Collection Latomus* 101, edited by J. Bibauw. Brussels, 1969: 622–33.

Putnam, Michael C. J. "The Languages of Horace Odes 1.24," *Classical Journal* 88 (1992–93): 123–35.

Ode 1.25

Ancona, Ronnie. "Horace *Odes* 1.25: Temporality, Gender, and Desire." in *Collection Latomus: Studies in Latin Literature and Roman History* 6, edited by C. Deroux, 245–59. Brussels, 1992.

Anderson, William S. "The Secret of Lydia's Aging: Horace, Ode 1.25." in *Why Horace? A Collection of Interpretations*, edited by W. Anderson. Wauconda, Ill., 1999: 85–91.

Arkins, Brian. "A Reading of Horace, *Carm.* 1.25." *Classica et Mediaevalia* 34 (1983): 161–75.

Armstrong, Michael. "Hebro/Euro: Two Notes on Horace Carm. 1.25.20." *Philologus* 136 (1992): 313–15.

Catlow, L. W. "Horace, *Odes* I,25 and IV, 13: a Reinterpretation." *Latomus* 35 (1976): 813–21.

Esler, Carol Clemeau. "Horace's Old Girls: Evolution of a Topos." in *Old Age in Greek and Latin Literature*, edited by T. Falkner and J. de Luce, Albany, N.Y., 1989, 172–82.

Lee, M. Owen. "Horace, Odes 1.25: The Wind and the River." *The Augustan Age* 4 (1985): 39–44.

Watson, Lindsay. (see under Ode 1.23).

Odes 1.23–25

Fuqua, Charles. "Horace *Carm.* 1.23–25." *Classical Philology* 63 (1968): 44–46.

Ode 1.37

Commager, Steele. "Horace, *Carmina* 1.37." *Phoenix* 12 (1958): 47–58.

De Forest, Mary Margolies. "The Central Simile of Horace's Cleopatra Ode." *Classical World* 82 (1989): 167–73.

Hendry, Michael. "More on Puns in the Cleopatra Odes." *Mnemosyne* 45 (1992): 529–31.

Hendry, Michael. "Three Problems in the Cleopatra Ode." *Classical Journal* 88 (1992–93): 137–47.

Johnson, W. R. "A Quean, a Great Queen? Cleopatra and the Politics of Misrepresentation." *Arion* 6 (1967): 388–402.

Mader, G. "Heroism and Hallucination: Cleopatra in Horace C. 1.37 and Propertius 3.11." *Grazer Beiträge* 16 (1989): 183–201.

Nussbaum, G. B. "A Study of Odes I, 37 and 38: The Psychology of Conflict and Horace's *Humanitas*." *Arethusa* 4 (1971): 91–97.

Ode 1.38

Fitzgerald, William. "Horace, Pleasure and the Text." *Arethusa* 22 (1989): 81–103.

Gold, Barbara (see under Ode 1.5).

Nussbaum, G. B. (see under Ode 1.37).

Sklenář, Robert. "Multiple Structural Divisions in Horace, Odes 1.38." *La Parola del Passato* 46 (1991): 444–47.

Toohey, P. G. "A Note on Horace, Odes I.38." *Maia* 32 (1980): 171–74.

Ode 2.3

Gold, Barbara (see under Ode 1.5).

Witke, Charles. "Questions and Answers in Horace *Odes* 2.3." *Classical Philology* 61 (1966): 250–52.

Woodman, A. J. "Horace, *Odes*, II,3." *American Journal of Philology* 91 (1970): 165–80.

Ode 2.7

Moles, John L. "Politics, Philosophy, and Friendship in Horace Odes 2,7." *Quaderni Urbinati di Cultura Classica* 25 (1987): 59–72.

Ode 2.10

Levin, D. N. "Horace, Carm. 2.10: Stylistic Observations." *Classical Journal* 54 (1958–59): 169–71.

Reagan, Christopher. "Horace, Carmen 2.10: The Use of Oxymoron as a Thematic Statement." *Rivista di Studi Classici* 18 (1970): 177–85.

Ode 2.14

Anderson, William. "Two Odes of Horace's Book Two." *California Studies in Classical Antiquity* 1 (1968): 35–61.

Roberts, Michael. "Reading Horace's Ode to Postumus (2.14)." *Latomus* 50 (1991): 371–75.

Ode 3.1

Cairns, Francis. "Horace's First Roman Ode (3.1)." *Papers of the Leeds International Latin Seminar* 8 (1995): 91–142.

Schenker, David. "Poetic Voices in Horace's Roman Odes." *Classical Journal* 88 (1992–93): 147–66.

Silk, E. T. "Towards a Fresh Interpretation of Horace *Carm.* III.1." *Yale Classical Studies* 23 (1973): 131–45.

Solmsen, F. "Horace's First Roman Ode." *American Journal of Philology* 68 (1947): 337–52.

Thom, Sjarlene. "Lyric Double Talk in Horace's Roman Odes (Odes 3.1–6)." *Akroterion* 43 (1998): 52–66.

Witke, Charles (chapter on Ode 3.1; see General Works, above).

Ode 3.9

Nielsen, Rosemary. "Catullus 45 and Horace *Odes* 3.9: The Glass House." *Ramus* 6 (1977): 132–38.

Putnam, Michael C. J. "Horace Odes 3.9: The Dialectics of Desire." In *Ancient and Modern: Essays in Honor of Gerald F. Else*, edited by John D'Arms and John Eadie. Ann Arbor, 1977, 139–57. Reprinted in Michael C. J. Putnam, *Essays on Latin Lyric, Elegy, and Epic* (Princeton, 1982).

Ode 3.13

Brown, Jerrold C. "Poetic Grammar in Horace's Ode to the Fountain at Bandusia." *Helios* 18 (1991): 137–46.

Coffta, David J. "Programmatic Synthesis in Horace 'Odes' III,13." In *Collection Latomus: Studies in Latin Literature and Roman History* 9, edited by C. Deroux, 268–81. Brussells, 1998.

Fitzgerald, William (see under Ode 1.38).

Hexter, Ralph. "O Fons Bandusiae: Blood and Water in Horace, Odes 3.13." in *Homo Viator: Classical Essays for J. Bramble*, edited by M. Whitby, P. Hardie, M. Whitby, 131–39. Bristol, 1987.

Jameson, Virginia. "What Words Can Do: Horace, C. 3,13, 'O Fons Bandusiae'." *Helios* 24 (1997): 44–59.

Mader, G. "That St(r)ain Again: Blood, Water, and Generic Allusion in Horace's Bandusia Ode." *American Journal of Philology* 123 (2002): 51–59.

Ode 3.30

Nielsen, R. M., and R. H. Solomon. "Horace, Strabo, and Ezra Pound: The Lie of the Final Poem ('Odes' 3.30)." *Revue Belge de Philologie et d' Histoire* 72 (1994): 62–77.

Putnam, Michael, C. J. "Horace C.3.30: The Lyricist as Hero." *Ramus* 2 (1973): 1–19. Reprinted in Michael C. J. Putnam, *Essays on Latin Lyric, Elegy, and Epic* (Princeton, 1982).

Simpson, Christopher. "The Tomb, Immortality, and the 'Pontifex': Some Realities in Horace Carm. 3.30." *Athenaeum* 90 (2002): 89–94.

Woodman, Tony. "Exegi Monumentum: Horace, Odes 3.30." in *Quality and Pleasure in Latin Poetry*, edited by Tony Woodman and David West, 115–28. Cambridge, 1975.

Ode 4.7

Woodman, A. J. "Horace's Odes *Diffugere niues* and *Soluitur acris hiems.*" *Latomus* 31 (1972): 752–78.

HORACE

SELECTED ODES
AND SATIRE 1.9

SATIRE 1.9

In Satire 1.9 Horace explores both literary and social values. Horace (or, more precisely, the character he takes on in this poem) encounters a man who aggressively keeps after him in an effort to gain access to Horace's literary friend and supporter, Maecenas. The poem is filled with irony and humor as this unwanted companion pursues Horace and Horace tries to escape. The intentional failure of Horace's friend, Aristius Fuscus, to save him adds to the poem's wit. On one level, the person Horace encounters is his opposite: they have completely different literary values. However, while Horace wants to distance himself from the aggressive, ambitious position the man represents, it should be noted that elsewhere (Satire 1.6) Horace shares his own social anxiety when he feels the need to defend himself, as the son of a freedman, against the charge of being an overly ambitious social climber because of his relationship to Maecenas.

Meter: dactylic hexameter

Ibam forte via sacra, sicut meus est mos,
nescio quid meditans nugarum, totus in illis.

---

1 **forte, adv.,** *by chance, as luck would have it, as it so happened*

Ibam forte...: a fragment of Lucilius (died 102/101 BCE), the inventor of the Latin genre of satire according to the satirists, Horace, Persius, and Juvenal, begins: **Ibat forte aries.** Horace is echoing his predecessor here.

via sacra: The Via Sacra, or Sacred Way, was the main street in Rome. It went through the Forum and on to the Capitolium.

mos, moris, m., *custom, tradition;* (plural) *character, habits*

2 **nescio, nescire, nescivi, nescitum,** *not know, be ignorant of, not to know how to, not to be able to*

nescio: the "o" is regularly short in poetry

nescio quid: *something or other,* literally, "I do not know what"

meditor, meditari, meditatus sum, *think over, contemplate, practice*

nugae, -arum, f. pl., *trifles, nonsense, things of no importance;* cf. Catullus' use of the word to refer to his own literary work in lines 3–4 of the first poem of his collection: **Corneli, tibi: namque tu solebas/meas esse aliquid putare nugas. Nugae** can refer to a literary work of light character.

totus in illis: elliptical; *totally* (involved) *in it*

accurrit quidam notus mihi nomine tantum,
arreptaque manu: 'quid agis, dulcissime rerum?'
'suaviter, ut nunc est' inquam, 'et cupio omnia, quae vis.'   5
cum adsectaretur: 'numquid vis?' occupo, at ille
'noris nos' inquit, 'docti sumus.' hic ego: 'pluris
hoc' inquam 'mihi eris.' misere discedere quaerens
ire modo ocius, interdum consistere, in aurem
dicere nescio quid puero, cum sudor ad imos   10

3   **accurro, accurrere, accurri/accucur-**
     ri, accursum, *run or hurry up to*

     tantum, adv., *so much, only*

     notus mihi nomine tantum: notice
     that he is never named

4   **arripio, arripere, arripui, arreptum,**
     seize, take hold of, arrest, bring before
     a court

     quid agis: idiomatic, "how are you?"

     dulcissime rerum: cf. Horace's char-
     acterization of Maecenas as **dulce**
     decus meum in Ode 1.1.2

     rerum: partitive genitive with super-
     lative adjective, "in the world"

5   **suaviter,** adv., *pleasantly, delightfully,*
     nicely

     inquam, inquit, defective verb, only
     a few forms occur, most often used
     parenthetically or before or after a
     quotation, *say*

     inquam: present indicative active,
     first person singular

     cupio omnia quae vis: common po-
     lite phrase

6   **adsector, adsectari, adsectatus sum,**
     follow closely, attend, escort

     numquid, interrogative particle,
     introduces question where a nega-
     tive answer is expected, *surely...not;*
     you don't, do you?

     occupo, occupare, occupavi, occupa-
     tum, *seize, forestall, take the lead over*

     occupo: here, *take the lead over,* in
     sense of breaking into the conver-
     sation

7   **nosco, noscere, novi, notum,** *get to*
     know, learn; know (in perfect tense)

noris: noris is the syncopated form
     of **no(ve)ris,** perfect subjunc-
     tive; **noris nos** is the answer to
     numquid vis?; normally the an-
     swer contains a statement of what
     the person wants in the subjunc-
     tive with **ut** understood.

nos, docti, sumus: all plural for sin-
     gular, as often in Latin

inquit: see **inquam** above; present
     indicative active, third person sin-
     gular

doctus, -a, -um, adj., *learned, taught*

docti: *learned,* especially as it applies
     to poetry; cf. Ode 1.1.29–30: **me**
     doctarum hederae praemia fron-
     tium/dis miscent superis; and
     Ode 3.9.10: **dulcis docta modos et**
     citharae sciens.

hic: the "i" is long

pluris: genitive of indefinite value

8   **hoc:** ablative of cause

     inquam: see line 5

9   **ire:** historical infinitive, as are **consis-**
     tere (9) and **dicere** (10)

     modo, adv., *only, just now*

     ocius, adv., *sooner, quicker*

     interdum, adv., *at times*

     consisto, consistere, constiti, *stop,*
     pause, stand still, take a position

10   **nescio quid:** see line 2 for meaning
     and meter

     puero: Horace is being accompanied
     by a slave to whom he whispers.

     sudor, sudoris, m., *sweat*

     imus, -a, -um, adj., *lowest, bottom of*

manaret talos. 'o te, Bolane, cerebri
felicem' aiebam tacitus, cum quidlibet ille
garriret, vicos, urbem laudaret. ut illi
nil respondebam: 'misere cupis' inquit 'abire;
iam dudum video. sed nil agis; usque tenebo.   15
persequar hinc, quo nunc iter est tibi.' 'nil opus est te
circumagi: quendam volo visere non tibi notum;

---

11   **mano, manare, manavi, manatum,**
      flow, spread

      talus, -i, m., *ankle bone, ankle, knuckle*
      bone used in games

      te: accusative of exclamation, as is **fe-**
      licem (12)

      Bolanus, -i, m., *Bolanus,* Roman cog-
      nomen; identity unknown

      cerebrum, -i, n., *brain, seat of intelli-*
      gence, seat of anger, anger

      cerebri: genitive of reference, stating
      respect with which the adjective,
      felicem, is applicable; in Classical
      Latin an ablative of respect would
      be used more typically

12   **aio**, defective verb, *say yes, say*

      aiebam: imperfect tense, first person
      singular

      tacitus, -a, -um, adj., *silent*

      quilibet, quaelibet, quidlibet, pron.,
      whoever or whatever you please, any-
      one or anything whatever

13   **garrio, garrire, garrivi,** *talk rapidly,*
      chatter, (do this in writing)

      vicus, -i, m., *group of dwellings, village;*
      block of houses, street, group of streets,
      often forming a social or admin-
      istrative unit (used of specific dis-
      tricts in Rome)

14   **nil: nil = nihil**

      inquit: see line 7

15   **dudum**, adv., *some time ago, previously,*
      just now; for a long time (with **iam**)

      video: present tense with **iam du-**
      dum; translate into English pres-
      ent perfect

nil: see line 14

nil agis: colloquial, *it's no use*

usque, adv., *continuously, continually,*
all the way

tenebo: **teneo** has the sense "persist"
here

16   **persequor, persequi, persecutus**
      sum, *pursue, chase*

      iter, itineris, n., *journey*

      nil: see line 14

      nil: used adverbially here

      opus, operis, n., *work, business, task,*
      genre; with **esse**, *be necessary, be*
      needed; here, with accusative and
      infinitive (**te circumagi**)

17   **circumago, circumagere, circumegi,**
      circumactum, *drive or lead around,*
      lead around in circles

      volo: the second "o" is short here,
      perhaps in imitation of early Latin
      comedy, which employed the met-
      rical law of **brevis brevians**, or
      iambic shortening. (An iamb is a
      short syllable followed by a long
      syllable.) According to this law,
      a long syllable, if preceded by a
      short syllable, may be counted as
      short if the word's natural accent
      falls on the syllable directly pre-
      ceding or following it. Here, **volo**
      ($\cup$ —) can become ($\cup$ $\cup$) because
      the word is accented on the first
      syllable, i.e., the syllable preceding
      the change.

      viso, visere, visi, *look at, go and see*

trans Tiberim longe cubat is prope Caesaris hortos.'
'nil habeo, quod agam, et non sum piger: usque sequar te.'
demitto auriculas, ut iniquae mentis asellus,   20
cum gravius dorso subiit onus. incipit ille:

18   **Tiberis, Tiberis,** m., *the river Tiber*
      longe, adv., *far, far off, far away in time*
      cubo, cubare, cubui, cubitum, *lie
      down or be lying down, recline, be in
      bed or on one's couch, be confined to
      bed by illness, recline at table*
      Caesar, Caesaris, m., *Caesar;* here,
      Julius Caesar, (100–44 BCE), Roman
      general who defeated Pompey at
      the battle of Pharsalus in 48 BCE
      and was made dictator for life in
      44 BCE, shortly before his assas-
      sination in the conspiracy led by
      Brutus and Cassius. Cf. notes to
      Ode 2.7 for Horace's association
      with Brutus.
      hortus, -i, m., *garden;* usually in plu-
      ral, *pleasure grounds or gardens*
      Caesaris hortos: an estate on the Ja-
      niculum left by Julius Caesar in his
      will as a public park for the people.
19   **nil:** see line 14
      agam: subjunctive in relative clause
      of characteristic

      piger, pigra, pigrum, adj., *inactive,
      lazy*
      usque: see line 15
20   **demitto, demittere, demisi, demis-
      sum,** *let fall, lower*
      demitto auriculas: the sense of **de-
      mittere aures ad,** *deign to listen to,*
      (*OLD* under **demitto,** 10. c) may be
      relevant here. He shows his feeling
      of defeat. The elision between the
      two words calls attention to the
      gesture.
      auricula, -ae, f., *ear*
      iniquus, -a, -um, adj., *uneven, unfavor-
      able, treacherous, discontented*
      asellus, -i, m., *young ass, young donkey*
21   **dorsum, -i,** n., *back*
      subeo, subire, subii, subitum, *go un-
      der, undergo*
      subiit: the second "i" is long, as is
      typical with compounds of **eo** in
      the perfect tense
      onus, oneris, n., *burden*
      onus: accusative

'si bene me novi, non Viscum pluris amicum,
non Varium facies: nam quis me scribere pluris
aut citius possit versus? quis membra movere

22   novi: see line 7

si bene me novi: idiomatic, *as certainly as I know myself*

Viscus, -i, m., *Viscus*; there were two brothers with this name; both were literary figures and friends of Horace and Maecenas. In Satire 1.10.83 they are mentioned along with several others, including Varius (cf. line 23 below), Vergil, Maecenas (cf. line 43 below), and Aristius Fuscus (cf. line 61 below) as people whose approval of his writing mattered greatly to Horace. One of them is also mentioned as a guest, along with Varius, at a dinner in honor of Maecenas described in Satire 2.8.

pluris: genitive of indefinite value

22–23 Note the anaphora with asyndeton, **non Viscum...non Varium**, which emphasizes the names.

non Viscum...facies: facies (*regard*) plus accusative (**amicum**) plus genitive of indefinite value (**pluris**), *you will not regard Viscus, Varius, as a friend of more value*

23   **Varius, Varii**, m., *L. Varius Rufus*, epic and tragic poet, a very significant figure to Horace. He, along with Vergil, introduced Horace to his future friend and supporter, Maecenas (cf. Satire 1.6.55). In Satire 1.6.52–55 Horace emphasizes the fact that his relationship with Maecenas was not a product of chance, but rather of his friends' introduction and Maecenas' careful choice. Contrast that process with the chance encounter (**Ibam *forte* via sacra**) of this satire and the desire of Horace's unwanted companion to become part of Horace's literary

circle. In addition, compare his lack of literary credentials (cf. note below on lines 23–24). In Satire 1.5.39–42 Horace says that no one is more attached to Varius, Vergil, and Plotius Tucca than he is and that there are no people better than they are. (Varius and Plotius Tucca served as Vergil's literary executors.) In Ode 1.6 Horace begs off from writing epic (while he simultaneously appropriates epic for lyric) and Varius is the epic writer whom he suggests in his place for singing the praises of Agrippa, who commanded the fleet of Augustus at the battle of Actium in 31 BCE in which the forces of Antony and Cleopatra were defeated. Cf. the notes to Ode 1.37.

pluris: **-is** ending, alternate accusative plural ending for **-es**; modifies **versus** (24); since the final syllable in the line can be considered either long or short, there may be a sense of the genitive of indefinite value as well (see line 22).

23–24 **nam...versus**: Cf. Satire 1.4.11 ff. for Horace's dislike of writing that is done too quickly or at too great length. He criticizes Lucilius (cf. note on line 1) for these very qualities. What Horace's unwanted companion sees as his literary credentials are the very literary qualities Horace abhors.

24   **citius**, adv., *quicker, sooner*

possit: potential subjunctive

versus, -us, m., *line of verse*

membrum, -i, n., *limb or member of the body, limb, member, part of anything*

movere: understand **possit** again

mollius? invideat quod et Hermogenes ego canto.'   25
interpellandi locus hic erat: 'est tibi mater,
cognati, quis te salvo est opus?' 'haud mihi quisquam;
omnis composui.' 'felices! nunc ego resto.
confice! namque instat fatum mihi triste, Sabella
quod puero cecinit divina mota anus urna: 30

25 **mollis, -e**, adj., *soft, gentle, flexible, voluptuous*

 invideo, invidere, invidi, invisum, *envy, begrudge, refuse*

 invideat: potential subjunctive

 quod: relative pronoun, direct object of **canto**, antecedent understood

 et: *even*

 Hermogenes, Hermogenis, m., *Hermogenes.* In Satire 1.10.80 Horace places a Hermogenes Tegellius in a group of people whose opinions do not matter to him as opposed to those of his literary friends (cf. note on **Viscus,** line 22).

 canto, cantare, cantavi, cantatum, *sing, sing about, recite*

 canto: cf. line 10 of Ode 1.22

 mollius...canto: this line is completely dactylic except for the obligatory last foot that has a long syllable followed by a syllable that can be either long or short. Line 31 is the only other equally dactylic line in the poem. The heavily dactylic meter of line 25 echoes the value the speaker places on quick writing.

26 **interpello, interpellare, interpellavi, interpellatum,** *interrupt, break in on, impede*

 interpellandi: notice how this word's five long syllables in a row put a halt to the chattering of the heavily dactylic previous line

 hic: the "i" is long

27 **cognatus, -a, -um,** adj., *related;* here, as noun, *relative*

 cognati: understand the verb "to be" again from **est** (26)

 quis: alternate form for **quibus** (dative and ablative plural of relative pronoun); here, dative of person who has the need, with **est opus**

 te: ablative with **est opus** (see line 16)

 salvus, -a, -um, adj., *safe, alive, well*

 salvo: ablative modifying **te**

 haud, adv., *not*

 mihi: dative of possession, understand **est**

28 **omnis:** -**is** ending, alternate accusative plural ending for -**es**

 compono, componere, composui, compositum, *put together, arrange, compose, calm, bury*

 resto, restare, restiti, *remain, remain to be dealt with*

29–34 These lines are a parody of epic passages in which the hero's death is foretold. Of course, the fate proclaimed for Horace is not a heroic one: he will be killed by an excessive talker!

29 **conficio, conficere, confeci, confectum,** *complete, destroy, finish off, kill*

 confice: understand a **me** as the direct object

 insto, instare, institi, *be pressing, loom, threaten*

 fatum, -i, n., *fate;* plural, *the Fates*

 mihi: dative with **insto**

 tristis, -e, adj., *sad*

 Sabellus, -a, -um, adj., *Sabine;* the Sabines were a people of central Italy.

30 **puero:** understand **mihi,** *for me when I was a boy*

 divina mota...urna: ablative absolute

 anus, -us, f., *old woman*

 urna, -ae, f., *urn*

hunc neque dira venena, nec hosticus auferet ensis,
nec laterum dolor aut tussis, nec tarda podagra:
garrulus hunc quando consumet cumque. loquaces,
si sapiat, vitet, simul atque adoleverit aetas.'
ventum erat ad Vestae, quarta iam parte diei   35
praeterita, et casu tum respondere vadato

---

31   **dirus, -a, -um**, adj., *terrible, awful, dire*

     venenum, -i, n., *poison, magical or medicinal potion*

     hosticus, -a, -um, adj., *belonging to an enemy*

     aufero, auferre, abstuli, ablatum, *take away, carry off, kill*

     ensis, ensis, m., *sword*

32   **latus, lateris**, n., *side, extreme part or region, flank, lungs, body*

     dolor, doloris, m., *pain, anguish, grief*

     tussis, tussis, f., *cough*

     tardus, -a, -um, adj., *slow, late, moving slowly, dull*

     podagra, -ae, f., *gout*

33   **garrulus, -a, -um**, adj., *talkative, loquacious*

     quandocumque, adv., *at some time or other*

     quando...cumque: tmesis, **quandocumque**

     consumo, consumere, consumpsi, consumptum, *consume, destroy, kill*

     loquax, loquacis, adj., *talkative, loquacious, talking*

34   **sapio, sapere, sapivi**, *have taste, be wise*

     vito, vitare, vitavi, vitatum, *avoid, shun*

     simul, conj., *as soon as* (also with **atque**); adv., *at the same time, together*

     adolesco, adolescere, adolevi, adultum, *grow up*, (of a season or time) *reach its peak*

     aetas, aetatis, f., *time, age*

35   **ventum erat**: intransitive verb used impersonally in the passive, literally, *it had been come*, i.e., *we had come*; person and number for translation supplied from context; this impersonal construction allows the speaker to avoid joining himself "grammatically" in the first person plural with this person he finds so distasteful.

     Vesta, -ae, f., *Vesta*, Roman goddess of the domestic hearth; *temple or shrine of Vesta*; she was served by the Vestal Virgins, who were chosen by the pontifex maximus (cf. Ode 3.30 for the image of Vestal Virgin and pontifex ascending the Capitolium)

     Vestae: genitive; the accusative **templum** is the understood object of **ad**; *temple of Vesta*

     quartus, -a, -um, adj., *fourth*

35–36   **quarta...praeterita**: ablative absolute; about 9 a.m., when business went on in the law courts

36   **praetereo, praeterire, praeterii, praeteritum**, *go by, go past, pass by, go beyond, omit*

     casus, -us, m., *fall, event, misfortune, chance*

     respondeo, respondere, respondi, responsum, *answer, reply*; technical sense, *appear in court*

     vador, vadari, vadatus sum, (of a plaintiff) *to accept a guarantee from the other party that the party will appear or reappear in court at an appointed date*

     vadato: impersonal ablative absolute, or dative of perfect participle as noun, *the plaintiff*

debebat, quod ni fecisset, perdere litem.
'si me amas' inquit, 'paulum hic ades.' 'interim, si
aut valeo stare aut novi civilia iura,
et propero, quo scis.' 'dubius sum, quid faciam' inquit,   40
'tene relinquam, an rem.' 'me, sodes.' 'non faciam' ille
et praecedere coepit. ego, ut contendere durum
cum victore, sequor. 'Maecenas quomodo tecum?'

---

37 **ni**: ni = nisi

nisi, conj., *if not, unless*

perdo, perdere, perdidi, perditum, *destroy, lose*

perdere: understand **debebat**

lis, litis, f., *quarrel, lawsuit*

38 **si me amas**: colloquial expression for "please" found, e.g., in Roman comedy and Cicero's letters

me: monosyllabic hiatus (no elision with **amas**) with shortening of the long vowel; **me amas** scans, ∪ ∪ —

inquit: see line 7

paulum, adv., *for a short while*

adsum, adesse, adfui, *be present;* in technical sense, *be present in court as a friend or adviser*

ades: present imperative singular of **adsum**

intereo, interire, interii, interitum, *perish, die*

interiam: *may I perish...* (hyperbolic)

39 **valeo, valere, valui, valitum,** *be powerful, be strong enough to, be well*

stare: literally, *stand,* or can have technical sense of **adsum** given above (Plautus, the Roman comic playwright, uses the word in this sense)

novi: see line 7; the long "o" makes this form the verb, not the adjective, **novus, -a, -um**

civilis, -e, adj., *civil*

ius, iuris, n., *law, right, court*

40 **propero, properare, properavi, properatum,** *hurry, hasten*

dubius, -a, -um, adj., *uncertain, indecisive*

faciam: subjunctive in indirect question

inquit: see line 7

41 **ne**, interrogative enclitic particle, in direct questions; in indirect questions with alternatives, often used with **an**, *whether...or*

rem: here, in the technical sense of a legal matter; it would go by default if he did not appear

sodes: sodes = si audes, *please;* **audeo** typically means "wish" in Plautus

42 **praecedo, praecedere, praecessi, praecessum,** *go in front, go on ahead*

coepi, coepisse, coeptum, typically appears in perfect system; *begin*

contendo, contendere, contendi, contentum, *stretch, hasten, compete, contend*

durum: understand **est**

43 **victor, victoris,** m., *victor, winner, conqueror*

Maecenas, Maecenatis, m. *Gaius Cilnius Maecenas,* friend and supporter of Horace and of other contemporary poets, including Vergil

quomodo, interr., rel. adv., *how, in the manner in which*

Maecenas...tecum: elliptical because a verb is lacking; the sense is, "how are things with you and Maecenas?" This kind of ellipsis is common in colloquial Latin.

hinc repetit, 'paucorum hominum et mentis bene sanae;
nemo dexterius fortuna est usus. haberes   45
magnum adiutorem, posset qui ferre secundas,
hunc hominem velles si tradere. dispeream, ni
summosses omnis.' 'non isto vivimus illic,
quo tu rere, modo. domus hac nec purior ulla est,

---

44   **repeto, repetere, repetivi, repetitum**,
     seek again, recall, resume

     sanus, -a, -um, adj., *healthy, sane*

     **paucorum hominum...mentis...sa-
     nae**: genitives of description

     paucorum...sanae: commentators dif-
     fer about who is speaking here, but
     agree that Maecenas is the one to
     whom the speaker refers. Cf. Satire
     1.6.51 ff. for Maecenas' selectivity
     in choosing those with whom he
     would associate.

45   **fortuna**: ablative with **usus est (utor)**

     fortuna: cf. the note on Varius, line
     23, for the lack of chance involved
     in his becoming part of Maecenas'
     circle of friends

     nemo...usus: some attribute these
     lines to Horace and take him to be
     speaking about Maecenas, while
     others (including the editor of the
     text printed here) attribute the
     lines to Horace's follower; these
     latter disagree as to whether the
     follower is referring to Maecenas
     or to Horace.

     haberes: apodosis of a present con-
     trary to fact condition; cf. **velles**
     (47) below

46   **adiutor, adiutoris**, m., *helper*

     posset qui: postposition; the relative
     pronoun **qui**, the subject of the
     clause, is placed after **posset**

     ferre: here, has the sense of "play" a
     part

     secundus, -a, -um, adj., *following, sec-
     ond, favorable*

     secundas: understand **partes**; the
     second actor supports the primary
     actor

     pars, partis, f., *part, party; stage role*
     (usually in plural)

47   **hunc hominem**: colloquial for **me**

     velles: protasis of present contrary to
     fact condition

     si: postposition; note how late in its
     clause this word appears

     trado, tradere, tradidi, traditum,
     hand over, deliver, introduce

     dispereo, disperire, disperii, *perish,
     be destroyed* (frequently hyperbolic)

     dispeream: *may I perish...* (hyperbol-
     ic)

     ni: see line 37

48   **summoveo, summovere, summovi,
     summotum**, *move away, remove,
     ward off, banish*

     summosses: syncopated form of
     summo(vi)sses; the pluperfect,
     rather than the imperfect, may em-
     phasize the idea of completion

     omnis: **-is** ending, alternate accusa-
     tive plural ending for **-es**

     omnis: all those competing for Mae-
     cenas' attention

49   **reor, reri, ratus sum**, *think*

     rere: alternate form of second person
     singular, **reris**

     quo...modo: see line 43

     purior: cf. the beginning of Ode 1.22,
     Integer vitae scelerisque *purus*

nec magis his aliena malis. nil mi officit, inquam,   50
ditior hic aut est quia doctior: est locus uni
cuique suus.' 'magnum narras, vix credibile.' 'atqui
sic habet.' 'accendis, quare cupiam magis illi
proxumus esse.' 'velis tantummodo: quae tua virtus,
expugnabis, et est, qui vinci possit, eoque   55
difficilis aditus primos habet.' 'haud mihi dero:
muneribus servos corrumpam; non, hodie si
exclusus fuero, desistam; tempora quaeram,

---

50 **alienus, -a, -um**, adj., *of another, alien,*
  strange (with ablative or dative)

nil: see line 14; used adverbial here;
  not at all

mi: mi = mihi

officio, officere, offeci, offectum, *im-*
  pede, interfere with (with dative)

inquam: see line 5

51 **dis, ditis**, adj., *rich, wealthy;* comparative, **ditior**

hic: long "i" here for the nominative
  singular masculine of **hic, haec,**
  hoc

quia: postposition; note the postponement of this conjunction

doctus, -a, -um, *learned, taught*

52 **credibilis, -e**, adj., *believable*

atqui, conj., *but, nevertheless*

53 **sic habet**: habeo, used impersonally
  with adv. of manner, *be in (such and*
  such) a way; it is so; a similar expression is **sic se res habet**

accendo, accendere, accendi, accen-
  sum, *kindle, arouse, ignite*

54 **proxumus, -a, -um**, adj., *nearest, next*

tantummodo, adv., *only*

velis tantummodo: ironic; literally,
  you would wish it only; the sense is,
  you only need to wish for it

quae tua virtus: an example of the

antecedent incorporated into the
relative clause, *such is your valor*
(literally, *which is your valor*)

55 **expugno, expugnare, expugnavi, ex-**
  pugnatum, *storm, conquer, overcome*

possit: subjunctive in relative clause
  of characteristic

eo, adv., ablative of **is**, *therefore*

56 **difficilis**: **-is** ending, alternate accusative plural ending for **-es**

aditus, -us, m., *approach, access*

haud: see line 27

desum, deesse, defui, *be missing, fail*
  (with dative of person)

dero: dero = deero, from **desum**; the
  dee- usually contracted to de- in
  poetry

57 **munus, muneris**, n., *service, duty, gift,*
  entertainment

corrumpo, corrumpere, corrupi, cor-
  ruptum, *damage, spoil, bribe, seduce*

58 **excludo, excludere, exclusi, exclu-**
  sum, *shut out, exclude*

exclusus fuero: exclusus fuero = exclusus ero; alternate form for the
  future perfect passive

exclusus fuero: the language here
  is similar to that of the "shut-out"
  lover who cannot gain access to
  the house of the one he desires

desisto, desistere, destiti, *cease, desist*

occurram in triviis, deducam. nil sine magno
vita labore dedit mortalibus.' haec dum agit, ecce   60
Fuscus Aristius occurrit, mihi carus et illum
qui pulchre nosset. consistimus. 'unde venis?' et
'quo tendis?' rogat et respondet. vellere coepi
et pressare manu lentissima brachia, nutans,

59　occurro, occurrere, occurri/occucur-
　　ri, occursum, *meet, hurry to meet,*
　　　arrive, turn up

　　trivium, trivii, n., *meeting place of*
　　　three roads, crossroads

　　deduco, deducere, deduxi, deduc-
　　　tum, *lead away, lead down, escort,*
　　　bring a person or army back with one
　　　to Rome, bring home in procession as
　　　a bride, spin, compose, adapt

　　deducam: understand Maecenas as
　　　the direct object

　　nil: see line 14

60　ecce, interj., *look, behold*

61　Fuscus, -i, m., *Aristius Fuscus,*
　　　Horace's literary friend in Satire
　　　1.10.83, the person to whom Epistle
　　　1.10 is addressed—and there he
　　　and Horace are linked as "twins,"
　　　but separated by their love for
　　　the city and the country, respec-
　　　tively—as well as the character
　　　who refuses to save Horace from
　　　his unwanted companion, here, in
　　　Satire 1.9. Porphyrio, the ancient
　　　commentator on Horace (third and
　　　fourth centuries CE), calls Aristius
　　　Fuscus a very outstanding **gram-**
　　　maticus (philologist or grammar-
　　　ian) and a writer of comedies. His
　　　appearance in Ode 1.22 (see later
　　　in this text), a poem about the
　　　poet's invulnerability, can be seen
　　　as an "answer" to his refusal to
　　　help the poet in Satire 1.9. In the
　　　city the poet needs help and does
　　　not receive it from Fuscus; later, in
　　　the ode, he claims his invulnera-
　　　bility in the country and in remote
　　　lands. **Fuscus, -a, -um** is an adjec-
　　　tive meaning "dark." For punning

on Fuscus' name, cf. the note on
Apollo, line 78 below. For further
punning on Fuscus, cf. the note
on **Hydaspes**, Ode 1.22.8. Putting
Fuscus before **Aristius** and at the
beginning of the line calls attention to the word.

Aristius, Aristii, m., see **Fuscus,** line
　61

occurrit: see line 59

carus, -a, -um, adj., *dear, beloved*

62　qui: postposition; **qui** placed after
　　illum, which belongs to the same
　　clause

　　pulchre: colloquial for **bene**; com-
　　mon in the comedies of Plautus
　　and Terence

　　nosset: syncopated form of
　　　no(vi)sset; subjunctive in relative
　　　clause of characteristic with an ac-
　　　cessory notion of cause

　　consistimus: see line 9

63　quo, adv., *where, for what purpose*

　　tendo, tendere, tetendi, tentum/ten-
　　　sum, *stretch out, extend, proceed,*
　　　direct one's course

　　rogat et respondet: they each ask and
　　　answer each other

　　respondet: see line 36

　　vello, vellere, velli, vulsum, *pull, tug*
　　　at

　　coepi: see line 42

64　presso, pressare, pressavi, pressa-
　　　tum, *press*

　　lentus, -a, -um, adj., *slow, lingering,*
　　　unresponsive

　　brachium, brachii, n., *arm*

　　nuto, nutare, nutavi, nutatum, *nod*
　　　with the head, nod, hesitate

distorquens oculos, ut me eriperet. male salsus   65
ridens dissimulare, meum iecur urere bilis:
'certe nescio quid secreto velle loqui te
aiebas mecum.' 'memini bene, sed meliore
tempore dicam: hodie tricesima sabbata. vin tu
curtis Iudaeis oppedere?' 'nulla mihi' inquam   70
'religio est.' 'at mi! sum paulo infirmior, unus

---

65 **distorqueo, distorquere, distorsi, distortum**, *twist this way and that, distort, torment*

eripio, eripere, eripui, ereptum, *snatch away, rescue*

male, adv., *badly, insufficiently, wickedly, scarcely*

salsus, -a, -um, adj., *salted, witty, funny*

66 **dissimulo, dissimulare, dissimulavi, dissimulatum**, *pretend that something is not what it is, pretend not to notice, ignore*

dissimulare: historical infinitive

iecur, iecoris, n., *liver, the seat of the feelings*

uro, urere, ussi, ustum, *burn*; in pass., *be on fire*

urere: historical infinitive

bilis, bilis, f., *gall, bile, anger*

meum...bilis: cf. the language of Ode 1.13

67 **certus, -a, -um**, adj., *certain, definite*

nescio quid: see line 2 for meaning and meter

secreto: adv., *secretly*

68 **aiebas**: see line 12; imperfect tense, second person singular

memini, meminisse, perfect with present meaning; *remember, recollect*

melior, melius, adj., *better*

69 **tricesimus, -a, -um**, adj., *thirtieth*

sabbata, sabbatorum, n. pl., *the Jewish sabbath*

tricesima sabbata: this refers to no known Jewish celebration and is likely an invention on Fuscus' part. Just as Horace creates obstacles for his unwanted companion, so Fuscus does the same for Horace.

vin: vin = visne

70 **curtus, -a, -um**, adj., *having a part missing, mutilated, circumcised*

curtis: male circumcision is a Jewish practice

Iudaeus, -i, m., *Jew*

oppedo, oppedere, *fart in the face of* (with dative)

inquam: see line 5

71 **religio, religionis**, f., *religious awe or conscience, religious practice, particular set of religious observances, cult, religious feeling, superstition*

mi: see line 50

at mi: elliptical; understand with **religio est**

paulum, -i, n., *a little*

infirmus, -a, -um, adj., *weak, lacking strength of purpose, not resolute*

multorum. ignosces; alias loquar.' huncine solem
tam nigrum surrexe mihi! fugit inprobus ac me
sub cultro linquit. casu venit obvius illi
adversarius et 'quo tu, turpissime?' magna   75
inclamat voce, et 'licet antestari?' ego vero

72   multorum: cf. **paucorum hominum**,
      line 44. Horace, the writer (as op-
      posed to the persona in the satire)
      has Fuscus humorously identify
      himself as one of the "many" in
      contrast to Maecenas who is a per-
      son of "few" people.

      ignosco, ignoscere, ignovi, ignotum,
      forgive, pardon

      alias, adv., *at another time*

      huncine: huncine = huncne

      -ne, here, affirmative particle with in-
      finitive in exclamation; see **surrexe**
      below

72–73 **huncine solem...nigrum**: accusa-
      tives of exclamation with infinitive
      in exclamation

      solem: sol can have the meaning of
      "a day," as determined by the ris-
      ing of the sun

73   **niger, nigra, nigrum**, *black, dark,*
      gloomy, black as a color of ill omen,
      evil

      nigrum: pun in connection with the
      meaning of Fuscus' name; Aristius
      Fuscus is the "dark sun," or un-
      lucky day.

      surgo, surgere, surrexi, surrectum,
      get up, rise (of heavenly bodies)

      surrexe: syncopated form of
      surrex(iss)e; infinitive in exclama-
      tion

      fugit: present tense, short "u"

      inprobus, -a, -um, adj., *unprincipled,*
      immoderate, unruly, relentless, shame-
      less

74   **culter, cultri**, m., *knife*

      sub cultro: *under the knife,* i.e., like
      a sacrificial victim with the knife

ready to fall, or like a warrior with
the opponent's weapon about to
fall

linquo, linquere, liqui, *go away from,*
abandon, leave behind

casu: see line 36

venit: present tense, short "e"

obvius, -a, -um, adj. (with dative), *in*
the way, placed so as to meet, situated
so as to confront

75   **adversarius, adversarii**, m., *adver-*
      sary, opponent

      adversarius: the plaintiff; see line 36

      quo: see line 63

      quo tu turpissime: elliptical; under-
      stand a verb of going

      turpissime: cf. **dulcissime**, line 4

      turpis, -e, adj., *ugly, shameful, disgrace-*
      ful

76   **inclamo, inclamare, inclamavi, in-**
      clamatum, *call out, cry out*

      licet, licere, licuit/licitum est, imper-
      sonal verb, *it is permitted*

      antestor, antestari, antestatus sum,
      call as a witness

      licet antestari: elliptical; *is it permit-*
      ted (to me) *to call* (you) *as a witness?*
      The context makes it clear that this
      is a question even though there is
      no question word or enclitic; stan-
      dard legal phrase; this is the ques-
      tion asked by a plaintiff who wants
      a witness to the legal seizure of a
      defendant who fails to appear in
      court.

      vero, adv., *in fact, indeed, certainly,*
      truly

      vero: possibly with ironic force here

oppono auriculam. rapit in ius: clamor utrimque, undique concursus. sic me servavit Apollo.

77 oppono, opponere, opposui, op-
    positum, *place against, place in front,*
    especially put before someone for ac-
    ceptance, proffer

auricula: see line 20

oppono auriculam: letting the plaintiff touch one's ear was the sign
that one agreed to serve as a witness

oppono auriculam: cf. what is signified by the ears in line 20

ius: see line 39

clamor, clamoris, m., *shout, shouting,*
clamor

utrimque, adv., *on both sides*

clamor utrimque: elliptical; understand est

78 undique, adv., *on all sides, everywhere*

concursus, -us, m., *running to and fro*

undique concursus: elliptical; understand est

Apollo, Apollinis, m., *Apollo,* son of
Jupiter and Latona, brother of Diana, god of archery, music, poetry,
etc.

Apollo: the mention of Apollo, who
is associated with the sun, continues the pun on Fuscus' name.
Fuscus (the dark one) abandons
him, while Apollo (the bright one)
seems to save him. Apollo's connections with poetry and justice
are important as well. Horace, the
poet, appears to be saved by the
intervention of a legal case. It has
been argued, though, that the ending of the poem is ironic and that
by agreeing to serve as a witness
Horace is not saved, but rather, is
caught up in the affairs of his unwanted companion since he will
have to accompany the litigants to
the magistrate.

sic me servavit Apollo: a translation
of the Greek of Homer, *Iliad* 20.443,
where Apollo rescues Hector,
quoted in Greek by Lucilius in his
sixth satire. Horace criticizes Lucilius in Satire 1.10.20 ff. for his use
of Greek words in his Latin satires.

ODE 1.1

Horace begins his lyric collection with this ode addressed to his friend and supporter, Maecenas. In the course of the poem he gives an extended description of the pursuits other people choose to follow. He ends with his own choice, the writing of lyric poetry.

Meter: first or lesser Asclepiadean

**Maecenas atavis edite regibus,
o et praesidium et dulce decus meum:**

---

1   **Maecenas, Maecenatis,** m., *Gaius Cilnius Maecenas,* friend and supporter of Horace and of other contemporary poets, including Vergil; friend and adviser to Augustus (Octavian); vocative. Note the emphatic position of Maecenas' name here. It begins the first poem of Horace's initial lyric collection (*Odes,* Books 1–3). Horace's *Epodes, Satires* Book 1, and *Epistles* Book 1 also begin with an address to Maecenas.

2   **atavus, -i,** m., *a great-great-great grandfather,* or (here) *a remote ancestor*

    editus, -a, -um, adj., "descended from," perfect passive participle of **edo, edere, edidi, editum,** *put forth, give out, give birth to*

rex, regis, m., *king,* here used adjectivally, meaning "royal." Cf. Vergil *Aeneid* 1.273, **regina sacerdos,** for another example of two nouns in apposition where one (**regina**) is used adjectivally, "royal priestess."

atavis edite regibus: Maecenas traced his family background to Etruscan kings.

o, interj., *O* (with vocative)

o et: hiatus (lack of elision) between **o** and **et.**

praesidium, praesidii, n., *protection, defense*

dulcis, -e, adj., *sweet,* (of persons) *dear, beloved;* vocative

decus, decoris, n., *that which adorns or beautifies, honor, glory*

sunt, quos curriculo pulverem Olympicum
collegisse iuvat metaque fervidis

3   **sunt quos: Illi** is the understood antecedent of the relative pronoun **quos**. "There are those whom..." Such a relative clause of characteristic normally takes the subjunctive in prose, but here takes the indicative (**iuvat**). Cf. lines 19, 21 below, **est qui...spernit. Sunt quos** begins a catalog of various occupations (racing, politics, trade, farming, relaxation, war, hunting), which continues through line 28. Understand **iuvat** with **hunc** (7) and **illum** (9) below, which are its direct objects along with **quos**. **Me,** the first word of line 29 signals the shift from others' occupations to that of the speaker of the poem.

curriculum, -i, n., *a running, course, race, racing chariot*

pulvis, pulveris, m., *dust*

Olympicus, -a, -um, adj., *Olympic, Olympian;* Olympia, in Elis, Greece, was the site of the ancient Olympic games, held every four years in honor of Olympian Zeus. The games, founded in 776 BCE, were still held in Horace's lifetime. Olympus was the name of several mountains in Greece, including one in Thessaly considered the home of the gods and another in the region of Elis.

4   **colligo, colligere, collegi, collectum,** *to gather or bring together, collect;* with **pulverem** (3) the idea is the raising of dust in the track through high speed racing.

iuvat: from **iuvo;** used here impersonally; the infinitive **collegisse** is the subject of **iuvat, quos** is the direct object.

meta, -ae, f., *turning point, end.* This is the turning post at either end of the race track. Take **meta...evitata** either as a second subject of **iuvat** (4) or as a subject of **evehit** (6) along with **palma** (5).

fervidus, -a, -um, adj., *boiling, burning, hot, impetuous*

evitata rotis palmaque nobilis   **5**
terrarum dominos evehit ad deos;

hunc, si mobilium turba Quiritium
certat tergeminis tollere honoribus,

---

5   **evitata**: The chariot must go around
the **meta** without hitting it.

rota, -ae, f., *wheel*

palma, -ae, f., *palm tree, palm branch,
palm wreath, token of victory;* subject
of **evehit** (6); metonymy for "victory."

nobilis: transferred epithet; the adjective grammatically modifies
palma rather than the victor.

6   **terrarum**: in plural, "the world."

dominus, -i, m., *master, lord, ruler*

eveho, evehere, evexi, evectum,
carry out, lift up, raise

terrarum dominos: **Dominos** looks
to both the victors in the chariot
race and to the gods and can be
seen as in apposition to another
quos understood from line 3 or as
in apposition to **deos** (6). While the
former may be more appealing in
terms of the general sense of the
poem—the victors become masters
of the world—it is important when
reading Latin, and Horace's poetry
in particular, to preserve such ambiguities. This kind of ambiguity
concerning what modifies what is
very typical of Horace and should
be understood not as lack of clarity
but rather as the poet's attempt to
say more than he could if he narrowed his possibilities to just one
option. Notice the position of **terrarum dominos** between **quos** (3)
and **deos** (6). Remember that Latin
word order is flexible because of

the inflected nature of Latin. Horace exploits this flexibility perhaps
more than any other Latin poet.

3–6   The shifts in construction in lines
3–6, from **collegisse**, an infinitive, as an impersonal subject of
iuvat, to **meta**, a noun, as a second
subject of **iuvat** or as a possible
subject of **evehit**, to **palma** as definite subject of **evehit**, are typical of
Horace's style. Where parallelism
of construction might be expected,
Horace often avoids it. This may
present some initial difficulties,
but the reader who remains open
to these shifts will quickly be on
the road to understanding a basic
feature of the poet's style.

7   **mobilis, -e**, adj., *moveable, changeable,
inconstant, pliant*

turba, -ae. f., *crowd*

Quiris, Quiritis, m., *Roman citizen*

8   **certo, certare, certavi, certatum**, *contend, strive*

tergeminus, -a, -um, *triple*

tollo, tollere, sustuli, sublatum, *lift,
raise, extol, take away, destroy;* understand an **eum** as direct object of
tollere.

honor (honos), honoris, m., *honor, office*

tergeminis...honoribus: "triple offices" (aedile, praetor, consul) or
possibly "reiterated applause," the
suggestion of Porphyrio, the ancient commentator on Horace.

illum, si proprio condidit horreo,
quicquid de Libycis verritur areis.   **10**

gaudentem patrios findere sarculo
agros Attalicis condicionibus

numquam demoveas, ut trabe Cypria
Myrtoum pavidus nauta secet mare;

9   **proprius, -a, -um**, adj., *one's own, personal*

   condo, condere, condidi, conditum, *found, establish, store up*

   horreum, -i, n., *storehouse, granary*

10   **Libycus, -a, -um**, adj., *Libyan*, sometimes *African*, in general

   verro, verrere, versum, *sweep together, collect*

   area, -ae, f., *open space, threshing floor*

11   **gaudeo, gaudere, gavisus sum**, *delight in, rejoice*

   patrius, -a, -um, adj., *of a father, ancestral, native, inherited, belonging to one's country*

   findo, findere, fidi, fissum, *split, separate, divide*

   sarculum, -i, n., *hoe*

12   **Attalicus, -a, -um**, adj., *of King Attalus or his dynasty, rich, splendid;* King Attalus III of Pergamum, in Asia Minor, known as the other Attalids before him for his wealth, left his territory to the Romans in 133 BCE. The wealth of the Attalids was proverbial for the Romans, like that of Croesus for the Greeks.

   condicio, condicionis, f., *condition, term, agreement*

   Attalicis condicionibus: suggests a huge amount of money

13   **ut:** with subjunctive, **secet** (see below, line 14)

   trabs, trabis, f., *beam of wood, trunk of tree, ship*

   Cyprius, -a, -um, adj., *Cyprian, of the island of Cyprus;* Cyprus was famous for its trees and its shipbuilding.

14   **Myrtous, -a, -um**, adj., *Myrtoan;* **Myrtoum...mare**, Myrtoan Sea; southwestern part of the Aegean Sea between the Peloponnese and the Cyclades; note how **Myrtoum... mare** surrounds **pavidus nauta**, the frightened sailor. Horace often uses word order as a vehicle for meaning. While the idea is that no one could get the one who is enjoying working his ancestral fields to go to sea, the Latin "shows" the reader through word order a "picture" of a sailor enveloped by the sea. Horace often images what he is negating. Cf. the note on line 34 below, as well as notes on Ode 1.23.

   pavidus, -a, -um, adj., *frightened, terrified, trembling, fearful*

   seco, secare, secui, sectum, *cut, divide, traverse;* subjunctive because of indirect command introduced by **demoveas**, which functions here as a verb of persuading

luctantem Icariis fluctibus Africum 15
mercator metuens otium et oppidi

laudat rura sui, mox reficit rates
quassas indocilis pauperiem pati.

est, qui nec veteris pocula Massici
nec partem solido demere de die 20

spernit, nunc viridi membra sub arbuto
stratus, nunc ad aquae lene caput sacrae;

---

15 **luctor, luctari, luctatus sum**, *wrestle, struggle, contend*

Icarius, -a, -um, adj., *of Icarus, Icarian;* Icarus, the son of Daedalus, drowned in the Aegean Sea while flying from Crete with wings his father had made. He gives his name to the area where he landed, the Icarian Sea, which is part of the Aegean. Cf. Horace Ode 2.20.13 for Horace's comparison of himself to Icarus.

Icariis fluctibus: dative case, with **luctor**

Africus (ventus) or **Africus**, *south-western, stormy wind*

16 **mercator, mercatoris**, m. *merchant*

otium, otii, n., *free time, leisure, peace*

oppidum, -i, n., *town*

17 **reficio, reficere, refeci, refectum**, *make again, repair*

ratis, ratis, f., *raft, boat, ship*

18 **quatio, quatere, quassum**, *shake, beat upon*

indocilis, -e, adj., *untrained, hard to instruct*

pauperies, pauperiei, f., *poverty*

pati: epexegetical infinitive explaining the adjective **indocilis**

19 **vetus, veteris**, adj., *old*

poculum, -i, n., *cup, drink*

Massicus, -a, -um, adj., *Massic;* **Massicum (vinum)**, *wine from the area of* **Mons Massicus**, in the Campanian region of Italy

20 **demo, demere, dempsi, demptum**, *take away, subtract*

21 **sperno, spernere, sprevi, spretum**, *remove, reject, spurn*

viridis, -e, adj., *green, fresh, young*

membrum, -i, n., *limb or member of the body, limb, member, part of anything*

arbutus, -i, f., *the wild strawberry or arbutus tree*

22 **sterno, sternere, stravi, stratum**, *stretch out, spread out, level, overthrow*

lenis, -e, adj., *smooth, gentle, mild*

caput, capitis, n., *head, person, person's life;* (here) *source*

multos castra iuvant et lituo tubae
permixtus sonitus bellaque matribus

detestata; manet sub Iove frigido   25
venator tenerae coniugis inmemor,

seu visa est catulis cerva fidelibus,
seu rupit teretes Marsus aper plagas.

me doctarum hederae praemia frontium
dis miscent superis, me gelidum nemus   30

---

23   **multos castra iuvant**: Notice how
      simply stated this is: direct object,
      subject, verb. It contrasts with
      the much more extended phrases
      found with **iuvat** (4) earlier in the
      poem. This kind of stylistic varia-
      tion is typical of Horace.

      lituus, litui, m., *curved cavalry trum-
      pet*

      lituo: dative or ablative case with
      permixtus

      tuba, -ae, f., *straight war trumpet*

24   **permisceo, permiscere, permiscui,
      permixtum**, *mix together, confuse*

      sonitus, -us, m., *sound*

      matribus: dative of agent with per-
      fect passive participle

25   **detestor, detestari, detestatus sum**,
      pray against, curse; **detestata**, al-
      though deponent, is passive in
      sense here

      Iuppiter, Iovis, m., *Jupiter,* supreme
      god of the Romans, god of sky and
      weather; here, by metonymy, *air,
      sky*

      sub Iove: under the open air

26   **venator, venatoris**, m., *hunter*

      tener, tenera, tenerum, adj., *tender,
      delicate, soft, young*

      coniunx, coniugis, c., *spouse, wife,
      husband*

inmemor, inmemoris, adj., *forgetful,
unmindful*

27   **catulus, -i**, m., *a young animal*, espe-
      cially *a young dog*

      cerva, -ae, f., *deer, female deer*

      fidelis, -e, adj., *faithful*

28   **rumpo, rumpere, rupi, ruptum**,
      break, shatter, destroy

      teres, teretis, adj., *rounded, smooth,
      polished*

      Marsus, -a, -um, adj., *Marsian, of the
      Marsi,* a people of central Italy

      aper, apri, m., *wild boar*

      plaga, -ae, f., *hunting net, trap*

29   **doctus, -a, -um**, adj., *learned, taught*

      hedera, -ae, f., *ivy*

      hederae: poetic plural

      praemium, praemii, n., *prize, reward*

      frons, frontis, f., *forehead, brow, front*

30   **dis**: dative plural; alternate form for
      deis

      misceo, miscere, miscui, mixtum,
      mix, mingle

      superus, -a, -um, adj., *upper, higher*

      gelidus, -a, -um, adj., *cold, icy*

      nemus, nemoris, n., *grove, forest*

Nympharumque leves cum Satyris chori
secernunt populo, si neque tibias

Euterpe cohibet, nec Polyhymnia
Lesboum refugit tendere barbiton.

quodsi me lyricis vatibus inseres,   35
sublimi feriam sidera vertice.

31 **nympha, -ae**, f., *nymph*, semi-divine
    female spirit of nature

    levis, -e, adj., *light, swift, gentle, unim-
    portant, fickle*

    Satyrus, -i, m., *satyr;* demi-god of
    wild places, especially forests, hav-
    ing the form of a man with some
    animal characteristics

    chorus, -i, m., *choral dance, people sing-
    ing and dancing, crowd, troop*

32 **secerno, secernere, secrevi, secre-
    tum**, *separate, distinguish*

    tibia, -ae, f., *shin bone, tibia, pipe, flute*

33 **Euterpe, Euterpes** f., *Euterpe,* one of
    the Muses. The Muses, daughters
    of Zeus and Mnemosyne, were
    goddesses who presided over the
    arts.

    **cohibeo, cohibere, cohibui, cohibi-
    tum**, *hold together, hold back, confine*

    Polyhymnia, -ae, f., *Polyhymnia,* one
    of the Muses

34 **Lesbous, -a, -um**, adj., *Lesbian,* of the
    Greek island of Lesbos, birthplace
    of the poets Sappho and Alcaeus

    refugio, refugere, refugi, *run away,
    avoid*

**tendo, tendere, tetendi, tentum/ten-
sum**, *stretch out, extend, proceed*

barbitos, barbiti, m., *lyre*

barbiton: Greek accusative singular

Lesboum...barbiton: Notice how
this phrase, which encompasses
the whole line, imitates the idea
of "stretching." The word order
here, as in line 14 above, is bound
up with the meaning of the line.
The words themselves enact the
stretching that the speaker needs
from Polyhymnia.

35 **quodsi**, conj., *but if*

    lyricus, -a, -um, adj., *of the lyre, lyric*

    vates, vatis, c., *prophet, singer, poet*

    insero, inserere, inserui, insertum,
    introduce, insert, put in or among

    inseres: the subject is "you, Maece-
    nas," the poem's addressee, but,
    perhaps, "you, the reader" as well

36 **sublimis, -e**, adj., *high, raised, elevated,
    sublime, lofty*

    ferio, ferire, *strike, hit*

    sidus, sideris, n., *star, sky* (plural)

    vertex, verticis, m., *head, summit*

ODE 1.5

In this ode sea, fire, and storm combine as images for erotic engagement. Pyrrha, the youth, and the speaker become entangled in a vision of love present, past, and future. While the more specific involvement of the speaker revealed in the final stanza is something of a surprise, his presence is felt from the beginning of the poem where he interrogates the present relationship between Pyrrha and her young man.

Meter: fourth Asclepiadean

Quis multa gracilis te puer in rosa
perfusus liquidis urget odoribus
    grato, Pyrrha, sub antro?
        cui flavam religas comam

---

1   **quis**: used here as interrogative adjective modifying **puer**

      gracilis, -e, adj., *slender, thin*

      rosa, -ae, f., *rose*

      rosa: singular as collective

      multa...rosa: chiastic arrangement of words with **te** in the middle; the young man and the roses surround or embrace the direct object

2   **perfundo, perfundere, perfudi, perfusum**, *pour over, fill with*

      urgeo, urgere, ursi, *push, press upon*

3   **gratus, -a, -um**, adj., *pleasing*

      Pyrrha, -ae, f., *Pyrrha*, woman's name; the Greek word for fire (**pyr**) contained in this name may suggest a fiery nature or flame-colored hair.

      sub: possible meaning here, *down in* (Cf. *OLD* A.2.)

antrum, i, n., *cave, hollow space*

1–3 Note the word order in these lines. In line 1, **te** is surrounded by the **gracilis...puer**, which in turn is surrounded by **multa...rosa**. Mystery begins the line, with an interrogative word (**quis**), and then two adjectives (**multa** and **gracilis**). The rest of the line, which follows the diaeresis, completes the meaning of these initial words. The addressee's name is not revealed until line 3, and once again, as in line 1, she is enclosed within a frame (**grato...antro**).

4   **flavus, -a, -um**, adj., *yellow, golden, blonde, auburn*

      religo, religare, religavi, religatum: *tie, fasten behind; untie* (occasionally), cf. Catullus 63, line 84

simplex munditiis? heu quotiens fidem   5
mutatosque deos flebit et aspera
    nigris aequora ventis
        emirabitur insolens,

qui nunc te fruitur credulus aurea,
qui semper vacuam, semper amabilem   10
    sperat, nescius aurae
        fallacis. miseri, quibus

---

5   **simplex, simplicis**, adj., *simple, artless, plain*

    munditia, -ae, f., *neatness, elegance*

    quotiens, adv., *how often*

    fides, fidei, f., *trust, belief, faith, honesty, honor*

    fidem: understand **mutatos** (changed) with **fidem** as well as **deos**

6   **fleo, flere, flevi, fletum**, *weep for, lament*

    asper, aspera, asperum, adj., *rough, violent*

6–7   **aspera / nigris aequora ventis**: an example of synchysis, or interlocked word order

7   **niger, nigra, nigrum**, *black, dark, gloomy*

    aequor, aequoris, n., *a flat level surface, the flat surface of the sea*, (often used in plural)

8   **emiror, emirari**, *wonder at exceedingly, be astonished at*

    insolens, insolentis, adj., *unaccustomed, excessive*

9   **fruor, frui, fructus sum**, *enjoy* (with ablative)

    credulus, -a, -um, adj., *credulous, trustful*

    aureus, -a, -um, adj., *golden, splendid*

10   **vacuus, -a, -um**, adj., *empty, free, available*

11   **nescius, -a, -um**, adj., *ignorant, unaware*

    aura, -ae, f., *breeze*

12   **fallax, fallacis**, adj., *deceitful, deceptive*

    miseri: understand **sunt** (*unhappy are they...*)

intemptata nites. me tabula sacer
votiva paries indicat uvida
  suspendisse potenti
   vestimenta maris deo.   **15**

[handwritten annotations: "sacred votive", "the wall shows wet from the sea", "clothes hung up to powerful god"]

13 **me**: Note the emphatic position of this word which shifts attention from the young man and Pyrrha to the speaker of the poem. It begins a sentence and appears right after the diaeresis in the line.

 intemptatus, -a, -um, adj., *untried, unattempted*

 niteo, nitere, nitui, *shine, be radiant with beauty*

 tabula, -ae, f., *board, plank, writing tablet, (votive) tablet*

13–16 **me...deo**: These final lines add a complication to the poem, namely, the involvement of the speaker. Their almost convoluted word order reflects this complication.

14 **votiva, -a, -um**, *votive, relating to a vow*

 tabula...votiva: meter shows both are ablative

 paries, parietis, m., *wall*

 indico, indicare, indicavi, indicatum, *point out, show, declare*

 uvidus, -a, -um, *wet*

 suspendo, suspendere, suspendi, suspensum, *hang up*

 suspendisse: those who escaped from being shipwrecked often made a votive offering to Neptune, god of the sea. Here the wet garments, themselves, are hung up.

 potens, potentis, *able, powerful, potent*

16 **vestimentum, -i**, n., *clothes, garments*

ODE 1.9

This poem travels from a wide, opening vista of Mount Soracte to a final focus on the specificity of a finger—or is it the arms? Contrasts abound: youth and age, green and white, warm and cold. While the advice given to Thaliarchus (and the reader), and the speaker himself (?) may at first seem clear, the final "spin-off" of the poem does not provide closure.

Meter: Alcaic

**Vides, ut alta stet nive candidum
Soracte, nec iam sustineant onus
   silvae laborantes, geluque
      flumina constiterint acuto?**

---

1   **vides**: questions sometimes do occur in Latin without the enclitic, **-ne,** or another question indicator; some texts punctuate this sentence with a period instead of a question mark.

ut: (here) interrogative adverb, *how*

ut: introducing dependent exclamatory clauses in the subjunctive, **stet, sustineant, constiterint** (*OLD*, under **ut**, A.2.b)

nix, nivis, f., *snow*

candidus, -a, -um, adj., *bright, radiant, white*

2   **Soracte, Soractis**, n., *Soracte,* mountain in the south of Etruria

sustineo, sustinere, sustinui, sustentum, *hold up, support, withstand*

onus, oneris, n., *burden*

3   **gelu, -us**, n., *frost, cold, chill*

4   **flumen, fluminis**, n., *river, waters of a river*

consto, constare, constiti, *stand together, stand still*

acutus, -a, -um, *sharp, severe*

dissolve frigus ligna super foco 5
large reponens atque benignius
   deprome quadrimum Sabina,
     o Thaliarche, merum diota.

permitte divis cetera, qui simul
stravere ventos aequore fervido 10
   deproeliantis, nec cupressi
     nec veteres agitantur orni.

5   **dissolvo, dissolvere, dissolvi, disso-**
       lutum, *dissolve, free*
     frigus, frigoris, n., *cold*
     lignum, -i, n., *wood* (often in plural)
     super, preposition with ablative,
       above
     focus, -i, m., *hearth, fireplace*

6   **large**, adv., *generously, plentifully*
     repono, reponere, reposui, reposi-
       tum, *put down, place*
     benigne, adv., *lavishly, liberally*
     benignius: comparative adverb

7   **depromo, depromere, deprompsi,**
       depromptum, *bring out, produce*
     quadrimus, -a, -um, *four-year-old*
     Sabinus, -a, -um, adj., *Sabine;* the Sa-
       bines were a people of central Italy.

8   **Thaliarchus, -i**, m., *Thaliarchus,* man's
       name, whose Greek roots mean
       "festivity" (**thalia**) and "ruler"
       (**arch**).

     merus, -a, -um, *pure, unmixed;* with
       vinum, or with **vinum** under-
       stood, *wine not mixed with water*
     diota, -ae, f., *two-handled wine jar*

9   **divus, -a, -um**, adj., *divine;* as noun,
       divus, -i, m., *god*

10   **sterno, sternere, stravi, stratum**,
       stretch out, spread out, level, over-
       throw
     aequore = (in) aequore
     fervidus, -a, -um, adj., *boiling, burn-*
       ing, hot, impetuous

11   **deproelior, deproeliari,** *fight fiercely,*
       struggle violently; verb appears only
       here in Latin literature
     cupressus, -i, f., *cypress;* the cypress
       had funereal associations

12   **agito, agitare, agitavi, agitatum,**
       drive, agitate, excite
     ornus, -i, f., *flowering ash tree*

quid sit futurum cras, fuge quaerere, et
quem Fors dierum cumque dabit, lucro
    adpone, nec dulcis amores   **15**
       sperne puer neque tu choreas,

donec virenti canities abest
morosa. nunc et campus et areae
    lenesque sub noctem susurri
       composita repetantur hora,   **20**

---

13   **quid...cras**: indirect question dependent on **quaerere**; **futurum** is a predicate adjective agreeing with **quid**

    fuge quaerere: functionally equivalent to negative imperative, **noli** + infinitive, however considering the importance of time and its flight in this poem and others of Horace, it is best to retain the sense of "fleeing" in **fuge**.

14   **quem...cumque**: tmesis, **quemcumque**

    fors, fortis, f., *chance, luck*

    dierum: partitive genitive with **quemcumque**

    lucrum, -i, n., *profit, gain*

15   **adpono, adponere, adposui, adpositum**, *add; treat as, count as* (with **lucrum**); **lucro**: dative; **lucro adpone**, *add to gain, count as gain*

    amores: literally "loves," can mean "love affairs"

16   **sperno, spernere, sprevi, spretum**, *remove, reject, scorn*

    puer: vocative; likely refers to Thaliarchus, but lines 13 ff. seem to offer more generalizing advice as well as advice to the specific addressee.

    chorea, -ae, f., *dance*

    choreas: direct object of **sperne**, along with **amores**

17   **vireo, virere, virui**, *be green, fresh, youthful*

canities, canitiei, f., *white or grey coloring, grey or white hair*; by metonymy, *old age*

virenti canities: example of **callida iunctura**, or clever arrangement, a device used often by Horace. The term comes from Horace's Ars Poetica: Epistle 2.3.47–48. The juxtaposition of these two words captures the contrasts in the poem between green and white, young and old, etc.

18   **morosus, -a, -um**, adj., *difficult*

    nunc: note the emphatic position of this monosyllabic word as it begins a sentence mid-line, a sentence that extends until the end of the poem (line 24). The two **nunc**s, along with the connective words, structure these lines (18–24). The outline is: **nunc et...et...-que; nunc et...-que**.

    campus, -i, m., *plain, level surface; plain, field*; often refers specifically to the Campus Martius in Rome

    area, -ae, f., *open space, threshing floor*

18–19   **campus, areae, susurri**: all subjects of **repetantur**

19   **lenis, -e**, adj., *smooth, gentle, mild, soft*

    sub noctem: just before night

    susurrus, -i, m., *whispering*

20   **compono, componere, composui, compositum**, *put together, arrange, compose, calm, bury*

    repeto, repetere, repetivi, repetitum, *seek again, recall, resume*

nunc et latentis proditor intumo
gratus puellae risus ab angulo
pignusque dereptum lacertis
aut digito male pertinaci.

21   **lateo, latere, latui,** *lie hidden;* **latentis** modifies **puellae**

proditor, proditoris, m., *betrayer, traitor;* in apposition to **risus**

intumus, -a, -um, adj., *innermost, most secret*

21–22   **intumo...angulo:** hyperbaton; wide separation between adjective and modifier. Note also how the adjective precedes the noun, a common practice in Horace that differs from typical Latin prose word order. The hyperbaton, here, creates a framing effect.

22   **gratus:** modifies **risus**

risus, -us, m., *laughter*

angulus, -i, m., *angle, corner*

22–23   **risus, pignus:** additional subjects of **repetantur**

23   **pignus, pigneris/pignoris,** n., *pledge, token, symbol*

deripio, deripere, deripui, dereptum, *tear down, snatch away;* **dereptum** modifies **pignus**

lacertus, -i, m., *upper arm;* **lacertis** and **digito,** datives of separation with **dereptum**

24   **digitus, -i,** m., *finger*

male, adv., *badly, insufficiently, wickedly, scarcely*

pertinax, pertinacis, adj., *very tenacious, holding fast, persisting*

male pertinaci: literally, *badly holding fast.* Some take **male** here as a quasi-negative almost equivalent to **non.** While such a use of **male** is not uncommon, the adverb's literal meaning, "badly," is significant, for it would suggest not that the girl puts up hardly any resistance, but rather that her resistance is not very successful.

18–24   Lines 18–24 contain a kind of "spin-off" ending for the poem. There is a furtive, elusive, and indeterminate quality to these final lines. **Repetantur** suggests both "things to be sought" and "things to be recalled or remembered." The speaker simultaneously gives injunctions about behavior as well as topics for recollection. **Composita...hora** suggests both a quiet time (which could occur in the solitude of recollection) as well as an arranged "date." The possible suggestion of a game between boy and girl is countered by the violence of the language of their interaction (**dereptum**). The poem ends with the ambiguous **male pertinaci.**

ODE 1.11

This ode to Leuconoe has elements of a serious, philosophical statement of Epicurean values (e.g., it is better not to foresee the future, it is better to endure whatever will be) as well as elements of an attempted seduction of Leuconoe. How one reads this poem will depend in part on how one interprets the role and interests of the speaker. Is he attempting to impart wisdom for its own sake? Or is he developing a rhetorical strategy whose purpose is winning over Leuconoe for himself? The long, yet rapidly moving, greater Asclepiadean line emphasizes the theme of the speed with which time proceeds.

Meter: fifth or greater Asclepiadean

Tu ne quaesieris (scire nefas), quem mihi, quem tibi
finem di dederint, Leuconoe, nec Babylonios

---

1   **ne**: with perfect subjunctives, **quaesieris** and **temptaris** in prohibition, or negative command; this construction is equivalent to **noli(te)** plus infinitive

    nefas, n., indeclinable, *crime, offense against divine law, sacrilege*

    nefas: understand **est**

    quem mihi, quem tibi: note the word order, which joins and makes parallel the speaker and his addressee

2   **finem**: take with each **quem**

    di: alternate form of **dei**, nominative plural

dederint: perfect subjunctive in indirect question dependent on **quem finem**

Leuconoe, Leuconoes, f., *Leuconoe,* woman's name, vocative. The name, from Greek **leukos** (clear, bright, white) and **nous** (mind) may suggest equally, "clear-minded" or "empty-minded."

2–3   **Babylonios...numeros**: Babylonian numbers; astrological tables predicting the future

temptaris numeros. ut melius, quidquid erit, pati!
seu pluris hiemes, seu tribuit Iuppiter ultimam,

quae nunc oppositis debilitat pumicibus mare   5
Tyrrhenum: sapias, vina liques et spatio brevi

3   **temptaris**: syncopated form of
    tempta(ve)ris

    ut, interrogative adverb, *how* (exclam-
    atory use, cf. *OLD*, under **ut**, A.2.)

    melior, melius, comparative adjec-
    tive, *better*

    ut melius: understand **est**

    quidquid erit: direct object of **pati**

4   **pluris: -is = -es** (accusative plural)

    hiems, hiemis, f., *winter, storm;* me-
    tonymy for "year," but the sense of
    "winter" as a way of reckoning the
    years is significant for the theme of
    death that pervades the poem. Cf.
    Ode 1.9, where winter also leads
    to thoughts of what to enjoy in the
    moment.

    pluris hiemes: understand **tribuit**
    (present) or a future form of the
    verb

    tribuo, tribuere, tribui, tributum,
    allot, assign; **tribuit** (present or per-
    fect)

    ultimam: understand **hiemem**

5   **oppositus, -a, -um**, adj., *placed against,
    hostile*

**debilito, debilitare, debilitavi, de-
bilitatum**, *weaken*

pumex, pumicis, m., *pumice-stone*

oppositis...pumicibus: note that the
stones are what make the sea become weakened, not the reverse

6   **Tyrrhenus, -a, -um**, adj., *Tyrrhenian,
    Etruscan;* **mare Tyrrhenum**, *Tyrrhe-
    nian Sea*, the sea lying between the
    west coast of Italy, and Sardinia,
    and Sicily; direct object of **debilitat**

    sapio, sapere, sapivi, *have taste, be
    wise;* **sapias** operates on both a
    sensory and an intellectual level

    sapias, liques: jussive subjunctives

    vina: plural for singular

    liquo, liquare, liquavi, liquatum,
    melt, strain; the Romans strained
    their wine before drinking it to re-
    move the sediment.

    spatium, spatii, n., *space, period of
    time*

    spatio brevi: probably best taken as
    a causal ablative (because of the
    brief time [of our lives]) or (be-
    cause of the brief time [appropriate
    for our hopes])

**spem longam reseces. dum loquimur, fugerit invida
aetas: carpe diem, quam minimum credula postero.**

7   **reseco, resecare, resecui, resectum**,
cut back, prune, restrain

reseces: jussive subjunctive, like **sapias, liques**

fugerit: effective use of the future
perfect tense; while the conversation takes place, time "will have
fled."

invidus, -a, -um, adj., *envious, jealous;*
invida personifies time; **invida
aetas** almost becomes a third party
jealous of Leuconoe and the speaker

8   **aetas, aetatis**, f., *time, age*

carpo, carpere, carpsi, carptum,
pluck, seize

carpe diem: this Horatian phrase has
become very famous. For poems in
English that utilize the **carpe diem**
theme, see Marvell's "To his Coy
Mistress," and Herrick's "To the
Virgins, to make much of Time."

quam minimum: **quam** with the superlative (*as...as possible*); *to the least
extent possible*

credulus, -a, -um, adj., *credulous,
trustful;* takes dative

posterus, -a, -um, adj., *next, following,
future, later*

postero: this adjective does not mod-
ify a noun; understand **diei**, (because of **diem** earlier in the line)
or, somewhat more humorously,
viro

ODE 1.13

In this poem the speaker's desire for Lydia is mediated by the relationship Lydia has with Telephus. Her enthusiastic praise of Telephus' body and the evidence upon her body of their sexual activity are what drive the speaker's reactions. While he attempts to dissuade Lydia from her relationship with Telephus, the wildness of his own reactions makes him seem little different from his version of Telephus. The poem ends on a somewhat ambiguous note. Who are the happy ones? And how do they relate to the trio of Lydia, Telephus, and the speaker?

Meter: second Asclepiadean

Cum tu, Lydia, Telephi
    cervicem roseam, cerea Telephi
laudas brachia, vae meum
    fervens difficili bile tumet iecur.

tunc nec mens mihi, nec color   5
    certa sede manet, umor et in genas
furtim labitur arguens,
    quam lentis penitus macerer ignibus.

---

1   **Lydia, -ae**, f., *Lydia*, woman's name
      Telephus, -i, m., *Telephus*, man's name; note the repetition of his name at the end of the next line

2   **cervix, cervicis**, f., *neck*
      roseus, -a, -um, adj., *rosy*
      cereus, -a, -um, adj., *waxen, supple*

3   **brachium, brachii**, n., *arm*
      vae, interjection, *alas, woe*

3–4 **meum...iecur**: hyperbaton; cf. note on Ode 1.9.21–22

4   **fervens, ferventis**, adj., *boiling, seething*
      bilis, bilis, f., *gall, bile, anger*
      tumeo, tumere, tumui, *swell*
      iecur, iecoris, n., *liver, the seat of the*

feelings; bile, secreted by the liver, was thought to produce anger

6   **certus, -a, -um**, adj., *certain, definite*
      sedes, sedis, f., *seat, site, home*
      umor, umoris, m., *moisture, liquid*
      gena, -ae, f., *cheek*

7   **furtim**, adv., *secretly*
      labor, labi, lapsus sum, *glide, slip, pass*
      arguo, arguere, argui, argutum, *prove, show*

8   **quam**: modifies **penitus**
      lentus, -a, -um, adj., *slow, lingering, unresponsive*
      penitus, adv., *deeply*
      macero, macerare, maceravi, maceratum, *soften, make weak, torment*

uror, seu tibi candidos
    turparunt umeros inmodicae mero   10
rixae, sive puer furens
    inpressit memorem dente labris notam.

non, si me satis audias,
    speres perpetuum dulcia barbare
laedentem oscula, quae Venus   15
    quinta parte sui nectaris imbuit.

---

9   **uro, urere, ussi, ustum**, *burn;* in passive, *be on fire*

    seu: correlative with **sive** (11)

    candidus, -a, -um, adj., *bright, radiant, white*

10   **turpo, turpare, turpavi, turpatum**, *make ugly*

    turparunt: syncopated form of **turpa(ve)runt**

    umerus, -i, m., *shoulder*

    merus, -a, -um, adj., *pure, unmixed*

11   **rixa, -ae**, f., *fight*

    puer, pueri, m., *boy, non-adult male, male beloved,* (young) *male slave*

    furens, furentis adj., *mad, wild*

12   **inprimo, inprimere, inpressi, inpressum**, *press upon*

    memor, memoris, adj., *mindful, remembering*

labrum, -i, n., *lip*

nota, -ae, f., *mark, sign, wine of a specified quality or vintage*

14   **perpetuus, -a, -um**, adj., *continuing, permanent, connected*

    barbare, adv., *roughly, cruelly*

15   **laedo, laedere, laesi, laesum**, *harm, strike*

    osculum, -i, n., *kiss, mouth, lips* (as used in kissing)

    venus, veneris, f., *Venus,* Roman goddess of love; *love, charm, sexual activity; best throw at dice*

16   **quinta...parte**: fifth part = one-fifth

    nectar, nectaris, n., *nectar,* drink of the gods

    imbuo, imbuere, imbui, imbutum, *wet, fill, inspire*

    imbuit: present or perfect

felices ter et amplius,
    quos inrupta tenet copula, nec malis
divolsus querimoniis
    suprema citius solvet amor die.   20

17–20   Commentators have traditionally taken **inrupta** to mean "unbroken" and have understood **nec** twice, once with **divolsus** and again with **solvet**. **Inrupta**, as "unbroken," is unprecedented in Latin and taking **nec** twice, while possible, is not necessary. A traditional reading of the last four lines yields the following: "Happy three times and more are those whom an *unbroken* bond holds, and whose love, torn apart by *no* serious complaints, will *not* loosen them sooner than the final day!" Another possible reading, which allows for the standard meaning of **inrupta**, would be: "Happy three times and more are those whom an *interrupted* bond holds and a love torn apart by serious complaints will *not* loosen sooner than the final day!" The former reading describes an idealized love with no difficulties that lasts until the "final day." The latter reading describes a love whose power is based not on its problem-free nature, but rather on its ability to endure despite difficulties. Cf. Ancona, *Time and the Erotic in Horace's Odes*, 121–28, for an argument in favor of the latter reading.

17   **ter**, adv., *three times*

     amplius, adv., *more*

18   **inruptus, -a, -um**, *broken into, interrupted; unbroken*

     copula, -ae, f., *bond, link*

19   **divello, divellere, divelli, divolsum**, *tear apart*

     querimonia, -ae, f., *complaint*

20   **citius**, adv., *quicker, sooner*

     solvo, solvere, solvi, solutum, *loosen, break up*

     suprema...die: *final day*, i.e., *death*

ODE 1.22

Catullus wrote only two poems in the Sapphic meter, Poems 11 and 51. Poem 51 is Catullus' translation or adaptation of Sappho's famous Poem 31, which details the experiencing of desire. Catullus adapts that poem for his own purposes, in part by making "Lesbia" its addressee. Poem 11, his only other poem in Sapphics, is a blunt farewell to his girlfriend. Horace clearly had Sappho 31 and Catullus Poems 11 and 51 in mind when composing this poem. As is mentioned below in the notes, there are specific echoes of their language. The poet/lover, though, in this poem is very different from those in Sappho and Catullus. This poet/lover is not overwhelmed by desire, but rather constructs a love that incorporates the notion of invulnerability.

Meter: Sapphic

Integer vitae scelerisque purus
non eget Mauris iaculis neque arcu,
nec venenatis gravida sagittis,
   Fusce, pharetra,

---

1   **integer, integra, integrum**, adj., *whole, untouched, upright*

   vitae: genitive of reference, stating respect with which the adjective, **integer**, is applicable; in classical Latin an ablative of respect would be used more typically

   scelus, sceleris, n., *wrongdoing, crime, affliction*

   sceleris: genitive of reference with **purus**; see definition of this genitive above (note on **vitae**)

   integer...purus: note the chiastic arrangement of the words,
   a   b   b   a
   integer vitae scelerisque purus.

2   **egeo, egere, egui**, *need, want* (with ablative)

   Maurus, -a, -um, adj., *Moorish, African*

   iaculum, -i, n., *javelin*

   arcus, -us, m., *bow*

3   **venenatus, -a, -um**, adj., *poisonous*

   gravidus, -a, -um, adj., *laden, weighed down*

4   **Fuscus, -i**, m., *Aristius Fuscus,* Horace's literary friend in Satire 1.10.83, the person to whom Epistle 1.10 is addressed—and there he and Horace are linked as "twins," but separated by their love for the city and the country, respectively—and the character who refuses to save Horace from his unwanted companion in Satire 1.9 (**Ibam forte via sacra**). His appearance here in a poem about the poet's invulnerability can be seen as an "answer" to his refusal to help the poet in Satire 1.9. In the city the poet needed help and did not receive it from Fuscus; here, in the country and in remote lands he claims he is invulnerable.

   pharetra, -ae, f., *quiver*

· 41 ·

sive per Syrtis iter aestuosas   5
sive facturus per inhospitalem
Caucasum, vel quae loca fabulosus
   lambit Hydaspes.

namque me silva lupus in Sabina,
dum meam canto Lalagen et ultra   10
terminum curis vagor expeditis,
   fugit inermem,

---

5   **Syrtis, Syrtis**, f., *Syrtis* (especially plural), name of two areas of sandy flats on the coast between Carthage and Cyrene; whole desert region next to this coast. Cato the Younger, the anti-Caesarian Stoic who chose to commit suicide rather than give in to the opposition, made a famous march across the Syrtes in 47 BCE. The integrity for which Cato was known may be suggested by the first word of this poem, **integer.**

    iter, itineris, n., *journey*

    aestuosus, -a, -um, adj., *very hot, agitated*

5–6 **sive...sive**: The form in which the catalog of places is presented recalls Catullus Poem 11 whose geographical catalog also repeats the word **sive** in enumerating alternatives.

7   **Caucasus, -i**, m., *Caucasus Mountains.* The Caucasus may evoke Pompey the Great, the first Roman general to have reached the area, or perhaps Alexander the Great who, while not reaching the Caucasus, did reach the Hindu-Kush, which was later identified with the Caucasus.

    quae loca: here, the antecedent (**loca**) is incorporated into the relative clause

    fabulosus, -a, -um, adj., *legendary, storied*

8   **lambo, lambere, lambi**, *lick, wash*

    Hydaspes, Hydaspis, m., *Hydaspes,* tributary of river Indus, the Jhelum; Horace calls this river **fuscus** in Satire 2.8.14. **Fuscus, -a, -um** is an adjective meaning "dark." Hydaspes, then, would recall Aristius Fuscus. For further punning on Fuscus' name, cf. note on Apollo, line 78 of Satire 1.9. That Horace calls the Hydaspes **fabulosus** is self-referential, for the river is "storied" in part because Horace has *written* about it before, in Satire 2.8. The river Hydaspes is associated with Alexander the Great, who in 326 BCE won a great military victory there and sailed down the river.

9   **lupus, -i**, m., *wolf*

    silva...in Sabina: Horace's country home, his Sabine farm, was located in Sabine territory.

10   **canto, cantare, cantavi, cantatum**, *sing, sing about, recite*

    Lalage, Lalages, f., *Lalage,* woman's name; Greek for "chatterer"

    Lalagen: Greek accusative

    ultra, preposition with accusative, *beyond*

11   **terminus, -i**, m., *boundary line, limit*

    cura, -ae, f., *care, concern, worry, a person or thing constituting an object of care*

    vagor, vagari, vagatus sum, *wander*

    expedio, expedire, expedivi, expeditum, *free, extricate, release*

12   **fugit**: perfect tense, not present, because the "u" is long

    inermis, -e, adj., *unarmed*

quale portentum neque militaris
Daunias latis alit aesculetis,
nec Iubae tellus generat, leonum   15
    arida nutrix.

pone me, pigris ubi nulla campis
arbor aestiva recreatur aura,
quod latus mundi nebulae malusque
    Iuppiter urget,   20

---

13 **portentum, -i**, n., *portent, abnormal phenomenon*

quale portentum: accusative, direct object of **alit** (14)

14 **Daunias, Dauniadis**, f., *Apulia*, region of southeastern Italy; Daunus was a legendary king of Apulia; Horace comes from the town of Venusia on the border between Apulia and Lucania.

alo, alere, alui, altum, *nourish*

aesculetum, -i, n., *oak forest*

15 **Iuba, -ae**, m., *Juba*, Juba I, Numidian king who supported Pompey in the civil war; Juba II, son of Juba I, fought for Octavian (Augustus) at the battle of Actium, made king of Maurentania by Augustus, known for his learning

tellus, telluris, f., *land, earth, country, ground*

genero, generare, generavi, generatum, *produce, create*

16 **aridus, -a, -um**, adj., *dry*

nutrix, nutricis, f., *nurse*, especially a *wet-nurse*

arida nutrix: oxymoron

17 **pone**: repeated as the first word of line 21; the anaphora makes more emphatic the bold commands

piger, pigra, pigrum, adj., *inactive, lazy*

campus, -i, m., *plain, level surface; plain, field*

18 **aestivus, -a, -um**, adj., *summer*

recreo, recreare, recreavi, recreatum, *recreate, restore, revive*

aura, -ae, f., *breeze*

19 **latus, lateris**, n., *side, extreme part or region, flank, lungs, body*

quod latus mundi: parallel to **ubi... aura** (17–18); the antecedent, **latus (mundi)**, is incorporated into the relative clause; cf. **quae loca** (7) above

mundus, -i, m., *world*

nebula, -ae, f., *mist, fog*

20 **Iuppiter**: (with **malus**, line 19), *bad weather* (by metonymy)

pone sub curru nimium propinqui
solis in terra domibus negata:
dulce ridentem Lalagen amabo,
    dulce loquentem.

---

21   **pone** (understand **me** again)

    currus, currus, m., *chariot*. The chariot of the sun is driven across the sky each day by the god of the sun; the Tropics would represent the area where his chariot gets too near the earth.

    nimium, adv., *too, too much, very*

    propinquus, -a, -um, adj., *near, neighboring*

    propinqui is genitive, modifying **solis** (22); understand the idea of **terra** (22) with **nimium propinqui** (too near the earth), as well as in its own phrase

22   **domibus**: dative because of **negata** (22)

23   **dulce**: adverb

23–24   These two lines echo both Catullus 51.5 (**dulce ridentem** "sweetly laughing") and Sappho 31.3–5 (**adu phoneisas...kai gelaisas imeroen** "sweetly speaking...and laughing in a lovely manner"). Note that Horace "reintroduces" Sappho's "sweetly speaking" which Catullus chooses not to follow in his adaptation of Sappho 31.

24   **dulce**: adverb

ODE 1.23

In this poem the speaker's rhetorical goal is to persuade Chloe that she has nothing to fear from him. He describes her fears as "empty." Yet the language he uses to persuade her is filled with violent and aggressive imagery, e.g., lions and tigers chasing her to break her. What is the effect of this clash between the literal meaning of his words and the emotions that his words evoke?

Meter: fourth Asclepiadean

Vitas inuleo me similis, Chloe,
quaerenti pavidam montibus aviis
   matrem non sine vano
     aurarum et siluae metu.

1   **vito, vitare, vitavi, vitatum,** *avoid, shun*

   in(n)uleus, -i, m., *fawn*

   inuleo: dative because of **similis**

   Chloe, Chloes, f., *Chloe,* woman's name; the **oe** is not a diphthong in the name; two syllable word. Chloe in Greek means "green bud" or "shoot." The name appears as an epithet of the Greek goddess of agriculture, Demeter, while there is inscriptional evidence of a festival of Demeter Chloe and Kore (which refers to her daughter, Persephone) at Eleusis in Greece. Thus through its association with Demeter, the name Chloe suggests simultaneously both female youth (Persephone) and female maturity (Demeter). Horace's use of this name in the poem evokes both the image of spring, and the life cycle of women.

vitas...Chloe: Note the word order; **me** is in the center, surrounded immediately by **inuleo** and **similis** (words related to Chloe), and further surrounded by more Chloe words (**vitas** and **Chloe**).

2   **pavidus, -a, -um,** adj., *frightened, terrified, trembling, fearful*

   montibus: ablative of place where; **in** frequently omitted in poetry

   avius, -a, -um, adj., *pathless, remote*

3   **non sine**: litotes

   vanus, -a, -um, adj., *empty, groundless, imaginary*

4   **aura, -ae,** f., *breeze*

   siluae: three syllables here; the letter *v/u* is being treated as a vowel, not a consonant

   metus, -us, m., *fear*

nam seu mobilibus veris inhorruit   5
adventus foliis, seu virides rubum
   dimovere lacertae,
      et corde et genibus tremit.

atqui non ego te tigris ut aspera
Gaetulusve leo frangere persequor: 10
   tandem desine matrem
      tempestiva sequi viro.

---

5   **mobilis, -e**, adj., *moveable, changeable, inconstant, pliant*

     ver, veris, n., *spring*

     inhorresco, inhorrescere, inhorrui, *begin to tremble, bristle, become stiffly erect*

6   **adventus, -us**, m., *arrival, approach*

     folium, folii, n., *leaf*

     viridis, -e, adj., *green, fresh, young*

     rubus, -i, m., *bramble, prickly bush*

7   **dimoveo, dimovere, dimovi, dimotum**, *move apart, separate*

     dimovere: -ere, alternate form of the third person plural perfect tense ending, **-erunt**

     lacerta, -ae, f., *lizard*

6–7 **virides rubum/dimovere lacertae:** can be seen as sexual imagery

8   **cor, cordis**, n., *heart*

     genu, -us, n., *knee*

     tremo, tremere, tremui, *tremble, quiver*

9   **atqui**, conj., *but, nevertheless*

     tigris, tigris/tigridis, f., *tiger*

     asper, aspera, asperum, adj., *fierce, rough*

10 **Gaetulus, -a, -um**, adj., *Gaetulian, of Gaetulia*, region of northwest Africa known for its lions

frango, frangere, fregi, fractum, *break, crush*

frangere: infinitive expressing purpose

persequor, persequi, persecutus sum, *pursue, chase*

9–10 **atqui...persequor**: Note how the literal sense of these two lines (I am not chasing you etc.) is countered by the fierceness of the imagery (lion and tiger) and the word order, which has "I" following/pursuing "you" (**ego te**) and **persequor** as the final word, with its negative (**non**) long forgotten.

11 **desino, desinere, desii, desitum**, *stop, cease*

     desine: takes infinitive, **sequi**

     matrem: direct object of **sequi**

11–12 Note how the word order allows for words to affect each other that do not depend on each other grammatically: **desine** at first seems to have **matrem** as its direct object (stop the mother); **sequi viro** suggests following a man, even though **viro** is not its grammatical object.

12 **tempestivus, -a, -um**, adj., *timely, seasonable, ripe*

     viro: dative, with **tempestiva**

ODE 1.24

This ode is a lament for Quintilius, addressed to Vergil. Here we see death, a frequent theme in Horace, personalized by the specificity of a friend's death as well as generalized about through the use of the mythic figures, Mercury and Orpheus. Here, the power of song creates a space for Horace and Vergil to mourn. Perhaps Vergil's "patience" in part entails being open to the "lightening" effect of Horace's song.

Meter: third Asclepiadean

Quis desiderio sit pudor aut modus
tam cari capitis? praecipe lugubris
cantus, Melpomene, cui liquidam pater
    vocem cum cithara dedit.

---

1   **quis**: for **qui**, the interrogative adjective; modifies **pudor** and **modus**

    desiderium, desiderii, n., *desire, longing* (for something or someone lost or absent)

    sit: deliberative subjunctive

    pudor, pudoris, m., *restraint, feeling of shame*

    modus, -i, m., *limit, way, rhythmic pattern*; in plural, *poetry*

2   **caput, capitis**, n., *head, person, person's life*

    cari capitis: objective genitive, with **desiderio**

praecipio, praecipere, praecepi, praeceptum, *take beforehand, teach*

lugubris, -e, adj., *mournful*

lugubris: **-is** ending, alternate accusative plural ending for **-es**

3   **cantus, -us**, m., *singing, song, poetry*

    Melpomene, Melpomenes, f., *Melpomene*, one of the Muses

    liquidus, -a, -um, adj., *flowing, clear, melodious, liquid*

    pater: Jupiter; the Muses were daughters of Jupiter and Mnemosyne (Memory)

4   **cithara, -ae**, f., *lyre*

ergo Quintilium perpetuus sopor   **5**
urget? cui Pudor et Iustitiae soror,
incorrupta Fides nudaque Veritas
   quando ullum inveniet parem?

multis ille bonis flebilis occidit,
nulli flebilior, quam tibi, Vergili.   **10**
tu, frustra pius, heu, non ita creditum
   poscis Quintilium deos.

5   **ergo**, particle, *then, consequently*

   Quintilius, Quintilii, m., *Quintilius Varus*, friend of Horace and Vergil; he is the addressee of Ode 1.18 as well; Horace praises him in Epistle 2.3 (Ars Poetica) 438 ff. as an honest and frank critic of others' writing.

   perpetuus, -a, -um, adj., *continuing, permanent, connected*

   sopor, soporis, m., *sleep*

6   **urgeo, urgere, ursi**, *push, press upon*

   cui, connecting relative pronoun; dative because of **parem** (8)

   iustitia, -ae, f., *justice*

6–7   **Pudor, Fides, Veritas**: personified virtues

7   **fides, fidei**, f., *trust, belief, faith, honesty, honor*

   nudaque Veritas: cf. Quintilius' honest criticism mentioned above, line 5.

9   **multis...bonis**: datives, parallel with **nulli** and **tibi** (10)

   flebilis, -e, adj., *worthy of tears, lamentable*

   occido, occidere, occidi, occasum, *fall, die*

occidit: present or perfect tense

9–10 **flebilis...flebilior**: the figura etymologica underscores the idea of lament

10   **Vergilius, Vergilii**, m., *Publius Vergilius Maro* (70–19 BCE), Horace's friend and contemporary; author of the *Aeneid*, *Eclogues*, and *Georgics*; it was Vergil who introduced Horace to Maecenas, who became his friend and supporter.

11   **frustra**, adv., *in vain, to no purpose*

   pius, -a, -um, adj., *dutiful, devoted*

   pius: Note the use of this epithet of Aeneas' to describe Vergil, author of the *Aeneid*.

   heu, interjection expressing grief or pain, *oh, alas*

   credo, credere, credidi, creditum, *trust, believe, entrust*

   non ita creditum: i.e., not entrusted to you on the basis that the gods would return him if asked

12   **posco, poscere, poposci**, *demand*

   Quintilium, deos: both accusatives with **poscis**, which takes the accusative of the thing asked for and of the individual asked

quid, si Threicio blandius Orpheo
auditam moderere arboribus fidem,
num vanae redeat sanguis imagini,   15
   quam virga semel horrida

non lenis precibus fata recludere
nigro compulerit Mercurius gregi?
durum, sed levius fit patientia,
   quicquid corrigere est nefas.   20

13–18   Note the length and complexity of the long sentence that spans these six lines in contrast with the simple statement "**durum**" that follows it. The abruptness of **durum** and the brief words that follow underscores the theme of the finality of death.

13   **Threicius, -a, -um**, adj., *Thracian*

blandus, -a, -um, adj., *charming, persuasive, seductive*

Orpheus, -i, m., *Orpheus*; he was able to charm animals and nature with his music; Vergil tells the story of Orpheus and Eurydice in his fourth Georgic.

14   **moderor, moderari, moderatus sum**, *handle, control*; (here) *play*

moderere: alternate form of second person singular, **modereris**

arboribus: dative of agent with perfect passive participle

fides, fidis, f., *lyre*

15   **vanus, -a, -um**, adj., *empty, groundless, imaginary*

imago, imaginis, f., *image, likeness, shape*

16   **virga, -ae**, f., *staff, wand*

virga: Mercury's caduceus, with which he leads the dead to the underworld

horridus, -a, -um, adj., *rough, harsh, dreadful*

17   **non lenis**: litotes

lenis, -e, adj., *smooth, gentle, mild, soft*

prex, precis, f., *prayer*

precibus: dative, with **recludere**

fatum, -i, n., *fate*; plural, *the Fates*

recludo, recludere, reclusi, reclusum, *open up, undo*

recludere: epexegetical infinitive explaining the adjective **lenis**

18   **niger, nigra, nigrum**, adj., *black, dark, gloomy*

compello, compellere, compuli, compulsum, *bring together, drive together, round up*

Mercurius, Mercurii, m., *Mercury*, son of Jupiter and Maia

grex, gregis, m., *flock, herd, company, crowd*

19   **durum**: understand **est**

levis, -e, adj., *light, swift, gentle, unimportant, fickle*

levius: predicate adjective modifying **quicquid**

patientia: ablative of means

20   **corrigo, corrigere, correxi, correctum**, *make straight, correct, remedy*

nefas, n., indeclinable, *crime, offense against divine law, sacrilege*

ODE 1.25

The comparative word **parcius**, *the poem's first word, signals a major theme of the poem: change over time. This theme is picked up by* **minus et minus iam** *and then by* **invicem,** *which sends the poem careening off into a future imagined (hoped for?) by the speaker. It is worth thinking about the effect of comparing the "future" Lydia to a* mare *in heat and dry leaves, and associating her with winter and Bacchic revels. What does this suggest about cultural expectations regarding the decorousness of active desire in the older woman?*

Meter: Sapphic

**Parcius iunctas quatiunt fenestras
iactibus crebris iuvenes protervi,
nec tibi somnos adimunt, amatque
    ianua limen,**

---

1 **parce**, adv., *sparingly*

parcius: *more sparingly,* hence, *less often*

iungo, iungere, iunxi, iunctum, *join, yoke, mate*

iunctas...fenestras: windows with shutters, closed

quatio, quatere, quassum, *shake, beat upon*

2 **iactus, -us**, m., *throwing, hurling*

iactibus: the idea is that those interested in Lydia throw stones at her windows to get her attention

creber, crebra, crebrum, adj., *crowded together, frequent*

protervus, -am -um, adj., *bold, violent*

3 **tibi**: dative of separation

somnus, -i, m., *sleep*

adimo, adimere, ademi, ademptum, *take away*

nec tibi somnos adimunt: normally, not losing sleep might be thought of as positive; here, it is a sign of declining interest in Lydia

amatque: amo can mean "keep to," but maintaining the erotic sense of "loves" seems useful in this context of Lydia becoming a less sought-after object of others' desire; cf. the use of this same verb with an inanimate subject in Ode 2.3.9–10.

4 **ianua, -ae**, f., *door*

limen, liminis, n., *threshold*

quae prius multum facilis movebat   **5**
cardines. audis minus et minus iam:
'me tuo longas pereunte noctes,
   Lydia, dormis?'

invicem moechos anus adrogantis
flebis in solo levis angiportu,   **10**
Thracio bacchante magis sub inter-
   lunia vento,

---

5   **multum**, adv., *much*

    multum: can modify **facilis** or **movebat**

    facilis: can be nominative singular modifying **quae**, which has as its antecedent, **ianua**, or can modify **cardines**, as an accusative plural (**-is** for **-es**)

6   **cardo, cardinis**, m., *hinge*

7   **tuo**: substantive use of the adjective

    pereo, perire, perii, peritum, *perish, die*

    longas...noctes: accusative of extent of time

7–8   These are the words of a shut-out lover who pines away for his beloved in front of her house door. This type of serenade is called a **paraclausithyron**, Greek for "at the closed door."

8   **Lydia, -ae**, f., *Lydia,* woman's name

    dormis: notice the repetition of the idea of sleep from line 3

9   **invicem**, adv., *in turn*

    invicem: this word switches the poem into a future imagined by the speaker

    moechus, -i, m., *adulterer*

    anus, -us, f., *old woman*

    adrogans, adrogantis, adj., *arrogant, insolent*

10   **fleo, flere, flevi, fletum**, *weep for, lament*

    levis, -e, adj., *light, swift, gentle, unimportant, fickle*

    angiportus, -us, m., *alley*

    in solo...angiportu: Horace's language recalls the abusive description of Lesbia in Catullus 58.4–5, where Lesbia engages in sexual activity in crossroads and alleys: **nunc in quadriviis et angiportis/ glubit magnanimi Remi nepotes.**

11   **Thracius, -a, -um**, adj., *Thracian*

    bacchor, bacchari, bacchatus sum, *celebrate the festival of Bacchus, rave, rage*

    bacchante: note the diaeresis delayed until after the sixth syllable; this uncommon metrical variation heightens the sense of things out of control

11–12 **interlunium, interlunii**, n., *the period between the old moon and the new*

    inter-lunia: I vary from the text here, adding a hyphen between **inter** and **lunia**, as most other texts do, since **interlunia** is one word. For another line end separating a word in Sapphic meter, cf. **uxorius**, Ode 1.2.19–20. This is an example of synapheia, or the joining together of two lines as if they were one.

cum tibi flagrans amor et libido,
quae solet matres furiare equorum,
saeviet circa iecur ulcerosum,   15
    non sine questu,

---

13 **tibi**: dative of reference

flagrans, flagrantis, adj., *hot, blazing, passionate*

libido, libidinis, f., *desire, lust*

14 **matres...equorum**: the lust of mares in heat was a traditional theme

soleo, solere, solitus sum, *be accustomed*

furio, furiare, furiavi, furiatum, *madden*

15 **saevio, saevire, saevii, saevitum**, *rage, rave*

circa, preposition with accusative, *around*

iecur, iecoris, n., *liver, the seat of the feelings*

ulcerosus, -a, -um, adj., *full of ulcers or sores*

16 **non sine**: litotes; ironic or sarcastic

questus, -us, m., *complaint, lament*

laeta quod pubes hedera virenti
gaudeat pulla magis atque myrto,
aridas frondes hiemis sodali
    dedicet Hebro.   20

17 **laetus, -a, -um**, *happy, glad, fertile*

laeta: very strategic placing of the word **laeta**. Coming right after a lengthy description of Lydia, one expects it to describe *her*, however it belongs to the clause which the postpositive **quod** introduces and one discovers only after reaching the word **pubes**, which is feminine, that **laeta** modifies *it*. This placement of **laeta** *before* the word that would more typically introduce the clause to which **laeta** belongs is typical of Horace's style and can prove tricky for first-time readers of Horace.

pubes, pubis, f., *adult population, age of puberty, the pubic region*

hedera, -ae, f., *ivy*

vireo, virere, virui, *be green, youthful, fresh*

17–19 There are three items listed here (with their modifiers): ivy, myrtle, and (dry) leaves. Depending on how one takes **atque** (below), ivy *and* myrtle are enjoyed more by the youth, or ivy is enjoyed more *than* myrtle. In either scenario, the dry leaves are an object for dismissal. The latter may be a better interpretation for it continues the comparative idea that is so central to the poem, starting with **parcius** and

continuing with **minus et minus**. In any case, the ivy, myrtle, and dry leaves are metaphors for three stages of a woman's life: youth, maturity, and old age.

18 **gaudeo, gaudere, gavisus sum**, *rejoice, delight in* (with ablative)

gaudeat: subjunctive in implied indirect statement introduced by **quod**; cf. **dedicet** below, line 20

pullus, -a, -um, adj., *gray, somber*

pulla: ablative with **myrto**, which is feminine

atque, conj., *and*; after comparatives, *than* (*OLD* 15); some take **atque** as "and," others as "than."

myrtus, -i, f., *myrtle*

19 **aridus, -a, -um**, adj., *dry*

frons, frondis, f., *leaf*

hiems, hiemis, f., *winter, storm*

sodalis, sodalis, m., *companion*

20 **dedico, dedicare, dedicavi, dedicatum**, *dedicate*

dedicet: asyndeton; adds to the dismissive tone; cf. note on **gaudeat** above, line 18

Hebrus, -i, m., *Hebrus*, river in Thrace

Hebro: this is the manuscript reading; a conjecture that some texts adopt is **Euro**, from **Eurus, -i**, m., *Eurus, the east wind*

ODE 1.37

The historical context for this ode is the defeat of Octavian's enemy, Cleopatra VII of Egypt, at the battle of Actium off the west coast of Greece in 31 BCE. Cleopatra and Antony were the final obstacles standing in the way of Octavian's total power. After their defeat at Actium, Antony and Cleopatra returned to Alexandria, Egypt. When their land forces were defeated and Octavian entered Alexandria, both committed suicide. The fact that Horace does not mention Antony in the poem helps to portray the conflict not as a civil war, but rather as a foreign threat.

*The endings of Horace's odes are frequently a source of interest (and sometimes of surprise). In this ode Horace follows five stanzas of celebration about the defeat of a **fatale monstrum** with an extended evocation in the last three stanzas of Cleopatra's nobility in the face of defeat. What are we to make of this? Does this express ambivalence on the part of Horace about Octavian's defeat of his final obstacle to complete rule? Or does it make Octavian's conquest all the more outstanding because of the notable dignity of the one he has conquered?*

Meter: Alcaic

Nunc est bibendum, nunc pede libero
pulsanda tellus, nunc Saliaribus

---

1 **bibo, bibere, bibi,** *drink*

 est bibendum: passive periphrastic construction

 pede libero: suggests the physical freedom to dance unrestrained as well as the political freedom to exist unenslaved; there also may be a sense here of "metrical" freedom (cf. notes on **nefas**, line 5, and **lymphatam**, line 14, below)

1–2 **Nunc...nunc...nunc**: note the anaphora, which heightens the importance of the need for present celebration. The beginning of the poem echoes a fragment of Alcaeus (Lobel-Page Z,8) in which the

poet calls for drinking to celebrate the death of the tyrant, Myrsilus, on Lesbos.

2 **pulso, pulsare, pulsavi, pulsatum,** *beat, strike repeatedly*

 pulsanda: understand **est** from line 1; passive periphrastic construction

 tellus, telluris, f., *land, earth, country, ground*

 Saliaris, -e, adj., *of the Salii,* who were a group of priests (at Rome usually associated with Mars) who performed ritual dances on certain occasions. They were known for the sumptuousness of their banquets (**Saliaribus...dapibus,** 2–4).

ornare pulvinar deorum
tempus erat dapibus, sodales.

antehac nefas depromere Caecubum   5
cellis avitis, dum Capitolio
    regina dementis ruinas
        funus et imperio parabat

---

3   **orno, ornare, ornavi, ornatum,** *prepare, decorate, adorn, honor* (with ablative)

pulvinar, pulvinaris, n., *sacred couch on which the image of a god was placed;* images of the gods were put on these couches for a ceremony the Romans took over from the Greeks called the **lectisternium,** in which the gods were treated as guests at a meal.

4   **erat:** the imperfect tense with **nunc** implies that the appropriate moment for celebration has existed for some time

daps, dapis, f., *feast, banquet*

sodalis, sodalis, m., *companion*

5   **antehac,** adv., *previously*

antehac: two syllables, by synizesis

nefas, n., indeclinable, *crime, offense against divine law, sacrilege*

nefas: understand **erat**

nefas: Normally the first two lines of the Alcaic meter have a diaeresis after the fifth syllable. That pattern, which is broken here and in line 14 of this poem, seems to have the effect here of speeding up the line and thus hastening the bringing out of the wine.

depromo, depromere, deprompsi, depromptum, *bring out, produce*

Caecubum, -i, n., *choice wine from Caecubum,* a district in south Latium

6   **cella, -ae,** f., *storeroom, wine cellar*

avitus, -a, -um, adj., *of a grandfather, ancestral*

Capitolium, Capitolii, n., *Capitolium,* the Capitoline hill in Rome on which the Capitoline gods, Jupiter, Juno, and Minerva, were worshipped

6–7 **Capitolio/regina:** the juxtaposition of these two words emphasizes Cleopatra's threat to Roman rule

7   **demens, dementis,** adj., *out of one's senses, mad, insane*

dementis: accusative plural with **ruinas;** transferred epithet, in sense goes with **regina** as well

ruina, -ae, f., *collapse, ruin*

8   **funus, funeris,** n., *funeral, death, destruction*

et: postposition; note the postponement of the conjunction until after **funus.**

imperium, imperii, n., *power, command, government*

parabat: imperfect with **dum,** rather than the more common present; understand this verb twice, once with **dementis ruinas** as direct object, then with **funus** as direct object

contaminato cum grege turpium
morbo virorum, quidlibet inpotens   **10**
    sperare fortunaque dulci
      ebria; sed minuit furorem

vix una sospes navis ab ignibus,
mentemque lymphatam Mareotico
    redegit in veros timores   **15**
      Caesar ab Italia volantem

---

9   **contaminatus, -a, -um**, adj., *morally foul, impure*

grex, gregis, m., *flock, herd, company, crowd*

turpis, -e, adj., *ugly, shameful, disgraceful*

9–10 **contaminato...virorum**: contemptuous reference to Cleopatra's eunuchs who served as attendants at her court; note the use of the word "men" in connection with the eunuchs in light of the shifting vocabulary about gender roles in lines 22 and 32 below (**nec muliebriter, mulier**).

10   **morbus, -i**, m., *sickness, disease*

morbo: ablative explaining **turpium**

quilibet, quaelibet, quidlibet, pron., *anyone or anything whatever, whoever or whatever you please*

inpotens, inpotentis, adj., *powerless, weak, wild, violent*

11   **sperare**: epexegetical infinitive explaining the adjective **inpotens**

dulcis, -e, adj., *sweet*, (of persons) *dear, beloved*

12   **ebrius, -a, -um**, adj., *drunk*

minuo, minuere, minui, minutum, *make smaller, reduce, weaken*

minuit: perfect tense

13   **vix una sospes navis**: Horace exaggerates for effect; in fact, Cleopatra escaped with sixty ships. He continues his reworking of events in the poem by foreshortening the historical sequence. Almost a year elapsed between the battle of Actium and the final defeat of Antony and Cleopatra in Egypt.

sospes, sospitis, adj., *safe and sound, unhurt*

14   **lymphatus, -a, -um**, adj., *frenzied, distracted, frantic*

lymphatam: cf. notes on **nefas**, line 5, and **pede libero**, line 1, above. Here the displacement of the normal diaeresis underscores the distracted state of Cleopatra's mind.

Mareoticum, -i, n., *wine from Mareotis*, area around Alexandria in Egypt

15   **redigo, redigere, redegi, redactum**, *drive back, reduce*

16   **Caesar, Caesaris**, m., *Caesar*, Octavian (later Augustus)

ab Italia: literally, from Actium, not Italy; the idea is that she is compelled to flee from her goal

Italia: the initial "i" is lengthened here

remis adurgens, accipiter velut
mollis columbas aut leporem citus
venator in campis nivalis
Haemoniae, daret ut catenis   **20**

fatale monstrum, quae generosius
perire quaerens nec muliebriter
expavit ensem, nec latentis
classe cita reparavit oras,

---

17   **remus, -i**, m., *oar*

     remis: synecdoche, "oars" for the whole ship

     adurgeo, adurgere, *press hard upon, pursue closely*

     accipiter, accipitris, m., *hawk*

     velut: introduces a simile; postposition, notice the placement of **velut** after **accipiter**, which begins the simile

18   **mollis, -e**, adj., *soft, gentle, flexible, voluptuous*

     columba, -ae, f., *dove, pigeon*

     lepus, leporis, m., *hare, rabbit*

     citus, -a, -um, adj., *swift, quick*

19   **venator, venatoris**, m., *hunter*

     campus, -i, m., *plain, level surface; plain, field*

     nivalis, -e, adj., *snowy*

20   **Haemonia, -ae**, f., *Thessaly*

     daret ut: subjunctive in purpose clause; postposition, **ut** placed after **daret**

     catena, -ae, f., *chain*

20–21   **daret ut catenis/fatale monstrum**:

enjambment, emphasizes **fatale monstrum**

21   **fatalis, -e**, adj., *deadly, fatal*

     monstrum, -i, n., *portent, marvel, monster*

     fatale monstum: i.e., Cleopatra. Cleopatra VII (69 BCE–30 BCE)

     quae: note the switch in gender to feminine from the neuter of the antecedent, **monstrum**

     generose, adv., *nobly, with dignity*

22   **pereo, perire, perii, peritum**, *perish, die*

     muliebriter, adv., *like a woman*

     nec muliebriter: here, she is not "womanish"

23   **expavesco, expavescere, expavi**, *become frightened of, dread*

     ensis, ensis, m., *sword*

     lateo, latere, latui, *lie hidden*

24   **classis, classis**, f., *fleet, political class*

     reparo, reparare, reparavi, reparatum, *obtain in exchange for, recover*

23–24   **nec...reparavit**: the sense, here, is likely something like "did not reach"

ausa et iacentem visere regiam   25
voltu sereno, fortis et asperas
   tractare serpentes, ut atrum
     corpore combiberet venenum,

deliberata morte ferocior:
saevis Liburnis scilicet invidens   30
   privata deduci superbo
     non humilis mulier triumpho.

---

25   **viso, visere, visi**, *look at, go and see*

26   **voltus, -us**, m., *face, expression*

      asper, aspera, asperum, adj., *fierce, rough*

27   **tracto, tractare, tractavi, tractatum**, *handle*

      tractare: epexegetical infinitive explaining the adjective **fortis**

      ater, atra, atrum, adj., *black, dark, gloomy*

28   **combibo, combibere, combibi**, *drink up, drink completely*

      combiberet: subjunctive in purpose clause

      venenum, -i, n., *poison, magical or medicinal potion*

29   **delibero, deliberare, deliberavi, deliberatum**, *consider carefully, deliberate, decide*

30   **Liburna, -ae**, f., *light, fast sailing warship, galley;* name taken from the Liburnians, a people of Illyricum

      scilicet, adv., *evidently, of course, surely*

      invideo, invidere, invidi, invisum, *envy, begrudge, refuse*

30–32   Some commentators take **saevis Liburnis** as ablative of means with **deduci** and **superbo...triumpho**

as dative of purpose with **deduci**, while others take **saevis Liburnis** as dative with **invidens** and **deduci** as an infinitive dependent on **invidens** (epexegetical infinitive).

31   **privatus, -a, -um**, adj., *private, not in public life*

      deduco, deducere, deduxi, deductum, *lead away, lead down, escort, bring a person or army back with one to Rome, bring home in procession as a bride, spin, compose, adapt*

31–32   Note the portrayal of Cleopatra as well as the word order in these final two lines. She is described as a **non humilis mulier**. While **superbo** modifies **triumpho**, the placement of **mulier** directly before **triumpho**, in a kind of crescendo beginning with **non humilis,** lends a sense of triumph to the defeated queen. Some commentators have sensed an indirect admiration of Cleopatra here. On the other hand, the final word **triumpho** may look specifically towards Octavian, who celebrated a triple triumph in 29 BCE for his victories in Illyricum, at Actium, and in Alexandria.

32   **mulier**: cf. **mulier** with **nec muliebriter,** line 22 above

ODE 1.38

The simplicity of this poem is deceptive. Everything is said indirectly; there is not a single positive statement. It can function on various levels: the metapoetic, symposiac, and, perhaps, even amatory.

Meter: Sapphic

Persicos odi, puer, apparatus,
displicent nexae philyra coronae;
mitte sectari, rosa quo locorum
    sera moretur.

---

1   **Persicus, -a, -um**, adj., *Persian*

odi, odisse, osum, (perfect with present sense), *have an aversion to, hate*

odi: cf. Ode 3.1.1, **odi profanum volgus et arceo**, for another example of Horace's method of delineating what he likes via what he does not like.

puer, pueri, m., *boy, non-adult male, male beloved*, (young) *male slave*

puer: It should be noted that here, as in Satire 1.9, discussed above, Horace is being attended by a slave.

apparatus, -us, m., *preparation, show, sumptuousness, paraphernalia*

Persicos...apparatus: yet cf. the previous poem, Ode 1.37, for an example of Horace's use of rather extravagant literary style. Cicero, *Orator* 83, makes an analogy (using the phrase **epularum apparatu**) between elaborate banquest preparations and elaborate literary style.

1–2 asyndeton: lack of connective between the clauses of lines 1 and 2, perhaps meant to underscore the idea of simplicity contained in the poem

2   **displiceo, displicere, displicui, displicitum**, *displease*

necto, nectere, nexi, nexum, *tie, weave, bind, compose*

philyra, -ae, f., *fibrous membrane under the bark of the linden or lime tree, bast;* used to bind together elaborate garlands of flowers

corona, -ae, f., *crown, garland*

3   **mitto, mittere, misi, missum**, *release, let go, abandon, send*

mitte sectari: the use of **mitte** makes this more vivid than a simple negative imperative would (**noli sectari**); cf. Horace's similar use of **fuge** in Ode 1.9.13

sector, sectari, sectatus sum, *pursue, chase*

rosa, -ae, f., *rose*

rosa: the rose is associated with Venus

quo, adv., *where, for what purpose*

locorum, partitive genitive with **quo**

3–4 **rosa quo locorum/sera moretur**: as often in Horace, the image of what is rejected contrasts with the rejection itself: the rose that is not to be pursued lingers in the mind's eye. Cf. the images of the tiger and lion in Ode 1.23 above.

4   **serus, -a, -um**, adj., *late, blossoming after the normal time*

moror, morari, moratus sum, *delay, linger, be late in appearing*

moretur: subjunctive in indirect question

simplici myrto nihil adlabores   **5**
sedulus, curo: neque te ministrum
dedecet myrtus, neque me sub arta
    vite bibentem.

5   **simplex, simplicis**, adj., *simple, art-less, plain*

    myrtus, -i, f., *myrtle*

    myrto: myrtle is associated with Ve-nus

    simplici myrto: dative with **adla-bores**

    adlaboro, adlaborare, *add to by taking trouble*

6   **sedulus, -a, -um**, adj., *attentive, dili-gent*

    sedulus: can modify either the speaker or the second person sin-gular subject of **adlabores**; note its placement between the two words with which it can be construed

    curo, curare, curavi, curatum, *care about, take care of, attend to*

    curo: **curo (ut)** plus subjunctive in a substantive clause developed from the jussive subjunctive

    minister, ministri, m., *servant, assis-tant*

6–7   **neque...dedecet**: litotes

7   **dedecet, dedecere, dedecuit**, used in third person; *be unsuitable for, be unbecoming to*

    artus, -a, -um, adj., *close, thrifty, dense, economical*

    arta: this adjective has connotations of literary simplicity

8   **vitis, vitis**, f., *vine*

    bibo, bibere, bibi, *drink*

ODE 2.3

The themes of death, moderation, and enjoyment intertwine in this ode to Delius. The generalizing statements and questions of the first three stanzas and the future, death-oriented, final three stanzas are divided by a central stanza (lines 13–16) which attempts to carve out a moment of physical and temporal immediacy that can be captured despite the universal human fact of death. The poem's final image of death as "exile" makes us want to return again to the immediacy of the sympotic moment which may be the only "home" that we can call our own for all time.

Meter: Alcaic

Aequam memento rebus in arduis
servare mentem, non secus in bonis
    ab insolenti temperatam
      laetitia, moriture Delli,

---

1   **aequus, -a, -um**, adj., *equal, even, impartial, fair*

    memini, meminisse, (perfect with present meaning), *remember, recollect*

    memento: future active imperative, second person singular, from **memini**

    arduus, -a, -um, adj., *steep, towering, lofty, high, difficult*

    aequam...arduis: note the contrast in images of "even" and "steep"

1–2   **aequam...mentem**: hyperbaton; cf. note on Ode 1.9.21–22

2   **secus**, adv., *otherwise, not so*

    non secus: litotes and asyndeton

    in bonis: understand **rebus**

3   **insolens, insolentis**, adj., *unaccustomed, excessive*

  tempero, temperare, temperavi, temperatum, *moderate, hold back*

    temperatam: understand **mentem**

4   **laetitia, -ae**, f., *happiness, joy*

    morior, mori, mortuus sum, *die*

    moriture: future active participle of **morior**, vocative

    Dellius, Dellii, m., *Quintus Dellius*, who first joined Dolabella, then Cassius, then Antony, and finally Octavian, right before Actium. He was called the **desultor bellorum civilium** "the circus rider of the civil wars" by Messalla. (A **desultor** is the circus rider who jumps from one horse to another.) His alternating allegiances to political figures make him an appropriate addressee for a poem that deals with changing circumstances.

seu maestus omni tempore vixeris,   5
seu te in remoto gramine per dies
   festos reclinatum bearis
      interiore nota Falerni.

quo pinus ingens albaque populus
umbram hospitalem consociare amant   10
   ramis? quid obliquo laborat
      lympha fugax trepidare rivo?

---

5   **maestus, -a, -um**, adj., *sad, sorrowful, dejected, gloomy*

    omni tempore: ablative of time when

    vixeris: future perfect indicative

6   **removeo, removere, removi, remotum**, *move back, withdraw*

    gramen, graminis, n., *grass*

7   **festus, -a, -um**, adj., *festal, on holiday, festive*

    reclino, reclinare, reclinavi, reclinatum, *cause to lean back*

    reclinatum: perfect passive participle with middle sense; *having reclined*

    beo, beare, beavi, beatum, *bless, make happy*

    bearis: syncopated form of **bea(ve)ris**

    bearis: future perfect indicative, like **vixeris** (line 5)

8   **interior, interius**, adj., *inner, interior, private*

    interiore: a wine from the inner part of the wine cellar denoting an older, better wine

    nota, -ae, f., *mark, sign, wine of a specified quality or vintage*

    Falernum, -i, n., *Falernian wine*, wine from a district in northern Campania famous for its wine

9–12   The two questions that begin with **quo** and **quid** introduce contrasting personified images from nature of loving embrace and frenzied hurrying. The images suggest the erotic part of life (the trees embracing) as well as the brevity of life (the speed with which the water moves along). Cf. **fugerit**

invida/aetas, Ode 1.11.7–8 for the "fleeing" quality of time. While the images portray a pleasant setting for the party called for in the next lines, they introduce a disquieting element as well.

9   **quo**, adv., *where, for what purpose*

    pinus, -us, f., *pine*

    albus, -a, -um, adj., *white, bright*

    populus, -i, f., *poplar tree*

    populus: the long "o" and the feminine gender distinguish this from the other, more common noun, **populus**, "people."

    pinus ingens albaque populus: chiasmus

10   **hospitalis, hospitale**, adj., *hospitable, belonging to a host or guest*

    consocio, consociare, consociavi, consociatum, *unite, connect, share*

    amant: cf. the use of this verb with an inanimate subject in Ode 1.25.3–4.

11   **ramus, -i**, m., *branch*

    quid, adv., *why*

    obliquus, -a, -um, adj., *slanting, zigzag*

11–12   **obliquo...rivo**: ablative of place where, **in** frequently omitted in poetry

12   **lympha, -ae**, f., *water*

    fugax, fugacis, adj., *swift, fugitive, elusive*

    trepido, trepidare, trepidavi, trepidatum, *be agitated, hurry*

    trepidare: infinitive with **laborat**

    rivus, -i, m., *stream*

huc vina et unguenta et nimium brevis
flores amoenae ferre iube rosae,
    dum res et aetas et sororum   **15**
       fila trium patiuntur atra.

cedes coemptis saltibus et domo
villaque, flavos quam Tiberis lavit,
    cedes, et exstructis in altum
       divitiis potietur heres.   **20**

---

13   **vina**: plural for singular

unguentum, -i, n., *ointment, perfume*

nimium, adv., *too, too much, very*

nimium: modifies **brevis** (accusative plural), which modifies **flores**

amoenus, -a, -um, adj., *charming, pleasing*

rosa, rosae, f., *a rose*

13–14   tricolon crescendo: **vina, unguenta, nimium...rosae.** The length of the last element contrasts with the notion it contains of the brevity of the rose; the poet is extending through language what is desirable, but brief.

14   **ferre iube**: understand a word like **pueros** (slaves) as accusative with **iube**

15   **res**: recalls **rebus**, line 1

aetas, aetatis, f., *time, age*

15–16   tricolon crescendo: **res, aetas, fila...** (with the phrase containing the last element (**fila...atra**) longer than the first two); **sororum...atra** refers to the image of the thread of each human life that the three Fates spin, measure, and cut.

16   **filum, -i**, n., *thread*

ater, atra, atrum, adj., *black, dark, gloomy*

17   **cedes...cedes** (line 19): anaphora; emphasizes the idea of loss

coemo, coemere, coemi, coemptum, *buy up*

saltus, -us, m., *forest or mountain pasture, forest or mountain pass*

17–18   **saltibus, domo, villa**: ablatives with **cedes**

18   **villa, -ae**, f., *country-house, estate, farm*

flavos: earlier spelling for **flavus**

flavus, -a, -um, adj., *yellow, golden, blonde, auburn*

quam: postposition; **quam** is delayed to the second position in its clause

Tiberis, Tiberis, m., *the river Tiber*; often described as yellowish because of the mud it contained

lavo, lavare/lavere, lavi, lavatum/lautum/lotum, *wash*

lavit: present tense; Horace treats the verb as third conjugation here.

19   **exstruo, exstruere, exstruxi, exstructum**, *heap up, pile up, construct*

altum, -i, n., *high place or position, heaven, sea, the deep*

19–20   **exstructis...divitiis**: ablative with verb, **potior**

20   **divitiae, divitiarum**, f. pl., *wealth, riches*

potior, potiri, potitus sum, *get possession of, obtain, possess*

heres, heredis, c., *heir*

heres: note the final, emphatic position of this word

divesne prisco natus ab Inacho,
nil interest, an pauper et infima
   de gente sub divo moreris,
     victima nil miserantis Orci:

omnes eodem cogimur, omnium   25
versatur urna serius ocius
   sors exitura et nos in aeternum
     exilium inpositura cumbae.

21 **dives, divitis**, adj., *rich, wealthy*

priscus, -a, -um, adj., *ancient, former*

nascor, nasci, natus sum, *be born*

Inachus, -i, m., *Inachus*, first king of Argos

21–22 **divesne...an pauper**: in apposition to the subject of **moreris**

22 **nil**: **nil** = **nihil**; cf. **nil** line 24; used adverbially here and in line 24, *not, not at all*

intersum, interesse, interfui, when used impersonally, *it makes a difference, it matters, it is of importance*

pauper, pauperis, adj., *poor*

infimus, -a, -um, adj., *lowest, most humble*

23 **gens, gentis**, f., *clan, tribe, family*

divum, -i, n., *sky*

moror, morari, moratus sum, *delay, linger, be late in appearing*

moreris: more vivid than "live" in the poem's context of the quick passing of time

24 **victima, -ae**, f., *victim, sacrifice*

victima: understand **es**

miseror, miserari, miseratus sum, *pity, lament*

Orcus, Orci, m., *Orcus*, the god of the lower world, *the lower world, death*

25 **eodem**, adv., *to the same place*

cogo, cogere, coegi, coactum, *drive together, force*

omnes...cogimur, omnium: the switch from second person singular to first person plural and the repetition of **omnes...omnium** (figura etymologica) generalize the situation to that of all human beings

26 **verso, versare, versavi, versatum**, *keep turning, stir*

urna, -ae, f., *urn*

urna: ablative of place where; cf. on **obliquo...rivo**, above, 11–12.

serius, adv., *later*

ocius, adv., *sooner, quicker*

serius ocius: asyndeton

27 **sors, sortis**, f., *lot, share*

exeo, exire, exii, exitum, *go out, come out, emerge*

aeternus, -a, -um, adj., *eternal, everlasting*

aeternum: hypermetric line; **aeternum** elides with **exilium** in the next line

28 **exilium, exilii**, n., *exile*

inpono, inponere, inposui, inpositum, *place on or over, build on*

cumba, -ae, f., *small boat*, especially that in which Charon ferries the dead across the river Styx

cumbae: dative with **impositura**

ODE 2.7

*When Horace was studying at the university in Athens he joined the republican forces and served under Brutus as a **tribunus militum**, a senior legionary officer, until Brutus' defeat at the battle of Philippi. This poem welcomes home Pompeius, who served along with Horace at Philippi. In the description of leaving behind his shield ignobly, Horace echoes a literary tradition that goes back to the Greek poets, Archilochus, Alcaeus, and Anacreon. There is a joyful sense to this poem of welcome (despite its reference to having been on the "wrong" side in the civil wars). In addition, there is an almost playful quality evinced by the frequent repetitions of the same or similar words: **deducte/ duce**, **fregi/fracta**, **mecum/cum quo**, **celerem/celer**, **sustulit/tulit**, **coronatus/coronas**.*

Meter: Alcaic

O saepe mecum tempus in ultimum
deducte Bruto militiae duce,
**   quis te redonavit Quiritem**
**   dis patriis Italoque caelo,**

---

1   **o**, interjection, *O* (with vocative)

    tempus: "danger" is the meaning here

2   **deduco, deducere, deduxi, deductum**, *lead away, lead down, escort, bring a person or army back with one to Rome, bring home in procession as a bride, spin, compose, adapt*

    deducte/duce: figura etymologica; cf. the other wordplay noted in the introduction to the poem, above

    Brutus, -i, m., *Marcus Iunius Brutus*, one of the leaders, along with Cassius, of the conspiracy to kill Julius Caesar. His forces were defeated by those of Antony, Octavian's then ally, at the second battle of Philippi in 42 BCE.

    Bruto...duce: ablative absolute

    militia, -ae, f., *military service, war, army*

3   **redono, redonare, redonavi, redonatum**, *give back*

    Quiris, Quiritis, m., *Roman citizen*

    Quiritem: in apposition to **te**

4   **dis:** dative and ablative plural, alternate form for **deis**

    patrius, -a, -um, adj., *of a father, ancestral, native, inherited, belonging to one's country*

    Italus, -a, -um, adj., *Italian*

Pompei, meorum prime sodalium,   5
cum quo morantem saepe diem mero
    fregi coronatus nitentis
        malobathro Syrio capillos?

tecum Philippos et celerem fugam
sensi relicta non bene parmula,   10
    cum fracta virtus et minaces
        turpe solum tetigere mento.

5   **Pompeius, Pompeii,** m., *Pompeius;* his identity is unknown

Pompei: vocative; disyllabic by synizesis

sodalis, sodalis, m., *companion*

6   **cum quo:** more frequently in Latin, **quocum**

moror, morari, moratus sum, *delay, linger, be late in appearing*

merus, -a, -um, adj., *pure, unmixed;* with **vinum** or with **vinum** understood, *wine not mixed with water*

7   **frango, frangere, fregi, fractum,** *break, crush*

corono, coronare, coronavi, coronatum, *put a garland on, crown*

niteo, nitere, nitui, *shine, be radiant with beauty*

nitentis: -is ending, alternate accusative plural ending for **-es**

7–8   **coronatus nitentis...capillos:** take as perfect passive participle with accusative of respect, or middle use of perfect passive participle with direct object

8   **malobathrum, -i,** n., *the tree Cinnamomum tamala or its oil*

Syrius, -a, -um, adj., *Syrian*

9   **Philippi, -orum,** m. pl., *Philippi,* town in eastern Macedonia where Brutus and Cassius were defeated

fuga, -ae, f., *flight, rout*

10   **non bene:** litotes

parmula, -ae, f., *little shield;* this particular shield was obsolete by Horace's time

relicta...parmula: ablative absolute

relicta...parmula: Horace places himself here in the Greek literary tradition of Archilochus, Alcaeus, and Anacreon, all of whom wrote poems in which they speak of leaving behind their shields shamefully.

11   **fracta:** see line 7

fracta: understand **est**

minax, minacis, adj., *threatening, projecting*

11–12   **minaces...mento:** image of death or prostration

12   **turpis, -e,** adj., *ugly, shameful, disgraceful*

solum, -i, n., *ground, floor, land*

tango, tangere, tetigi, tactum, *touch*

tetigere: alternate form of the third person plural perfect tense ending, **-erunt**

mentum, -i, n., *chin*

sed me per hostis Mercurius celer
denso paventem sustulit aere,
   te rursus in bellum resorbens   **15**
      unda fretis tulit aestuosis.

ergo obligatam redde Iovi dapem,
longaque fessum militia latus
   depone sub lauru mea, nec
      parce cadis tibi destinatis.   **20**

---

13 **sed me...**: Horace is imitating the topos, found in Homeric epic, of the god whisking away a hero in a cloud.

    hostis, hostis, c., *enemy*

    hostis: **-is** ending, alternate accusative plural ending for **-es**

    Mercurius, Mercurii, m., *Mercury,* son of Jupiter and Maia

    Mercurius: perhaps Mercury because he is a protector of poets

14 **paveo, pavere,** *be frightened, be terrified*

    tollo, tollere, sustuli, sublatum, *lift, raise, extol, take away, destroy*

    aer, aeris, m., *air, weather, mist*

    aere: trisyllabic; "ae" is not a diphthong in the forms of **aer, aeris**

15 **rursus,** adv., *back, again*

    resorbeo, resorbere, *suck back, swallow again*

16 **unda, -ae,** f., *wave, water*

    fretum, -i, n., *strait, sea, violence*

    aestuosus, -a, -um, adj., *very hot, agitated*

    unda...aestuosis: notice the coincidence of meter and sense; the two dactyls that begin the fourth line of the Alcaic stanza play off the idea of a "wave"

    fretis...aestuosis: ablative of place where; **in** frequently omitted in poetry

17 **ergo,** particle, *then, consequently, therefore*

    obligo, obligare, obligavi, obligatum, *tie up, pledge, dedicate*

    daps, dapis, f., *feast, banquet*

18 **fessus, -a, -um,** adj., *tired, weary*

    militia: see line 2

    latus, lateris, n., *side, extreme part or region, flank, lungs, body*

19 **depono, deponere, deposui, depositum,** *lay down*

    laurus, -i/-us, f., *laurel tree*

    sub lauru mea: the laurel is associated both with those celebrating military triumphs and with poets

20 **parco, parcere, peperci, parsum,** *spare* (with dative)

    cadus, -i, m., *jar, flask* (especially for wine)

    destino, destinare, destinavi, destinatum, *fix, determine, intend, destine, earmark*

oblivioso levia Massico
ciboria exple, funde capacibus
   unguenta de conchis. quis udo
      deproperare apio coronas

curatve myrto? quem Venus arbitrum   25
dicet bibendi? non ego sanius
   bacchabor Edonis: recepto
      dulce mihi furere est amico.

21   **obliviosus, -a, -um**, adj., *producing forgetfulness, forgetful*

oblivioso: there may be an allusion here to the amnesty proclaimed by Octavian at the conclusion of the civil wars

levis, -e, adj., *smooth, smooth* (from polishing)

levia: note the long "e," which identifies this word as coming from the **levis, -e** given above, and not the other adjective, **levis, -e**, which has a short "e"

Massicum, -i, n., *Massic wine, wine from the area of* **Massicus**, a mountain in Campania

22   **ciborium, ciborii**, n., *a kind of drinking cup*

expleo, explere, explevi, expletum, *fill up*

fundo, fundere, fudi, fusum, *pour, spread, scatter, defeat*

capax, capacis, adj., *spacious, capable*

23   **unguentum, -i**, n., *ointment, perfume*

concha, -ae, f., *shell fish, sea shell, perfume dish*

udus, -a, -um, adj., *wet*, (here) *pliant*

24   **depropero, deproperare**, *hurry to complete*

apium, apii, n., *parsley, celery*

corona, -ae, f., *crown, garland*

25   **curo, curare, curavi, curatum**, *take care of, attend to, care about*

myrtus, -i, f., *myrtle*

venus, veneris, f., *Venus*, Roman goddess of love; *love, charm, sexual activity; best throw at dice*

arbiter, arbitri, m., *judge, overseer*

25–26   **quem...bibendi**: the head of the drinking party was chosen by using dice; the Venus throw, or highest throw, determined the winner

26   **bibo, bibere, bibi**, *drink*

sanus, -a, -um, adj., *healthy, sane*

27   **bacchor, bacchari, bacchatus sum**, *celebrate the festival of Bacchus, rave, rage*

Edonus, -a, -um, adj., *Thracian*; the **Edoni** were a tribe celebrated for their orgiastic worship of Bacchus

28   **dulcis, -e**, adj., *sweet*, (of persons) *dear, beloved*

furo, furere, *behave wildly, be crazy*

ODE 2.10

*This poem, which advocates following a "golden mean," is built around a series of antitheses. Notice how Horace creates variation within this basic framework. For example, the balance of the pattern laying out alternatives in line 13 contrasts with the expansion (through the **dum** clause) upon the second alternative in the first stanza. It is this variation upon one basic theme that makes the poem seem both simple and carefully crafted.*

Meter: Sapphic

**Rectius vives, Licini, neque altum
semper urgendo, neque – dum procellas
cautus horrescis – nimium premendo
    litus iniquum.**

---

1   **rectus, -a, -um**, adj., *straight, right, correct, proper*

    rectius: this comparative is echoed by the comparative, **saepius**, in line 9

    Licinius, Licinii, m., *Licinius;* this Licinius may have been Lucius Licinius Murena, brother-in-law of Maecenas, who was executed when trying to escape after his alleged participation in a conspiracy against Augustus. This Licinius was a patron of Athenaeus, a leading Peripatetic, or follower of Aristotle's school of philosophy. If this is the Licinius addressed, extra point is added to both the ethical and political advice Horace gives here.

altum, -i, n., *high place or position, heaven, sea, the deep*

altum: this nautical language introduces the metaphor of the "sea" of life or of politics

2   **urgeo, urgere, ursi**, *push, press upon*

    procella, -ae, f., *storm, trouble*

3   **cautus, -a, -um**, adj., *on one's guard, wary, cautious, prudent*

    horresco, horrescere, horrui, *shudder at, tremble at*

    nimium, adv., *too, too much, very*

    premo, premere, pressi, pressum, *press, follow closely*

4   **litus, litoris**, n., *shore, coast, beach*

    iniquus, -a, -um, adj., *uneven, unfavorable, treacherous, discontented*

auream quisquis mediocritatem 5
diligit, tutus caret obsoleti
sordibus tecti, caret invidenda
    sobrius aula.

saepius ventis agitatur ingens
pinus et celsae graviore casu 10
decidunt turres feriuntque summos
    fulgura montis.

---

5   **aureus, -a, -um**, adj., *golden, splendid*

    mediocritas, mediocritatis, f., *mean, moderation, keeping of a middle course*

    mediocritatem: Cf. Aristotle's notion in the *Nicomachean Ethics* that excellence in a particular thing lies somewhere (not necessarily midway) between the extremes of deficiency and excess.

6   **diligo, diligere, dilexi, dilectum**, *love, esteem, hold dear, have special regard for*

    tutus, -a, -um, adj., *safe, secure*

    careo, carere, carui, caritum, *lack, be without* (with ablative)

    obsoletus, -a, -um, adj., *worn out, shabby, ordinary*

6–8 Note the repetition of **caret**, which highlights the extremes, as well as the asyndeton, which makes the alternatives more stark.

7   **sordes, sordis**, f., often used in plural; *dirt, squalor, baseness*

tectum, -i, n., *roof, house*

caret: see line 6

invideo, invidere, invidi, invisum, *envy, begrudge, refuse*

8   **sobrius, -a, -um**, adj., *sober, moderate, sensible*

    aula, aulae, f., *noble residence, palace, hall*

9   **agito, agitare, agitavi, agitatum**, *drive, agitate, excite*

    ingens, ingentis, adj., *huge*

10 **pinus, -us**, f., *pine*

    celsus, -a, -um, adj., *high, lofty, proud*

    casus, -us, m., *fall, event, misfortune, chance*

11 **decido, decidere, decidi**, *fall down, die*

    turris, -is, f., *tower*

    ferio, ferire, *strike, hit*

12 **fulgur, fulguris**, n., *a flash of lightning, flash of light*

    montis: **-is** = **-es** (accusative plural)

sperat infestis, metuit secundis
alteram sortem bene praeparatum
pectus. informis hiemes reducit   **15**
Iuppiter, idem

submovet. non, si male nunc, et olim
sic erit: quondam cithara tacentem
suscitat Musam, neque semper arcum
tendit Apollo.   **20**

rebus angustis animosus atque
fortis appare: sapienter idem
contrahes vento nimium secundo
turgida vela.

---

13   **infestus, -a, -um**, adj., *dangerous, hostile, insecure*

     secundus, -a, -um, adj., *following, second, favorable*

     infestis...secundis: understand a word like **rebus** (circumstances); ablative of time when

     sperat...secundis: synchysis

14   **sors, sortis**, f., *lot, share*

     praeparo, praeparare, praeparavi, praeparatum, *prepare*

15   **pectus**: subject of **sperat** and **metuit** (13)

     informis, -e, adj., *shapeless, deformed, ugly*

     informis: **-is** = **-es** (accusative plural)

     hiems, hiemis, f., *winter, storm*

16–17   Note the enjambment between the fourth and fifth stanzas. All the other stanzas are end-stopped.

17   **submoveo, submovere, submovi, submotum**, *move away, remove, ward off, banish*

     olim, adv., *formerly, once, on an occasion, at some future date*

18   **quondam**, adv., *once, formerly, sometimes, in the future*

     cithara, -ae, f., *lyre*

19   **suscito, suscitare, suscitavi, suscitatum**, *rouse, awaken*

     Musa, -ae, f., *muse;* one of the nine Muses, goddesses who were daughters of Zeus and Mnemosyne and presided over the arts

     arcus, -us, m., *bow*

20   **tendo, tendere, tetendi, tentum/tensum**, *stretch out, extend, proceed*

     Apollo, Apollinis, m., *Apollo,* son of Jupiter and Latona, brother of Diana, god of archery, music, poetry, etc.

21   **rebus angustis**: ablative of time when

     angustus, -a, -um, adj., *narrow, limited, difficult* (of circumstances)

     animosus, -a, -um, adj., *spirited, bold*

22   **appareo, apparere, apparui, apparitum**, *appear*

     sapienter, adv., *wisely*

23   **contraho, contrahere, contraxi, contractum**, *draw together, narrow*

     nimium, adv., *too, too much, very*

     secundo: see line 13

24   **turgidus, -a, -um**, adj., *swollen, turgid*

     velum, -i, n., *sail*

ODE 2.14

*While educated Romans of Horace's time were sceptical about the reality of the kinds of images of what occurs after death we find in this poem (cf., e.g., Cicero Tusculan Disputations 1.10–12), such images still functioned effectively at the imaginative level. Death's necessity is underscored through the poem's three gerundives (**enaviganda, visendus, linquenda**), which define the journey to the underworld, show what it contains, and explain what it leaves behind. The recklessness of Postumus' heir, who spills the wine he enjoys, intensifies the poem's gloom and may suggest that his behavior is a less than ideal alternative to Postumus' senseless hoarding. At the imaginative level, death overshadows the figure who is associated with the Epicurean injunction to enjoy the moment.*

Meter: Alcaic

Eheu fugaces, Postume, Postume,
labuntur anni, nec pietas moram
    rugis et instanti senectae
        adferet indomitaeque morti,

---

1   **eheu**, interjection (expressing grief or pain), *alas*

      fugax, fugacis, adj., *swift, fugitive, elusive*

      Postumus, -i, m., *Postumus*; this name was often given to boys who were born after the death of their fathers; the identity of this Postumus is unknown; he may be the Postumus addressed by Propertius in Elegy 3.12.

2   **labor, labi, lapsus sum**, *glide, slip, pass*

      pietas, pietatis, f., *duty, devotion*

      mora, -ae, f., *delay, hindrance*

3   **ruga, -ae**, f., *wrinkle*

      instans, instantis, adj., *pressing, urgent*

      senecta, -ae, f., *old age*

4   **adfero, adferre, attuli, allatum**, *bring, add*

      indomitus, -a, -um, adj., *unconquered, unconquerable*

non, si trecenis, quotquot eunt dies,   5
amice, places inlacrimabilem
    Plutona tauris, qui ter amplum
      Geryonen Tityonque tristi

conpescit unda, scilicet omnibus,
quicumque terrae munere vescimur,   10
    enaviganda, sive reges,
      sive inopes erimus coloni.

---

5   **treceni, trecenae, trecena**, pl. adj., *three hundred each, three hundred at a time*

    quotquot, indeclinable adj., *however many*

6   **placo, placare, placavi, placatum**, *appease, calm*

    places: note that this verb form is from **placo**, not **placeo**

    inlacrimabilis, -e, adj., *pitiless*

5–7   **trecenis...tauris**: this sacrifice would be three times as large as the traditional hecatomb, the sacrifice of one hundred cattle

7   **Pluto, Plutonis**, m., *Pluto,* king of the underworld

    taurus, -i, m., *bull*

    ter, adv., *three times*

    amplus, -a, -um, adj., *large, spacious*

8   **Geryon, Geryonis**, m., *Geryon;* triple-headed or triple-bodied king whom Hercules killed when carrying off his cattle.

    Tityos, -i, m., *Tityus;* giant primarily known for attempting to rape Latona, mother of Apollo and Diana; punished in the underworld by being stretched over nine acres while two vultures or snakes ate his heart or liver.

    Geryon and **Tityon**: Greek accusatives

    tristis, -e, adj., *sad*

9   **compesco, compescere, compescui**, *confine, restrain, check*

    unda, -ae, f., *wave, water*

    unda: ablative with **enaviganda** (11)

    scilicet, adv., *evidently, of course, surely*

    omnibus: dative of agent with gerundive

10   **munus, muneris**, n., *service, duty, gift, entertainment*

    vescor, vesci, *enjoy, feed on, eat* (with ablative)

11   **enavigo, enavigare, enavigavi, enavigatum**, *sail across, sail forth*

    enaviganda, visendus (17), **linquenda** (21): gerundives

12   **inops, inopis**, adj., *lacking wealth, poor*

    colonus, -i, m., *farmer, settler*

frustra cruento Marte carebimus
fractisque rauci fluctibus Hadriae,
   frustra per autumnos nocentem   **15**
      corporibus metuemus Austrum:

visendus ater flumine languido
Cocytos errans et Danai genus
   infame damnatusque longi
      Sisyphus Aeolides laboris.   **20**

---

13   **frustra**, adv., *in vain, to no purpose*

      cruentus, -a, -um, adj., *bloody, gory, cruel*

      Mars, Martis, m., *Mars*, god of war

      Marte: *war*, by metonymy

      careo, carere, carui, caritum, *lack, be without* (with ablative)

14   **frango, frangere, fregi, fractum**, *break, crush*

      raucus, -a, -um, adj., *hoarse, noisy, raucous*

      Hadria, -ae, m., *Adriatic Sea*

      fractisque...Hadriae: synchysis

15   **frustra**: see line 13

      autumnus, -i, m., *autumn*

      autumnos: autumn was traditionally an unhealthy season in Italy

      noceo, nocere, nocui, nocitum, *harm* (with dative)

16   **Auster, Austri**, m., *south wind*

17   **viso, visere, visi**, *look at, go and see*

      visendus: takes its number and gender from **Cocytos** (masculine singular); **genus** and **Sisyphus** should be taken with it as well

      ater, atra, atrum, adj., *black, dark, gloomy*

flumen, fluminis, n., *river, waters of a river*

languidus, -a, -um, adj., *languid, sluggish, slow*

18   **Cocytos, Cocyti**, m., *Cocytus*, one of the rivers of the underworld

      Danaus, -i, m., *Danaus*; all but one of his fifty daughters, the Danaids, on instructions from their father, killed their husbands on their wedding night; they are punished in the underworld by having continuously to fill up leaky jars; story portrayed by Polygnotus at Delphi as well as at Augustus' Temple of Apollo on the Palatine.

19   **infamis, -e**, adj., *infamous, disreputable*

      damno, damnare, damnavi, damnatum, *condemn, sentence*

      longi: litotes

19–20 **longi...laboris**: genitive of penalty with **damnatus**

20   **Sisyphus, -i**, m., *Sisyphus*; son of Aeolus, committed various crimes and is punished in the underworld by forever having to roll a rock up a steep hill only to have it roll down again.

      Aeolides, Aeolidae, m., *a son or more remote descendant of Aeolus*

linquenda tellus et domus et placens
uxor, neque harum, quas colis, arborum
    te praeter invisas cupressos
        ulla brevem dominum sequetur,

absumet heres Caecuba dignior   25
servata centum clavibus et mero
    tinguet pavimentum superbo,
        pontificum potiore cenis.

---

21   **linquo, linquere, liqui**, *go away from, abandon, leave behind*

     tellus, telluris, f., *land, earth, country, ground*

     placeo, placere, placui, placitum, *please*

22   **colo, colere, colui, cultum**, *cultivate, cherish*

23   **praeter**, preposition with accusative, *except, beyond*

     invisus, -a, -um, adj., *hateful, odious*

     cupressus, -i, f., *cypress;* the cypress had funereal associations

24   **dominus, -i**, m., *master, lord, ruler*

25   **absumo, absumere, absumpsi, absumptum**, *spend, consume*

     heres, heredis, c., *heir*

     Caecubum, -i, n., *choice wine from Caecubum,* a district in south Latium

     dignus, -a, -um, adj., *worthy, worthy of, deserving* (with ablative)

dignior: because he uses and enjoys the wine rather than hoarding it, however there may be irony here

26   **clavis, clavis**, f., *key*

     merus, -a, -um, adj., *pure, unmixed;* with **vinum** or with **vinum** understood, *wine not mixed with water*

27   **tinguo, tinguere, tinxi, tinctum**, *wet, stain*

     pavimentum, -i, n., *pavement, floor*

     superbo: suggests both an excellent wine and perhaps arrogant disregard for wasting some wine while enjoying life's pleasures

28   **pontifex, pontificis**, m., *high priest, pontiff*

     potior, potius, adj., *better, preferable*

     pontificum potiore cenis: elliptical; wine being compared to *the wine* served at the dinners of the pontiffs

ODE 3.1

Some see in this ode an attempt to discourage personal ambition and to encourage contentment with one's situation. Whatever grand power and wealth one seeks does not differentiate one from the powerless and poor in the long run — all are subject to divinity and Necessity, powers beyond human control. Yet, it is in Horace's ambitous role as "priest of the Muses" that he makes these pronouncements, leading the reader to the paradoxical conclusion that it is his poetry (surely the product of intense ambition) that allows him to make these very pronouncements against personal ambition.

Meter: Alcaic

[handwritten: = uninitiated, don't read poetry]

Odi profanum volgus et arceo.   *[handwritten: frame]*
favete linguis: carmina non prius
    audita Musarum sacerdos
      virginibus puerisque canto.

[handwritten left margin: imperative; ritual language b/c "priest of the Muses"]

1–4 These lines function as an introduction to this poem and to the so-called Roman Odes (Book 3.1–6), a group of poems set apart by their Alcaic meter, solemn style, closely related themes, lack of individual addressees, and interest in the values necessary for a successful Augustan Rome. The **carmina non prius/audita** (2–3) refer to Latin lyric used for national song. Horace as "priest of the Muses" initiates the next generation into the sacral space of his song.

1 **odi, odisse, osum,** (perfect with present sense), *have an aversion to, hate*

  profanus, -a, -um, adj., *profane, secular, impious, uninitiated*

  volgus, -i, n., *the common people, the general public, crowd*

arceo, arcere, arcui, *contain, keep away, spurn*

2 **faveo, favere, favi, fautum,** *favor;* with **linguis** (ablative), *avoid words of ill omen, be silent*

  carmen, carminis, n., *solemn or ritual utterance, song, poem, lyric poetry*

3 **Musa, -ae,** f., *muse;* one of the nine Muses, goddesses who were daughters of Zeus and Mnemosyne and presided over the arts

  sacerdos, sacerdotis, c., *priest or priestess*

4 **puer, pueri,** m., *boy, non-adult male, male beloved,* (young) *male slave*

  canto, cantare, cantavi, cantatum, *sing, sing about, recite*

regum timendorum in proprios greges,   5
reges in ipsos imperium est Iovis,
   clari Giganteo triumpho,
     cuncta supercilio moventis.

est, ut viro vir latius ordinet
arbusta sulcis, hic generosior   10
   descendat in campum petitor,
     moribus hic meliorque fama

5–8   The kings who evince fear (**regum timendorum**) quickly give way to Jupiter who rules them in turn (**reges in ipsos imperium est Iovis**). Lines 7–8 expand upon the description of the power of Jupiter who rules with a nod of his head.

5   **regum timendorum**: understand **imperium est** from the next line

   proprius, -a, -um, adj., *one's own, personal*

   grex, gregis, m., flock, *herd, company, crowd*

5–6   **in**: in plus accusative in these two lines has the sense of "over"

   regum/reges: figura etymologica

6   **imperium, imperii**, n., *power, command, government*

6–7   With **imperium** and **triumpho** Horace uses words from the Roman political vocabulary to describe the power structure of the world.

7   **Giganteus, -a, -um**, adj., *of the Giants*, a mythical race, who fought and were defeated by the Olympian gods

   clari: modifies **Iovis**

   Giganteo triumpho: the adjective functions like an objective genitive with the noun; for more on Jupiter's victory over the Giants, cf. Ode 3.4.42–80

8   **supercilium, supercilii**, n., *eyebrow, nod*

   moventis: modifies **Iovis**

9–16   A successful landowner (**vir**) and three candidates for political office (**hic, hic, illi**) who excel, respectively, in noble birth, character and fame, and number of clients are shown to be subject to the impartial law of Necessity that determines the fates of high and low alike.

9–14   **Est, ut** introduces four subordinate verbs in the subjunctive in substantive clauses of result: **ordinet...descendat...contendat...sit**

9   **ordino, ordinare, ordinavi, ordinatum**, *set in order, arrange*

10   **arbustum, -i**, n., *wood, plantation*, (plural) *trees*

   sulcus, -i, m., *a furrow, trench, track*

   generosus, -a, -um, adj., *of noble birth, noble*

11   **descendo, descendere, descendi, descensum**, *come or go down, descend*

   campus, -i, m., *plain, level surface; plain, field*; often refers specifically to the Campus Martius in Rome; elections took place in the Campus Martius

   petitor, petitoris, m., *seeker, candidate*

12   **mos, moris**, m., *custom, tradition*; (plural) *character, habits*

   moribus and **fama**: ablatives of respect with **melior**

12–13   Notice the enjambment. The structure of the poem is as follows: 1–4 (introduction to this poem and the Roman Odes as a whole); 5–8; then pairs of stanzas joined by enjambment: 9–16; 17–24; 25–32; 33–40; 41–48.

contendat, illi turba clientium
sit maior: aequa lege Necessitas
   sortitur insignis et imos,   15
      omne capax movet urna nomen.

13   **contendo, contendere, contendi, contentum**, *stretch, hasten, compete, contend*

     turba, -ae, f., *crowd*

     cliens, clientis, m., *client;* one who attaches himself to a person of greater influence or political power (**patronus**) for protection

14   **aequuus, -a, -um**, adj., *equal, even, impartial, fair*

     The personifications of **Necessitas** (14), **Timor** (37), **Minae** (37), and **Cura** (40) create very strong images.

15   **sortior, sortiri, sortitus sum**, *cast lots over, choose*

sortitur: a significant verb to use directly following a political context where winners were not chosen by lot

insignis, -e, adj., *distinguished*

imus, -a, -um, adj., *lowest*

16   **capax, capacis**, adj., *spacious, capable*

     urna, -ae, f., *urn*

capax...urna: cf. Ode 2.3.25 ff. where fortunes are also tossed about in an urn

omne capax movet urna nomen: a golden line, i.e., two adjectives and two nouns with a verb between, in this case arranged chiastically, adj. a, adj. b, verb, noun b, noun a

destrictus ensis cui super impia
cervice pendet, non Siculae dapes
dulcem elaborabunt saporem,
  non avium citharaeque cantus   20

somnum reducent: somnus agrestium
lenis virorum non humilis domos
fastidit umbrosamque ripam,
  non Zephyris agitata Tempe.

17–24   Those who possess power and
wealth cannot enjoy them because
of the threat of their loss; sleep
eludes them unlike the humble
farmer, and those who enjoy the
shady bank and the wind-stirred
valley.

17–19   These lines are a reference to the
story of the sword of Damocles.
Dionysius, tyrant of Syracuse (430–
367 BCE), shows his subject, Damocles, that the life of the tyrant is
not the total enjoyment Damocles
thinks it is by placing before him
a magnificent banquet only to sus-
pend over his head a sword. In this
story, Dionysius teaches Damocles
a lesson about the anxieties inher-
ent in power and wealth. Horace,
in turn, uses the story for his own
moral purpose, which seems to be
to show the tyrant's greedy use of
power. The description of the neck
as **impia** suggests a grasping after
things beyond what is good. The
wise ruler, presumably, would not
be worried about what he person-
ally has to lose.

17   **destringo, destringere, destrinxi,
destrictum**, *strip off, scrape lightly,
draw or unsheathe* (a weapon)

ensis, ensis, m., *sword*

cui: dative of reference

impius, -a, -um, adj., *impious, undutiful, disloyal*

18   **cervix, cervicis**, f., *neck*

pendeo, pendere, pependi, *hang,
hover, hang down, be suspended*

Siculus, -a, -um, adj., *Sicilian*

daps, dapis, f., *feast, banquet*

19   **elaboro, elaborare, elaboravi, elabo-
ratum**, *strive, work out, develop, perfect*

sapor, saporis, m., *taste, flavor*

20   **avis, avis**, f., *bird*

cithara, -ae, f., *lyre*

cantus, -us, m., *singing, song, poetry*

21   **somnus, -i**, m., *sleep*

agrestis, -e, adj., *of the country, rustic,
rural*

22   **lenis, -e**, adj., *smooth, gentle, mild, soft*

humilis, -e, adj., *humble, low*

humilis: -is = -es (accusative plural)

23   **fastidio, fastidire, fastidivi, fastidi-
tum**, *show aversion to, scorn*

umbrosus, -a, -um, adj., *shady*

ripa, -ae, f., *bank of a river, shore*

24   **zephyrus, -i**, m., *west wind, zephyr*

agito, agitare, agitavi, agitatum, *stir,
drive, agitate, excite*

Tempe, n. pl., (here, accusative),
Tempe, valley of the Peneus river
between Ossa and Olympus in
Thessaly noted for its beauty; *any
beautiful valley*

desiderantem quod satis est neque   **25**
tumultuosum sollicitat mare,
   nec saevus Arcturi cadentis
      impetus aut orientis Haedi,

non verberatae grandine vineae
fundusque mendax, arbore nunc aquas   **30**
   culpante, nunc torrentia agros
      sidera, nunc hiemes iniquas.

25–32   The one who desires just what is enough is not bothered by various forces of nature that pose a danger to one's livelihood, whether merchant or farmer.

26   **tumultuosus, -a, -um**, adj., *full of commotion, turbulent*

sollicito, sollicitare, sollicitavi, sollicitatum, *rouse, excite, shake up, disturb with repeated attacks*

27–28   Haedus and Arcturus are constellations that appear in October, the stormy season.

27   **Arcturus, -i**, m., *Arcturus,* the brightest star of the constellation Boötes

cadentis: the verb **cado** is used of the setting of heavenly bodies

28   **impetus, -us**, m., *attack, onset, rapid motion*

orior, oriri, ortus sum, *rise, be born*

Haedus, -i, m., *young goat, kid;* two stars in the constellation **Auriga**

29   **verbero, verberare, verberavi, verberatum**, *beat, lash*

grando, grandinis, f., *hail*

vinea, -ae, f., *vineyard*

30–32   The farm and tree are personified; the farm is deceitful (**mendax**), while the tree (**arbore**) blames (**culpante**) the water, stars, and winters, presumably for its lack of productivity. Notice the repetition of **nunc** with each new reason for complaint.

30   **fundus, -i**, m., *bottom, farm, estate*

mendax, mendacis, adj., *lying, false*

31   **culpo, culpare, culpavi, culpatum**, *blame*

torreo, torrere, torrui, tostum, *burn, parch*

32   **sidus, sideris**, n., *star; sky* (plural)

hiems, hiemis, f., *winter, storm*

iniquus, -a, -um, adj., *uneven, unfavorable, treacherous, discontented*

contracta pisces aequora sentiunt
iactis in altum molibus: huc frequens
   caementa demittit redemptor   35
      cum famulis dominusque terrae

fastidiosus, sed Timor et Minae
scandunt eodem, quo dominus, neque
   decedit aerata triremi et
      post equitem sedet atra Cura.   40

33–40 The rich build houses out into the sea, overstepping natural bounds, with the master disdainful of the land. Yet fear and threats and concern follow the master wherever he goes.

33 **contraho, contrahere, contraxi, contractum**, *draw together, narrow*

piscis, piscis, m., *fish*

aequor, aequoris, n., *a flat level surface, the flat surface of the sea*, (often used in plural)

34 **iacio, iacere, ieci, iactum**, *throw, lay foundations*

altum, -i, n., *high place or position, heaven, sea, the deep*

moles, molis, f., *mass, bulk, massive structure*

frequens, frequentis, adj., *crowded, assiduous, constant, regular*

35 **caementum, -i**, n., *small stones, rubble*

demitto, demittere, demisi, demissum, *let down, sink, lower*

redemptor, redemptoris, m., *contractor*

36 **famulus, -i**, m., *servant, attendant, slave*

dominus, -i, m., *master, lord, ruler*

37 **fastidiosus, -a, -um**, adj., *critical, exacting, disdainful*

timor, timoris, m., *fear*

minae, -arum, f. pl., *threats, warning signs*

38 **scando, scandere**, *climb, ascend, mount*

eodem, adv., *to the same place*

quo, adv., *where, for what purpose*

dominus: see line 36

39 **decedo, decedere, decessi, decessum**, *go away, depart, withdraw* (with ablative)

aeratus, -a, -um, adj., *made of or fitted with bronze or brass*

triremis, triremis, f., *ship having three banks of oars; trireme*

39–40 The rich man engages in leisure activities by riding (**equitem**) and going out on a fancy boat (**aerata triremi**).

40 **eques, equitis**, m., *horseman, rider, member of the cavalry, member of the equestrian order*

ater, atra, atrum, adj., *black, dark, gloomy*

cura, -ae, f., *care, concern, worry, a person or thing constituting an object of care*

quodsi dolentem nec Phrygius lapis,
nec purpurarum sidere clarior
    delenit usus, nec Falerna
        vitis Achaemeniumque costum,

cur invidendis postibus et novo   **45**
sublime ritu moliar atrium?
    cur valle permutem Sabina
        divitias operosiores?

41–48 If excessive elaborateness does nothing to alleviate pain and entails excessive toil (**divitias operosiores**), how could it be preferable to the poet's Sabine home? These lines echo the first person singular used in the opening lines of the poem.

41 **quodsi**, conj., *but if*

doleo, dolere, dolui, dolitum, *suffer mental or physical pain, be in pain, grieve*

Phrygius, -a, -um, adj., *Phrygian*

lapis, lapidis, m., *stone*

Phrygius lapis: a kind of marble

42 **purpura, -ae,** f., *shellfish yielding a purple dye, the purple dye from the shellfish, purple-dyed cloth, purple*

sidere: (see line 32)

clarior: transferred epithet; grammatically modifies **usus** (43), but goes in sense with **purpurarum**

43 **delenio, delenire, delenivi, delenitum,** *soothe*

usus, -us, m., *use, enjoyment*

Falernus, -a, -um, adj., *Falernian, of a district in northern Campania famous for its wine*

44 **vitis, vitis,** f., *vine*

Achaemenius, -a, -um, adj., *Persian, Parthian*

costum, -i, n., *an aromatic plant*

45 **invideo, invidere, invidi, invisum,** *envy, begrudge, refuse*

postis, postis, m., *door-post, door*

46 **sublimis, -e,** adj., *high, raised, elevated, sublime, lofty*

ritus, -us, m., *ritual, custom, manner, style*

molior, moliri, molitus sum, *labor at, build*

moliar: deliberative subjunctive

atrium, atrii, n., *hall, first main room in a Roman-style house*

47 **valles, vallis,** f., *valley*

permuto, permutare, permutavi, permutatum, *exchange, receive in exchange for* (accusative of thing received and ablative of thing given up)

permutem: deliberative subjunctive, like **moliar** above

Sabinus, -a, -um, adj., *Sabine;* the Sabines were a people of central Italy.

valle...Sabina: where Horace had his Sabine farm

48 **divitiae, divitiarum,** f. pl., *wealth, riches*

operosus, -a, -um, adj., *toilsome, laborious, painstaking, industrious*

operosiores: Cf. Ode 4.2.31–32, where Horace describes his own poems as **operosa...carmina.**

ODE 3.9

This conversation between two lovers (former lovers, present lovers? future lovers?) is Horace's only lyric poem in dialogue form. Each of the lovers speaks the same number of lines. Each tries to outdo the other's previous words. Some see the woman each time outdoing the man; others see the man, who speaks first, as the one who gets to set the terms of the conversation. Some see the end of the poem as the lovers' reconciliation; others, more sceptical, see the competitive and tempestuous nature of the relationship as a sign that any reconciliation would contain the elements of its own destruction. This poem is frequently compared with Catullus 45, the Acme and Septimius poem. There, too, critics debate the believability of what seems to be an ideal love.

Meter: second Asclepiadean

Donec gratus eram tibi,
    nec quisquam potior brachia candidae
cervici iuvenis dabat,
    Persarum vigui rege beatior.

---

1   **donec**, conj., *as long as, while*
      gratus, -a, -um: adj., *pleasing*
2   **potior, potius**, adj., *more able, more powerful, preferable*
      brachium, brachii, n., *arm*
      candidus, -a, -um, adj., *bright, radiant, white*

3   **cervix, cervicis**, f., *neck*
      iuvenis, iuvenis, m., (f.), *young man, young woman*
4   **Persae, Persarum**, m. pl., *Persians*
      vigeo, vigere, vigui, *flourish, thrive*

'donec non alia magis   5
    arsisti, neque erat Lydia post Chloen,
multi Lydia nominis
    Romana vigui clarior Ilia.'

me nunc Thressa Chloe regit,
    dulcis docta modos et citharae sciens,   10
pro qua non metuam mori,
    si parcent animae fata superstiti.

---

5   **alia**: note the meter requires this to be a long **a**; ablative with **ardeo**, not ablative of comparison

6   **ardeo, ardere, arsi**, *be on fire, burn, be in love* (with ablative)

    Lydia, -ae, f., *Lydia*, woman's name

    post: after, in sense of "second to"

    Chloe, Chloes, f., *Chloe*, Greek woman's name; the **oe** is not a diphthong here.

    Chloen: Greek accusative singular; two syllables

7   **Lydia**: note how the repetition of the name **Lydia** from the previous line enacts the sense of **multi nominis**; the male speaker's name never appears in the poem; the names Chloe and Lydia each occur three times

    multi nominis: genitive of quality

8   **Ilia, -ae**, f., *Ilia* or *Rhea Silvia*, mother of Romulus and Remus

    Romana...Ilia: ablative of comparison

9   **Thressa, -ae**, f., *a Thracian woman*; here, as feminine adjective, *Thracian*

10   **dulcis**: **-is** = **-es** (accusative plural)

    doctus, -a, -um, *learned, taught*

    dulcis...modos: accusative of respect with **docta**

    modus, -i, m., *limit, way, rhythmic pattern*; in plural, *poetry*

    cithara, -ae, f., *lyre*

    citharae: genitive of reference (cf. notes to Ode 1.22.1) with **sciens**; here, the participle functions as an adjective, "knowing" plus the genitive

11   **metuam**: the form can be either future indicative or present subjunctive; probably best taken as future, considering the future tense of **parcent** (line 12)

    morior, mori, mortuus sum, *die*

12   **parco, parcere, peperci, parsum**, *spare* (with dative)

    anima, -ae, f., *breath, life, darling*

    fatum, -i, n., *fate*, pl., *the Fates*

    superstes, superstitis, adj., *standing over, surviving*

'me torret face mutua
  Thurini Calais filius Ornyti,
pro quo bis patiar mori,   15
  si parcent puero fata superstiti.'

quid si prisca redit Venus
  diductosque iugo cogit aeneo,
si flava excutitur Chloe,
  reiectaeque patet ianua Lydiae?   20

---

13   **torreo, torrere, torrui, tostum**, *burn, parch*

  fax. facis, f., *torch, torch used at funerals and marriages, marriage, death*

  mutuus, -a, -um, adj., *mutual, reciprocal*

14   **Thurinus, -a, -um**, adj., *pertaining to the town of Thurii in southern Italy*

  Calais, Calais, m., *Calais*, man's name

  Ornytus, -i, m., *Ornytus*, man's name

  Thurini...Ornyti: Lydia makes important the "naming" of her current flame; cf. lines 7–8 where she makes her own name important

15   **bis**, adv., *twice*

  patior, pati, passus sum, *suffer, undergo, experience, endure, allow*

  patiar: cf. **metuam**, line 11, for the form

  mori: see line 11

16   **parcent**: see line 12

  puer, pueri, m., *boy, non-adult male, male beloved,* (young) *male slave*

  fata: see line 12

  superstiti: see line 12

17   **priscus, -a, -um**, adj., *ancient, former*

  redeo, redire, redii, reditum, *go back, come back, return*

  venus, veneris, f., *Venus*, Roman goddess of love; *love, charm, sexual activity; best throw at dice*

18   **diduco, diducere, diduxi, diductum**, *separate, split*

  iugum, -i, n., *yoke, bond*

  cogo, cogere, coegi, coactum, *drive together, force*

  aeneus, -a, -um, adj., *of bronze;* the **ae** is not a diphthong here

19   **flavus, -a, -um**, adj., *yellow, golden, blonde, auburn*

  excutio, excutere, excussi, excussum, *shake out, drive out, banish*

  Chloe: see line 6

20   **reicio, reicere, reieci, reiectum**, *throw back, drive back, reject*

  pateo, patere, patui, *be open*

  ianua, -ae, f., *door*

  Lydiae: see line 6

  reiectae...Lydiae: dative, rather than genitive, in the context

'quamquam sidere pulchrior
   ille est, tu levior cortice et inprobo
iracundior Hadria,
   tecum vivere amem, tecum obeam libens.'

---

21   **quamquam**, conj., *although*

  sidus, sideris, n., *star; sky* (plural)

22   **levis, -e**, adj., *light, swift, gentle, unim-
     portant, fickle*

  cortex, corticis, m., *bark, rind, cork*

  inprobus, -a, -um, adj., *unprincipled,
     immoderate, unruly, relentless, shame-
     less*

23   **iracundus, -a, -um**, adj., *angry, hot-
     tempered, prone to anger*

  Hadria, -ae, m., *Adriatic Sea*

24   **amem, obeam**: potential subjunctive

  obeo, obire, obii, obitum, *go to, meet,
     die*

  libens, libentis, adj., *willing*

  tecum: note the repetition of this
     word in the last line of the poem

ODE 3.13

This hymn to a spring celebrates the complexity of the site of poetic creativity. On the one hand, a hymn involving a proposed dedication, the poem also functions as vehicle for the poet's self-praise. How do humility and pride operate in the poem? What is gained and lost in the sacrifice of the kid to the spring? What, finally, is the relationship between the spring and the poet?

Meter: fourth Asclepiadean

O fons Bandusiae splendidior vitro,
dulci digne mero non sine floribus,
    cras donaberis haedo,
        cui frons turgida cornibus

1   **o**, interjection, *O* (with vocative)

fons, fontis, m., *spring, source*

Bandusia, -ae, f., *Bandusia*, name of a spring perhaps at Horace's Sabine farm or near Apulia, the area on which his hometown bordered; Horace mentions a spring on his Sabine farm elsewhere, but not by name.

Bandusiae: appositional genitive, with **fons**

splendidus, -a, -um, adj., *bright, brilliant, glittering, illustrious*

vitrum, -i, n., *glass*

2   **dulcis, -e**, adj., *sweet,* (of persons) *dear, beloved*

dignus, -a, -um, adj., *worthy, worthy of, deserving* (with ablative)

digne: vocative with **fons**

merus, -a, -um, adj., *pure, unmixed;* with **vinum** or with **vinum** understood, *wine not mixed with water*

non sine: litotes

flos, floris, m., *flower*

mero, floribus: wine as a libation to the gods; flowers, perhaps in the form of garlands, which were used to decorate springs at the festival of the Fontinalia, the festival of the **Fons**

3   **dono, donare, donavi, donatum**, *present, endow, reward* (with), with ablative of thing given

haedus, -i, m., *young goat, kid;* two stars in the constellation **Auriga**

4   **cui**: dative of reference

frons, frontis, f., *forehead, brow, front*

turgidus, -a, -um, adj., *swollen, turgid*

cornu, -us, n., *horn, anything horn-shaped*

4–5   **cornibus/primis**: horns just beginning to grow

primis et Venerem et proelia destinat,   5
frustra: nam gelidos inficiet tibi
   rubro sanguine rivos
      lascivi suboles gregis.

te flagrantis atrox hora Caniculae
nescit tangere, tu frigus amabile   10
   fessis vomere tauris
      praebes et pecori vago.

---

5   **venus, veneris**, f., *Venus,* Roman goddess of love; *love, charm, sexual activity; best throw at dice*

    proelium, proelii, n., *battle*

    destino, destinare, destinavi, destinatum, *fix, determine, intend, destine, earmark*

    et Venerem et proelia destinat: "destines (him) for," with accusative of what he is destined for; **Venerem et proelia**, love and battles may be taken separately, or may refer to battling with rivals over sex (hendiadys)

6   **frustra**, adv., *in vain, to no purpose*

    gelidus, -a, -um, adj., *cold, icy*

    inficio, inficere, infeci, infectum, *dye, imbue, taint, stain*

7   **ruber, rubra, rubrum**, adj., *red*

    sanguis, sanguinis, m., *blood*

    rivus, -i, m., *stream*

8   **lascivus, -a, -um**, adj., *playful, frisky, wanton*

    suboles, subolis, f., *offspring*

    grex, gregis, m., *flock, herd, company, crowd*

9   **te, tu** (10, 13): the repetition in asyndeton of the personal pronoun is typical in outlining the characteristics of the divinity in a hymn

    flagrans, flagrantis, adj., *hot, blazing, passionate*

    atrox, atrocis, adj., *dreadful, fierce, cruel*

    canicula, -ae, f., *the Dog Star, Sirius,* in the constellation Canis Major, brightest star in the sky, thought to bring hot weather

10   **nescio, nescire, nescivi, nescitum**, *not know, be ignorant of, not to know how to, not to be able to*

    tango, tangere, tetigi, tactum, *touch*

    frigus, frigoris, n., *cold*

11   **fessus, -a, -um**, adj., *tired, weary*

    vomer, vomeris, m., *plowshare;* by metonymy, *the plow*

    taurus, -i, m., *bull*

12   **praebeo, praebere, praebui, praebitum**, *give, supply, provide*

    pecus, pecoris, n., *farm animal;* singular as collective, *farm animals, livestock, especially sheep and cattle*

    vagus, -a, -um, adj., *roaming, wandering*

fies nobilium tu quoque fontium
me dicente cavis inpositam ilicem
    saxis, unde loquaces   15
       lymphae desiliunt tuae.

13   **fontium**: see line 1

nobilium...fontium: ellipsis of **unus** and genitive of the whole; the fountain will become famous, like Hippocrene, Arethusa, Castalia

14   **me dicente**: causal ablative absolute

cavus, -a, -um, adj., *hollow, concave*

inpono, inponere, inposui, inpositum, *place on or over, build on*

inpositam, desiliunt (16): both these verbs can have sexual meanings in descriptions of the animal world; **inpono** can mean to place a male to a female for purposes of copulation (cf. *OLD* 8), while **desilio** can be used of an animal jumping or leaping down after copulation (cf. *OLD*).

ilex, ilicis, f., *holm oak, ilex*

ilicem: direct object of **dicente**

14–15   **cavis...saxis**: dative with **inpositam**

15   **saxum, -i**, n., *rock*

loquax, loquacis, adj., *talkative, loquacious, talking*

loquaces: personification; also, cf. the sense of **me dicente** above

15–16   The alliteration of the liquid consonant "l" in **loquaces, lymphae, desiliunt** imitates the sense of the lines

16   **lympha, -ae**, f., *water*

desilio, desilire, desilui, *leap or jump down*

poetry > immortality

epilogue
epitaph - gave bio + merita
prayer

ODE 3.30

With this ode Horace closes the lyric collection he published in 23 BCE. He frames the collection by repeating only here the first Asclepiadean meter he used in the first poem of the collection. In this poem he takes on a tone of supreme confidence and lays claim to an enduring literary achievement: the adaptation to the Latin language of the genre of Greek lyric poetry. There is a grandeur to this ode that gives one a sense of how much pride Horace must have had in his own work. This almost excessive pride is balanced by the reference to humble beginnings and the prayer-like address to the Muse whom he indirectly asks to approve of his work. It is difficult to read this ode without incorporating our knowledge that, in fact, Horace's work has endured, long past the time of Roman rule.

epitaph for himself

Meter: first or lesser Asclepiadean

only other = ode 1.1
framing collection

verb 1st unusual,
emphasize
himself

Exegi monumentum aere perennius
regalique situ pyramidum altius,

royal site/decay

1 **exigo, exigere, exegi, exactum**, *drive out, complete, execute*

monumentum, -i, n., *monument, memorial*

monumentum: anything that "reminds or tells" (the root in the word is the verb **moneo**); often refers to inscriptions in bronze or stone

aes, aeris, n., *copper, bronze, money*

perennis, -e, adj., *lasting throughout the year, lasting for many years, enduring*

2 **regalis, -e**, adj., *royal, regal*

situs, -us, m., *site*

situs, -us, m., *deterioration, neglect*

situ: can be from either **situs**; since both words make sense it is best to keep the ambiguity.

pyramis, pyramidis, f., *pyramid*

regali...pyramidum: the pyramids of Egypt; while the pyramids were very old there may be an allusion here to the end of Cleopatra's rule and threat to Roman power; cf. Ode 1.37

"eat, drink and be merry"
Epicurean —
avoid pain, seek pleasure
Horace's pleasure = avoid pain of pressures, power, wealth

· 95 ·

eating at bronze, rust
Latin obsolete
to grow old or
anaphora
asyndeton – urgency
could be "powerless" metrically
he IS "powerful"
long-lasting poetry

quod non imber edax non Aquilo inpotens
possit diruere aut innumerabilis

annorum series et fuga temporum.   5
non omnis moriar, multaque pars mei

goddess = metonymy
contrast

himself { vitabit Libitinam usque ego postera
crescam laude recens, dum Capitolium

"continually" alliding death + I will live on

---

3 **non...non**: anaphora with asyndeton

imber, imbris, m., *rain, rain shower, water*

edax, edacis, adj., *greedy, devouring, destructive*

Aquilo, Aquilonis, m., *the north wind*

inpotens, inpotentis, adj., *powerless, weak, wild, violent*

3–4 The Greek lyric poet, Pindar, also speaks in Pythian 6 of poems that cannot be destroyed by wind and rain.

4 **possit**: potential subjunctive

diruo, diruere, dirui, dirutum, *cause to fall in ruin, demolish*

innumerabilis, -e, adj., *countless, numberless*

5 **series, (-ei)**, f., *series, sequence, succession*

fuga, -ae, f., *flight, rout*

6 **omnis**: all, "completely"; English would use an adverb here where Latin uses an adjective; contrasts with **pars**

morior, mori, mortuus sum, *die*

mei: partitive genitive

7 **vito, vitare, vitavi, vitatum**, *avoid, shun*

Libitina, -ae, f., *Libitina, the goddess of funerals; funeral couch*

Libitinam: death, by metonymy; however, her specificity may wittily counteract some of the grandiosity of these lines, for it reminds us of the details of burial

usque, adv., *continuously, continually, all the way*

posterus, -a, -um, adj., *next, following, future, later*

8 **cresco, crescere, crevi, cretum**, *arise, multiply, expand, increase*

recens, recentis, adj., *fresh, recent, modern*

Capitolium, Capitolii, n., *Capitolium, the Capitoline hill in Rome on which the Capitoline gods, Jupiter, Juno, and Minerva, were worshipped*

8–9 **dum...pontifex**: The Pontifex Maximus, or chief priest, and the Vestal Virgins represent Rome's state religion. Their continued walk up the Capitolium symbolizes the continuity of Roman culture and institutions. Cf. note on Satire 1.9.35.

[handwritten: Horace = poetry]

[handwritten: "silent virgin" Vestal – i.e. silence separating from others]

[handwritten: as long as Rome]

scandet cum tacita virgine pontifex.
dicar qua violens obstrepit Aufidus   10
et qua pauper aquae Daunus agrestium
regnavit populorum, ex humili potens

[handwritten: GEN reference]

[handwritten: Florace]

[handwritten: "rustic" – hillbillies, his hometown reference to Apulia (coast) like "violent N. wind"]

9   **scando, scandere,** *climb, ascend, mount*

   tacitus, -a, -um, adj., *silent*

   tacita: Note the contrast between
   the Vestal Virgin's silence and the
   roaring Aufidus of the next line as
   well as Horace's voice as poet and
   the voice of posterity which will
   increase his fame.

   pontifex, pontificis, m., *high priest,
   pontiff*

10 **qua,** adv., *where*

   violens, violentis, adj., *violent, vehement*

   **obstrepo, obstrepere, obstrepui, ob-
   strepitum,** *make a loud noise, roar,
   drown by louder noise*

   Aufidus, -i, m., *Aufidus,* river in Apulia

10–12 He is powerful, although from
   humble origins (a reference,

perhaps, both to his status as a
freedman's son and his small town
beginnings), and his fame will exist in the Apulian area of his child-
hood.

11 **pauper, pauperis,** adj., *poor* (with
   genitive of reference; cf. notes to
   Ode 1.22.1)

   Daunus, -i, m., *Daunus,* legendary
   king of Apulia

   agrestis, -e, adj., *of the country, rustic,
   rural*

11–12 **agrestium...populorum:** genitive
   with **regnavit** (a Greek construction for verbs of ruling)

12 **humilis, -e,** adj., *humble, low;* neuter
   as noun, *low position;* masculine as
   noun, *humble person*

   potens, potentis, *able, powerful, potent*

handwritten annotations across top: "first citizen" v. imperator

handwritten: Augustus' title for himself

handwritten left margin: prayer to the Muses

handwritten left margin: 1.1 called on Polyhymnia + Euterpe

princeps Aeolium carmen ad Italos
deduxisse modos. sume superbiam

handwritten: prisoners led back to Rome in triumphal march / colonization,

quaesitam meritis et mihi Delphica *handwritten:* ABL means   15
lauro cinge volens, Melpomene, comam.

13 **princeps, principis**, adj., *first in time, leading, first*

princeps: suggests temporal priority as well as leadership. **Princeps** is also the title Augustus officially used of himself, so the term has Roman political resonance as well.

Aeolius, -a, -um, adj., *Aeolian, Aeolic*; referring to Aeolia, the Greek area of Asia Minor, including the island of Lesbos where the Greek poets Sappho and Alcaeus lived, as well as to the dialect of Greek in which they wrote.

carmen, carminis, n., *solemn or ritual utterance, song, poem, lyric poetry*

Italus, -a, -um, adj., *Italian*

Italos: Some take **Italos** as proleptic, in that the lyric meters were not "Italian" until Horace adapted them from the Greek. The initial "i" is long here.

13–14 **princeps...modos**: This is Horace's claim that he, first, adapted Aeolic poetry, that is, the Greek lyric poetry of Sappho and Alcaeus, to the Latin language. Of course, Catullus did write two poems in the Sapphic meter (11 and 51), but clearly Horace's accomplishment in this area is on a far greater scale.

14 **deduco, deducere, deduxi, deductum**, *lead away, lead down, escort, bring a person or army back with one to Rome, bring home in procession as a bride, spin, compose, adapt*

handwritten left margin: wedded Greek to Rome ("entwining threads")

deduxisse: the verb **deducere** can have the sense of "to settle" (leading down people to the ships to embark on a journey to the new colony) and therefore Horace is establishing an image of his being the leader of a Greek colonization of Italy (**ad Italos...**).

modus, -i, m., *limit, way, rhythmic pattern*; in plural, *poetry*

modos: The word **modos** operates on many levels, as "poetry," "rhythmic patterns or verse," and "ways."

sumo, sumere, sumpsi, sumptum, *take, take on*

superbia, -ae, f., *pride, arrogance*

superbiam: The Muse, Melpomene, deserves to be proud because of Horace's poetic achievement.

15 **meritum, -i**, n., *that which one deserves, due reward, service, meritorious action*

meritis: by not using a possessive adjective with this word, Horace leaves open whose "meritorious actions" have earned Melpomene her pride. Are they Horace's actions as evidenced in his lyric achievement or are they the "services" of inspiration provided by the Muse?

Delphicus, -a, -um, adj., *Delphic, of Delphi* (the site of the oracle of Apollo, god of poetry and the arts, among other things)

15–16 **Delphica...comam**: cf. Ode 1.1.29: **doctarum hederae praemia frontium**

16 **laurus, -i/-us**, f., *laurel tree*

lauro: the laurel tree was sacred to Apollo; cf. the story of Apollo and Daphne (Greek for laurel); triumphant Roman generals were crowned with laurel

cingo, cingere, cinxi, cinctum, *surround, encircle*

volens, volentis, adj., *willing*

volens: see note on **omnis** (line 6) above

Melpomene, Melpomenes, f., *Melpomene, one of the Muses*

ODE 4.7

In this poem thoughts of spring give way to thoughts of death. Here Horace articulates, perhaps more powerfully than in any other poem of his, the difference between what time means for nature and what it means for humankind: the repeated, cyclical, motion of time versus the inexorable one-way progression of time from human birth to human death.

Meter: first Archilochian

Diffugere nives, redeunt iam gramina campis
arboribusque comae,
mutat terra vices et decrescentia ripas
flumina praetereunt,

---

1 **diffugio, diffugere, diffugi,** *flee in several directions, disperse, scatter*

   diffugere: alternate form of the third person plural perfect tense ending, **-erunt**

   nix, nivis, f., *snow*

   redeo, redire, redii, reditum, *go back, come back, return*

   gramen, graminis, n., *grass*

   campus, -i, m., *plain, level surface; plain, field*

1–2 **gramina campis/arboribusque comae:** chiasmus

2 **comae:** *hair;* by extension, *leaves*

3 **mutat vices: mutare vices,** pass through one's cycle of changes

   vicis (genitive), f., *turn, succession, alternation*

   decresco, decrescere, decrevi, decretum, *decrease, grow smaller, shrink*

   ripa, -ae, f., *bank of a river, shore*

4 **flumen, fluminis,** n., *river, waters of a river*

   praetereo, praeterire, praeterii, praeteritum, *go by, go past, pass by, go beyond, omit*

Gratia cum Nymphis geminisque sororibus audet 5
  ducere nuda choros.
inmortalia ne speres, monet annus et almum
  quae rapit hora diem.

frigora mitescunt Zephyris, ver proterit aestas
  interitura, simul 10
pomifer autumnus fruges effuderit, et mox
  bruma recurrit iners.

---

5 **gratia, -ae**, f., *goodwill, kindness charm, attraction*, plural personified, *the Graces*, goddesses (usually three in number) embodying charm and beauty

nympha, -ae, f., *nymph,* semi-divine female spirit of nature

geminus, -a, -um, adj., *twin, double*

soror, sororis, f., *sister*

6 **nudus, -a, -um**, adj., *naked, bare, plain*

chorus, -i, m., *choral dance, people singing and dancing, crowd, troop*

ne speres: subjunctive in indirect command introduced by **monet**

7 **almus, -a, -um**, adj., *providing nurture, kindly, gracious*

7–8 **almum**: postposition, **quae** placed after **almum**; also, hyperbaton, with the separation of **almum... diem**; the postponement of the antecedent, **hora**, so that it follows rather than precedes the relative pronoun, **quae**, is an example of postposition, verging on hyperbaton. Compare the length of the statement and the complexity of the word order from **monet** to **diem** with the simplicity of **rapit hora diem**, which in a sense sums up the idea expressed from **monet** to **diem**.

9–12 The word order and vocabulary choice of this stanza are particularly noteworthy; summer is trampling on spring, so **ver** comes first and is gone by the time **aestas** is reached; but the fact that summer is about to die is immediately

introduced by **interitura**, and **simul** makes this even more immediate; the quickness of the change in seasons is heightened by **recurrit**, with its root "to run," while the emphasis on time is continued through the use of the word **bruma** for winter, rather than **hiems**, which refers to the shortest day of the year and is the superlative of the adjective **brevis, -e**, as well; **iners**, with its sense of inactivity effectively brings the cycle to a halt.

9 **frigus, frigoris**, n., *cold*

mitesco, mitescere, *become mild, soft, or ripe*

zephyrus, -i, m., *west wind, zephyr*

ver, veris, n., *spring*

protero, proterere, protrivi, protritum, *trample down, crush*

aestas, aestatis, f., *summer*

10 **intereo, interire, interii, interitum**, *perish, die*

11 **pomifer, pomifera, pomiferum**, adj., *fruit-bearing, fruitful*

autumnus, -i, m., *autumn*

frux, frugis, f. usually in plural, *fruit, crops*

effundo, effundere, effudi, effusum, *pour out, pour forth*

12 **bruma, -ae**, f., *the shortest day, winter, wintry weather*

recurro, recurrere, recurri, recursum, *run back, return*

iners, inertis, adj., *lacking skill, inactive, lazy, impotent*

damna tamen celeres reparant caelestia lunae:
  nos ubi decidimus,
quo pater Aeneas, quo Tullus dives et Ancus,   15
  pulvis et umbra sumus.

13 **damnum, -i**, n., *loss*

  reparo, reparare, reparavi, reparatum, *obtain in exchange for, recover*

  caelestis, -e, adj., *of the sky, celestial, divine*

  lunae: the use of the plural emphasizes the endless repeatability of nature as opposed to the "end" of human existence

  damna…celeres…caelestia lunae: synchysis

  damna…lunae: Horace is referring to the monthly cycle of the moon; his terminology of loss and recovery comes from the financial world; cf. the focus on material goods in lines 19–20 below.

13–16 Cf. Catullus 5.4–6 with these lines and with **cum semel occideris** (21), below, for a similar contrast between time in nature and in the human condition and the use of some similar vocabulary: **Soles occidere et redire possunt;/nobis cum semel occidit brevis lux,/nox est perpetua una dormienda.**

14 **decido, decidere, decidi**, *fall down, die*

15 **quo**, adv., *where, for what purpose*

  Aeneas, Aeneae, m., *Aeneas,* son of Venus and Anchises, Trojan leader who brought his followers to Italy after the Trojan War and founded what would become the Roman state; hero of Vergil's *Aeneid*; cf. note to lines 25–28 below.

  Tullus, -i, m., *Tullus Hostilius,* third king of Rome

  dives, divitis, adj., *rich, wealthy*

  dives: cf. the notes to lines 13 and 19–20 on financial language and material possessions

  Ancus, -i, m., *Ancus Martius,* fourth king of Rome

16 **pulvis, pulveris**, m., *dust*

  umbra: the use of the singular with the plural **sumus** is particularly effective here; the plural of **umbra** (shades, ghosts) would suggest at least individual continuity after death, whereas the singular gives the sense of all people becoming one undifferentiated mass of shade and dust.

quis scit, an adiciant hodiernae crastina summae
    tempora di superi?
cuncta manus avidas fugient heredis, amico
    quae dederis animo.   **20**

cum semel occideris, et de te splendida Minos
    fecerit arbitria,
non, Torquate, genus, non te facundia, non te
    restituet pietas:

---

17   **adicio, adicere, adieci, adiectum**, *throw to, add*

    adiciant: subjunctive in indirect question; the tense of the subjunctive denotes either present or future time

    hodiernus, -a, -um, adj., *of today*

    crastinus, -a, -um, adj., *of tomorrow*

    summa, -ae, f., *sum, the whole*

17–18   **hodiernae crastina summae/tempora**: synchysis

18   **di**: alternate form of **dei**, nominative plural of **deus**

    superus, -a, -um, adj., *upper, higher*

19   **cunctus, -a, -um**, adj., *the whole of, all*

    avidus, -a, -um, adj., *greedy, avaricious, eager*

    heres, heredis, c., *heir*

    amico: imitation of the use of the Greek adjective, **philos** (beloved, dear), which is comparable to **amicus, -a, -um**, as "one's own."

19–20   **amico/quae**: postposition, **quae** placed after **amico**

    The sense, here, is that whatever material goods you do not enjoy now will just go to your greedy heir.

20   **animus, -i**, m., *mind; mind, as standing for the whole person*

21   **semel**, adv., *once, once and for all*

    occido, occidere, occidi, occasum, *fall, die*

    splendidus, -a, -um, adj., *bright, brilliant, glittering, illustrious*

    Minos, Minois/Minonis, m., *Minos*, king of Crete, and later a judge in the underworld

22   **arbitrium, arbitrii**, n., *decision, judgement*

23   **Torquatus, -i**, m., *Torquatus*; identity uncertain; a Torquatus, an orator, also appears as addressee of Horace Epistle 1.5; may be a son of Lucius Manlius Torquatus, consul in 65 BCE, the year in which Horace was born; the Manlii Torquati were a famous family.

    facundia, -ae, f., *eloquence*

23–24   **non...non...non**: the anaphora makes emphatic the finality of death; note, though, that the repetition calls attention to the very qualities (**genus, facundia, pietas**) that will not be of help

24   **restituo, restituere, restitui, restitutum**, *restore, revive*

    pietas, pietatis, f., *duty, devotion*

infernis neque enim tenebris Diana pudicum   **25**
    liberat Hippolytum,
nec Lethaea valet Theseus abrumpere caro
    vincula Pirithoo.

25–28 These extremely compact lines need some elucidation. Chaste Hippolytus rejects love as represented by Venus and embraces the worship of chaste Diana. Theseus and Pirithous swear lifelong friendship and, among other things, attempt to steal Persephone from the underworld as wife for Pirithous. When Pirithous is compelled to stay in the underworld, Theseus attempts to save him. Theseus functions in these stories as intimate friend of Pirithous and as father who causes the death of his son, Hippolytus. There is a contrast between love by a divinity, Diana, and love by a mortal, Theseus. In lines 25–26 the pair involves male and female, in lines 27–28, male and male. Hippolytus is a symbol of chastity, Pirithous of lechery.

It should be noted that there are other versions in which Hippolytus is saved by Diana (cf. Vergil *Aeneid* 7.761 ff., esp., 769, **revocatum... amore Dianae**) and in which Theseus remains in the underworld (cf. Vergil *Aeneid* 6.617–18, but contrast 6.122). Horace's particular use of these stories underscores the notion of the finality of death and its accompanying end to love. The reference to **pater Aeneas** in line 15 suggests that Horace may be responding here to the *Aeneid*, which had recently been published.

Ode 4.7 is often compared with Ode 1.4 because they both deal with spring. The tone of 4.7 is much more grim and it is interesting to note that 1.4, which expresses much more ambivalence than grimness, ends with the next generation loving Lycidas who will be lost to Sestius after Sestius dies (cf. Ode 1.4.14–20).

25   **infernus, -a, -um**, adj., *lower, of the lower world, infernal*

    tenebrae, -arum, f. pl., *darkness*

    infernis...tenebris: ablative of separation

    Diana, -ae, f., *Diana,* the goddess, daughter of Jupiter and Latona

    pudicus, -a, -um, adj., *having a sense of modesty or shame, modest, honorable, chaste*

26   **Hippolytus, -i**, m., *Hippolytus,* son of Theseus, whose rejection of the sexual advances of his stepmother, Phaedra, resulted in his death

27   **Lethaeus, -a, -um**, adj., *relating to Lethe or the underworld;* Lethe is a place or river in the underworld whose waters, if drunk, were supposed to induce sleepiness or forgetfulness

    valeo, valere, valui, valitum, *be powerful, be strong enough to, be well*

    Theseus, Thesei/Theseos, m., *Theseus,* son of Aegeus or Poseidon; national hero of Athens; **Theseus** is disyllabic.

    abrumpo, abrumpere, abrupi, abruptum, *break, break apart*

    carus, -a, -um, adj., *dear, beloved*

27–28 **caro...Pirithoo**: ablative with **abrumpere** or dative of personal interest

28   **vinculum, -i**, n., *chain, bond*

    Pirithous, -i, m., *Pirithous,* a king of the Lapiths who fights with the Centaurs; son by Dia of Zeus or Ixion

    Pirithoo: on Pirithous, cf. Horace Ode 3.4.79–78: **trecentae/Pirithoum cohibent catenae.**

MAPS

Map of Rome

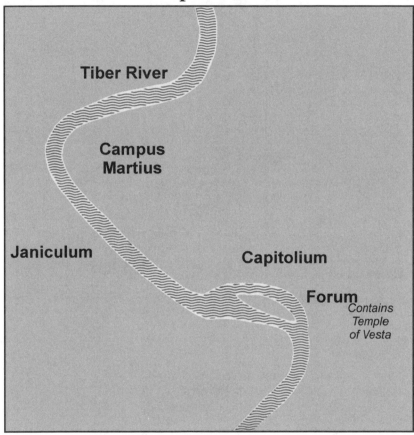

The Via Sacra, or Sacred Way, went through the Forum and on to the Capitolium.

Campus Martius (Odes 1.9 and 3.1)

Tiber River (Satire 1.9 and Ode 2.3)

Temple of Vesta (Satire 1.9)

Via Sacra (Satire 1.9)

Capitolium (Ode 1.37 and 3.30)

Map of Italy

Map of Greece

Map of the Mediterranean and Beyond

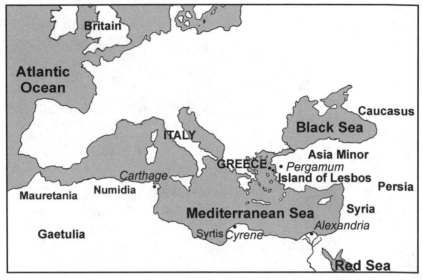

METERS OF THE POEMS

In English poetry metrical patterns are based on which syllables in a word are *stressed*, or said more emphatically. In Latin poetry, however, the metrical patterns are based on the *length* of the syllables in the Latin words, not on their stress. While the stress accent played some role in how Latin poetry sounded, the *length* of the syllables determined the particular meter being used in a given poem. For this reason the meters are called *quantitative meters*, that is, they are based on the length or *quantity* of the syllables. The student or teacher should consult the prosody or versification section in a basic Latin grammar or text for rules about determining syllable length, and, more generally, for rules about figuring out Latin meter.

The metrical patterns consist of arrangements of short syllables (∪) and long syllables (—). A syllable marked (X) is called *anceps* ("double-headed") and can be long or short. When pronounced, long syllables are said for a longer time than short ones.

The student should learn to write out the *scansion*, or the marking of the long and short syllables and elisions, of the poems. (Students taking the Advanced Placement* Latin Exam will be *required* to do this on the exam.) After gaining competence in writing out the scansion, the student should become familiar with the *sound* of the Latin poetry. The best way to accomplish this is to write out the scansion of a particular passage, e.g., about four lines that make sense as a metrical and grammatical unit, to practice reading it with the appropriate long and short syllables, elisions etc., and then to *memorize* it. Having such a "chunk" of Latin in one's head or on one's lips is the best way to reinforce the particular metrical patterns.

The following nine meters occur in the poems in this text: dactylic hexameter, Alcaic, Sapphic, first or lesser Asclepiadean, second Asclepiadean, third Asclepiadean, fourth Asclepiadean, fifth or greater Asclepiadean, and first Archilochian. (It should be noted that scholars have not adopted a consistent method for numbering the Asclepiadean meters in Horace. For example, what is called third Asclepiadean here may be called fourth Asclepiadean elsewhere. I have adopted the system that is used most commonly.)

---

* AP is a registered trademark of the College Entrance Examination Board, which was not involved in the production of, and does not endorse, this product.

Dactylic Hexameter

This meter occurs in Satire 1.9.

Horace's satires are composed in dactylic hexameter, the same meter used in Latin for Vergil's *Aeneid* and Ovid's *Metamorphoses*, and in Greek for Homer's *Iliad* and *Odyssey*. While perhaps best known as an epic meter, dactylic hexameter fits well the conversational style of satire.

There are six feet ("hex" is Greek for six) in a line or verse of dactylic hexameter poetry. (A foot is the smallest metrical unit of verse with a given sequence and number of short and long syllables.) The first five feet are either dactyls (— ∪ ∪) or spondees (— —) or any combination of these (i.e., the first foot could be a dactyl, the second a spondee etc.). A dactyl is one long syllable followed by two short syllables. A spondee is two long syllables. The sixth foot is treated as a spondee (— —), but the second syllable of the spondee is actually anceps (— X). The fifth foot is almost always a dactyl.

This is the metrical pattern of the line:

$$\underset{—\ —}{}\ \ \overset{∪∪}{—\ —}\ \ \overset{∪∪}{—\ —}\ \ \overset{∪∪}{—\ —}\ \ \overset{∪∪}{—\ —}\ \ \overset{∪∪}{—\ X}$$

The major pause in the line, called the principal caesura—a caesura (//) is a pause or break between words within a foot—usually occurs after the first syllable of the third foot or after the first syllable of the fourth foot.

example (Satire 1.9.1)

$$—\ —\ \ \ —\ ∪\ \ ∪—\ \ \ —\ —\ \ \ —\ —\ \ ∪∪\ \ \ —\ \ X$$

Ibam forte via   sacra, sicut meus est mos,

Alcaic

This meter is used in the following poems: Odes 1.9, 1.37, 2.3, 2.7, 2.14, 3.1.

The Alcaic meter is used in the *Odes* more often than any other meter. It is named after Alcaeus, the Greek lyric poet from the island of Lesbos.

This is the metrical pattern of the Alcaic stanza:

X — ∪ — — // — ∪ ∪ — ∪ X

X — ∪ — — // — ∪ ∪ — ∪ X

X — ∪ — — — ∪ — X

— ∪ ∪ — ∪ ∪ — ∪ — X

The first two lines have the same meter. Horace prefers to start the first three lines with a long syllable, but does not always do so. (Cf., e.g., Ode 1.9.1). (Students taking the Advanced Placement Latin Exam *will not* be tested on Alcaic lines that begin with a short syllable.) There is typically a diaeresis (//), or pause and break between words, after the fifth syllable in the first two lines, but cf. Ode 1.37.5 and 14.

example (Ode 1.9.22-24)

— — ∪ — — — ∪∪ — ∪ X
nunc et latentis proditor intumo

— — ∪ — — — ∪ ∪ — ∪ X
gratus puellae risus ab angulo

— — ∪ — — — ∪ — X
pignusque dereptum lacertis

— ∪ ∪— ∪ ∪ — ∪ — X
aut digito male pertinaci

Sapphic

This meter is used in the following poems: Odes 1.22, 1.25, 1.38, 2.10.

The Sapphic meter is named after Sappho, the Greek lyric poet from the island of Lesbos.

The following is the metrical pattern of the Sapphic stanza. The pattern is written as four lines, although the fourth line originally may have been thought of as just a lengthening of the third line:

$$- \cup - - - // \cup \cup - \cup - \text{X}$$

$$- \cup - - - // \cup \cup - \cup - \text{X}$$

$$- \cup - - - // \cup \cup - \cup - \text{X}$$

$$- \cup \cup - \text{X}$$

Occasionally the diaeresis will occur after the sixth syllable rather than the fifth (cf. Ode 1.25.11).

example (Ode 1.22.1-4)

$$- \quad \cup - \quad - - \quad \cup \cup - \quad \cup \quad - \text{X}$$
Integer vitae scelerisque purus

$$- \quad \cup - \quad - - \quad \cup \cup - \quad \cup \quad \quad - \text{X}$$
non eget Mauris iaculis nequ(e) arcu,
$$\underset{\cup}{}$$

$$- \quad \cup - - - \quad \cup \quad \cup - \cup - \text{X}$$
nec venenatis gravida sagittis,

$$- \quad \cup \quad \cup - \text{X}$$
Fusce, pharetra,

First or Lesser Asclepiadean

This meter is used in Odes 1.1 and 3.30.

This meter is named after the Hellenistic poet Asclepiades, who revived these meters used earlier by Sappho and Alcaeus.

This is the pattern for the first Asclepiadean line:

$$- \ - \ - \cup \cup - \ // \ - \cup \cup - \cup X$$

The first Asclepiadean line is a Glyconic (see under second Asclepiadean) lengthened through a choriamb ($-\cup\cup-$) placed between its sixth and seventh syllables.

example (Ode 3.30.16)

$$- \ -- \ \ \cup \cup - \ \ \ - \ \cup \ \cup - \ \cup X$$

lauro cinge volens, Melpomene, comam.

Second Asclepiadean

This meter is used in Odes 1.13 and 3.9.

$$- \ - \ - \cup \cup - \cup X$$

$$- \ - \ - \cup \cup - \ // \ - \cup \cup - \cup X$$

The first line is called a Glyconic. The Glyconic or a version of it is found in all the Asclepiadean meters. The second of the two lines is a first Asclepiadean line.

example (Ode 3.9.1–2)

$$- \ - \ \ - \cup \ \cup - \ \ \cup X$$

Donec gratus eram tibi,

$$- \ \ - \ \ - \ \ \ \ \cup \cup - \ \ - \cup \cup \ - \ \cup \ X$$

nec quisquam potior brachia candidae

Third Asclepiadean

This meter occurs in Ode 1.24.

The following is the pattern for the third Asclepiadean stanza:

$$- - - \cup\cup - // - \cup\cup - \cup X$$

$$- - - \cup\cup - // - \cup\cup - \cup X$$

$$- - - \cup\cup - // - \cup\cup - \cup X$$

$$- - - \cup\cup - \cup X$$

This stanza is composed of three first Asclepiadean lines followed by a Glyconic.

example (Ode 1.24.1–4)

$$- \quad - - \cup\cup - - \quad \cup \quad \cup \quad - \quad \cup X$$
Quis desiderio sit pudor aut modus

$$- \quad - - \cup\cup - \quad - \cup\cup - \cup X$$
tam cari capitis? praecipe lugubris

$$- \quad - \quad - \cup \cup - \quad - \cup\cup - \quad \cup X$$
cantus, Melpomene, cui liquidam pater

$$- - \quad - \quad \cup\cup - \cup X$$
vocem cum cithara dedit.

Fourth Asclepiadean

This meter occurs in Odes 1.5, 1.23, 3.13.

The pattern of the fourth Asclepiadean meter is as follows:

$$-\;-\;-\;\cup\cup\;-\;/\!/\;-\;\cup\cup\;-\;\cup\;X$$

$$-\;-\;-\;\cup\cup\;-\;/\!/\;-\;\cup\cup\;-\;\cup\;X$$

$$-\;-\;-\;\cup\cup\;-\;X$$

$$-\;-\;-\;\cup\cup\;-\;\cup\;X$$

The stanza consists of two first Asclepiadean lines, followed by a Pherecratean and a Glyconic.

example (Ode 1.23.1–4)

$$-\;-\;-\;\cup\cup-\;-\;\cup\;\cup-\qquad \cup X$$
Vitas inuleo me similis, Chloe,

$$-\;-\;-\;\cup\;\cup-\;\;\;-\;\cup\;\cup\;-\cup X$$
quaerenti pavidam montibus aviis

$$-\;-\;\;\;-\;\;\cup\cup\;-\;X$$
matrem non sine vano

$$-\;-\;\;\;\;-\;\;\cup\cup-\;\;\cup X$$
aurar(um) et siluae metu.

(note that "siluae" is trisyllabic here)

Fifth or Greater Asclepiadean

This meter occurs in Ode 1.11

This is the pattern for the fifth Asclepiadean meter:

$$- - - \cup\cup - \;/\!/\; - \cup\cup - \;/\!/\; - \cup\cup - \cup X$$

example (Ode 1.11.8)

$$- - \quad - \cup \cup\!- \quad - \quad \cup\cup - \quad - \cup\cup - \cup X$$
aetas: carpe diem, quam minimum credula postero.

First Archilochian

This meter occurs in Ode 4.7.

Archilochian meters are named after the Greek iambic and elegiac poet, Archilochus.

The pattern for the first Archilochian meter is as follows:

$$\overset{\cup\cup}{-\,-} \quad \overset{\cup\cup}{-\,-} \; -\;/\!/\; - \quad \overset{/\!/\cup\cup}{} \quad \overset{\cup\cup}{-\,-} \quad \overset{\cup\cup}{-\,-} \; - X$$

$$- \cup\cup - \cup\cup X$$

The first line is a dactylic hexameter. The second line is a hemiepes; the hemiepes repeats the dactylic hexameter line up to the caesura, but has two dactyls rather than dactyls or spondees.

example (Ode 4.7.1–2)

$$- - -\cup\cup - \quad \cup\cup - \quad - \quad - \cup\cup - X$$
Diffugere nives, redeunt iam gramina campis

$$\qquad\qquad - \cup\cup - \cup \cup X$$
arboribusque comae,

METRICAL TERMS, TROPES OR FIGURES OF THOUGHT, AND RHETORICAL FIGURES OR FIGURES OF SPEECH

The following is a list of definitions for terms used in this book that are important for (1) meter and (2) the figurative use of language, whether a departure from the standard meaning of a word (a trope) or a departure from the standard order of words (a rhetorical figure). References in parentheses are to examples from poems in this book.

alliteration: repetition of the same sound, usually initial, in two or more words. The term usually applies to consonants. (Ode 3.13.15–16) ...unde *loquaces* / *lymphae* desi*liunt* tuae

anaphora: repetition of a word, often at the beginning of successive clauses or phrases. (Ode 4.7.23–24) *non*, Torquate, genus, *non* te facundia, *non* te / restituet pietas

asyndeton: lack of a conjunction between words or clauses. (Ode 2.3.26) versatur urna *serius ocius*

caesura: pause or break between words within a metrical foot.

chiasmus: arrangement of words parallel in syntax with corresponding words reversed in an A B B A pattern like the Greek letter *chi* (X). (Ode 1.22.1) Integer vitae scelerisque purus

diaeresis: pause or break between words that coincides with the end of a metrical unit; except for those in the dactylic hexameter line, the pauses indicated in this book are diaereses. The same symbol (//) is used here to indicate either kind of pause.

elision: suppression, partial suppression, or blending of a final syllable of a word ending in a vowel (or a vowel followed by the letter "m") before another word beginning with a vowel (or the letter "h" followed by a vowel). Elision is indicated in scansion by writing the symbol (◡) from the end of the first word to the beginning of the second word as well as by crossing through with a single line (/) or putting in parentheses ( ) the elided letter(s).

ellipsis: omission of a word or words that must be understood from the context. (Satire 1.9.2) nescio quid meditans nugarum, *totus in illis*

enjambment: running over of a phrase, clause, or sentence from one line to the next. (Ode 1.37.20–21) Haemoniae, daret ut catenis / fatale monstrum, quae generosius

foot: the smallest metrical unit of verse with a given sequence and number of short and long syllables.

figura etymologica: the repetition of a word in a somewhat different form. (Ode 1.24.9–10) multis ille bonis *flebilis* occidit, / nulli *flebilior*, quam tibi, Vergili

golden line: two adjectives and two nouns with a verb between. (Ode 3.1.16) omne capax movet urna nomen

hendiadys: one idea expressed through two. (Ode 3.13.5) ...et Venerem et proelia destinat

hiatus: lack of elision. (Ode 1.1.2) *o et* praesidium et dulce decus meum

hyperbaton: disruption of normal prose word order, for example, through wide separation of noun and modifier. (Ode 1.9.21–22) nunc et *latentis* proditor *intumo* / gratus *puellae* risus ab *angulo*

hyperbole: extravagant exaggeration. (Satire 1.9.38) ...inteream si

hypermetric line: elision from one line to the next. (Ode 2.3.27) sors exitura et nos in aeternum / exilium...

irony: statement in which implied meaning is different from explicitly stated meaning. (Satire 1.9.54) ...velis tantummodo...

litotes: understatement, usually involving the assertion of something by denying its opposite. (Ode 1.23.3) matrem *non sine* vano / ...metu

metaphor: implied comparison in the form of an identity. The "tenor" is the subject to which the metaphoric language is applied, while the "vehicle" is the metaphoric language itself. (In Ode 1.25.17–19 the tenor consists of particular times of life, while the vehicle consists of the ivy, myrtle, or dry leaves.)

metonymy: application of a term for one thing to another with which it is closely associated. (Ode 1.1.5) evitata rotis *palmaque* nobilis

oxymoron: paradox expressed through juxtaposition of seemingly contradictory words. (Ode 1.22.16) arida nutrix

personification: application to inanimate objects of human qualities. (Ode 3.13.15–16) *loquaces* / lymphae

postposition: placement of a word later than the location expected in prose; often, the placement of a word second rather than first in its clause. (Ode 1.25.17) laeta *quod* pubes hedera virenti

simile: explicit comparison between two distinct things introduced by a word like **velut** (just as). (Ode 1.37.17 ff.) ...accipiter *velut*

stanza: division of a poem containing a series of lines repeating in a pattern.

strophe: stanza

synapheia: the joining together of two lines as if they were one. (Ode 1.25.11–12) Thracio bacchante magis sub inter- / lunia vento

synchysis or interlocked word order: arrangement of words parallel in syntax with an interlocking of the corresponding words in an A B A B pattern. (Ode 1.5.6–7) ...aspera / nigris aequora ventis

synecdoche: part of something used to signify the whole. (Ode 1.37.17) *remis* adurgens

synizesis: the joining of two successive vowels within a word into one long syllable. (Ode 2.7.5) Pomp*ei*

tmesis: separation of a compound word. (Satire 1.9.33) garrulus hunc *quando* consumet *cumque*...

transferred epithet (or hypallage): transfer of an adjective from the noun with which it goes "in sense" to another related noun. (Ode 1.1.5) evitata rotis palmaque *nobilis*

tricolon crescendo: arrangement of three phrases, clauses etc. with increasing length. (Ode 2.3.13–14) huc *vina* et *unguenta* et *nimium brevis* / *flores amoenae* ferre iube *rosae*

LATIN TEXT WITHOUT
NOTES AND VOCABULARY

Satire 1.9

Ibam forte via sacra, sicut meus est mos,
nescio quid meditans nugarum, totus in illis.
accurrit quidam notus mihi nomine tantum,
arreptaque manu: 'quid agis, dulcissime rerum?'
'suaviter, ut nunc est' inquam, 'et cupio omnia, quae vis.'   5
cum adsectaretur: 'numquid vis?' occupo, at ille
'noris nos' inquit, 'docti sumus.' hic ego: 'pluris
hoc' inquam 'mihi eris.' misere discedere quaerens
ire modo ocius, interdum consistere, in aurem
dicere nescio quid puero, cum sudor ad imos   10
manaret talos. 'o te, Bolane, cerebri
felicem' aiebam tacitus, cum quidlibet ille
garriret, vicos, urbem laudaret. ut illi
nil respondebam: 'misere cupis' inquit 'abire;
iam dudum video. sed nil agis; usque tenebo.   15
persequar hinc, quo nunc iter est tibi.' 'nil opus est te
circumagi: quendam volo visere non tibi notum;
trans Tiberim longe cubat is prope Caesaris hortos.'
'nil habeo, quod agam, et non sum piger: usque sequar te.'
demitto auriculas, ut iniquae mentis asellus,   20
cum gravius dorso subiit onus. incipit ille:
'si bene me novi, non Viscum pluris amicum,
non Varium facies: nam quis me scribere pluris
aut citius possit versus? quis membra movere
mollius? invideat quod et Hermogenes ego canto.'   25
interpellandi locus hic erat: 'est tibi mater,
cognati, quis te salvo est opus?' 'haud mihi quisquam;
omnis composui.' 'felices! nunc ego resto.
confice! namque instat fatum mihi triste, Sabella
quod puero cecinit divina mota anus urna: 30
hunc neque dira venena, nec hosticus auferet ensis,
nec laterum dolor aut tussis, nec tarda podagra:
garrulus hunc quando consumet cumque. loquaces,
si sapiat, vitet, simul atque adoleverit aetas.'

ventum erat ad Vestae, quarta iam parte diei   35
praeterita, et casu tum respondere vadato
debebat, quod ni fecisset, perdere litem.
'si me amas' inquit, 'paulum hic ades.' 'inteream, si
aut valeo stare aut novi civilia iura,
et propero, quo scis.' 'dubius sum, quid faciam' inquit,   40
'tene relinquam, an rem.' 'me, sodes.' 'non faciam' ille
et praecedere coepit. ego, ut contendere durum
cum victore, sequor. 'Maecenas quomodo tecum?'
hinc repetit, 'paucorum hominum et mentis bene sanae;
nemo dexterius fortuna est usus. haberes   45
magnum adiutorem, posset qui ferre secundas,
hunc hominem velles si tradere. dispeream, ni
summosses omnis.' 'non isto vivimus illic,
quo tu rere, modo. domus hac nec purior ulla est,
nec magis his aliena malis. nil mi officit, inquam,   50
ditior hic aut est quia doctior: est locus uni
cuique suus.' 'magnum narras, vix credibile.' 'atqui
sic habet.' 'accendis, quare cupiam magis illi
proxumus esse.' 'velis tantummodo: quae tua virtus,
expugnabis, et est, qui vinci possit, eoque   55
difficilis aditus primos habet.' 'haud mihi dero:
muneribus servos corrumpam; non, hodie si
exclusus fuero, desistam; tempora quaeram,
occurram in triviis, deducam. nil sine magno
vita labore dedit mortalibus.' haec dum agit, ecce   60
Fuscus Aristius occurrit, mihi carus et illum
qui pulchre nosset. consistimus. 'unde venis?' et
'quo tendis?' rogat et respondet. vellere coepi
et pressare manu lentissima brachia, nutans,
distorquens oculos, ut me eriperet. male salsus   65
ridens dissimulare, meum iecur urere bilis:
'certe nescio quid secreto velle loqui te
aiebas mecum.' 'memini bene, sed meliore
tempore dicam: hodie tricesima sabbata. vin tu
curtis Iudaeis oppedere?' 'nulla mihi' inquam   70
'religio est.' 'at mi! sum paulo infirmior, unus
multorum. ignosces; alias loquar.' huncine solem
tam nigrum surrexe mihi! fugit inprobus ac me
sub cultro linquit. casu venit obvius illi
adversarius et 'quo tu, turpissime?' magna   75
inclamat voce, et 'licet antestari?' ego vero
oppono auriculam. rapit in ius: clamor utrimque,
undique concursus. sic me servavit Apollo.

Ode 1.1

Maecenas atavis edite regibus,
o et praesidium et dulce decus meum:

sunt, quos curriculo pulverem Olympicum
collegisse iuvat metaque fervidis

evitata rotis palmaque nobilis   5
terrarum dominos evehit ad deos;

hunc, si mobilium turba Quiritium
certat tergeminis tollere honoribus,

illum, si proprio condidit horreo,
quicquid de Libycis verritur areis.   10

gaudentem patrios findere sarculo
agros Attalicis condicionibus

numquam demoveas, ut trabe Cypria
Myrtoum pavidus nauta secet mare;

luctantem Icariis fluctibus Africum   15
mercator metuens otium et oppidi

laudat rura sui, mox reficit rates
quassas indocilis pauperiem pati.

est, qui nec veteris pocula Massici
nec partem solido demere de die   20

spernit, nunc viridi membra sub arbuto
stratus, nunc ad aquae lene caput sacrae;

multos castra iuvant et lituo tubae
permixtus sonitus bellaque matribus

detestata; manet sub Iove frigido   25
venator tenerae coniugis inmemor,

seu visa est catulis cerva fidelibus,
seu rupit teretes Marsus aper plagas.

me doctarum hederae praemia frontium
dis miscent superis, me gelidum nemus   30

Nympharumque leves cum Satyris chori
secernunt populo, si neque tibias

Euterpe cohibet, nec Polyhymnia
Lesboum refugit tendere barbiton.

quodsi me lyricis vatibus inseres,   35
sublimi feriam sidera vertice.

Ode 1.5

Quis multa gracilis te puer in rosa
perfusus liquidis urget odoribus
    grato, Pyrrha, sub antro?
        cui flavam religas comam

simplex munditiis? heu quotiens fidem   5
mutatosque deos flebit et aspera
    nigris aequora ventis
        emirabitur insolens,

qui nunc te fruitur credulus aurea,
qui semper vacuam, semper amabilem   10
    sperat, nescius aurae
        fallacis. miseri, quibus

intemptata nites. me tabula sacer
votiva paries indicat uvida
    suspendisse potenti   15
        vestimenta maris deo.

Ode 1.9

Vides, ut alta stet nive candidum
Soracte, nec iam sustineant onus
    silvae laborantes, geluque
        flumina constiterint acuto?

dissolve frigus ligna super foco   5
large reponens atque benignius
    deprome quadrimum Sabina,
        o Thaliarche, merum diota.

permitte divis cetera, qui simul
stravere ventos aequore fervido   10
    deproeliantis, nec cupressi
        nec veteres agitantur orni.

quid sit futurum cras, fuge quaerere, et
quem Fors dierum cumque dabit, lucro
    adpone, nec dulcis amores   15
        sperne puer neque tu choreas,

donec virenti canities abest
morosa. nunc et campus et areae
    lenesque sub noctem susurri
        composita repetantur hora,   20

nunc et latentis proditor intumo
gratus puellae risus ab angulo
    pignusque dereptum lacertis
        aut digito male pertinaci.

Ode 1.11

Tu ne quaesieris (scire nefas), quem mihi, quem tibi
finem di dederint, Leuconoe, nec Babylonios

temptaris numeros. ut melius, quidquid erit, pati!
seu pluris hiemes, seu tribuit Iuppiter ultimam,

quae nunc oppositis debilitat pumicibus mare   5
Tyrrhenum: sapias, vina liques et spatio brevi

spem longam reseces. dum loquimur, fugerit invida
aetas: carpe diem, quam minimum credula postero.

Ode 1.13

Cum tu, Lydia, Telephi
    cervicem roseam, cerea Telephi
laudas brachia, vae meum
    fervens difficili bile tumet iecur.

tunc nec mens mihi, nec color   5
    certa sede manet, umor et in genas
furtim labitur arguens,
    quam lentis penitus macerer ignibus.

uror, seu tibi candidos
    turparunt umeros inmodicae mero   10
rixae, sive puer furens
    inpressit memorem dente labris notam.

non, si me satis audias,
    speres perpetuum dulcia barbare
laedentem oscula, quae Venus   15
    quinta parte sui nectaris imbuit.

felices ter et amplius,
    quos inrupta tenet copula, nec malis
divolsus querimoniis
    suprema citius solvet amor die.   20

Ode 1.22

Integer vitae scelerisque purus
non eget Mauris iaculis neque arcu,
nec venenatis gravida sagittis,
    Fusce, pharetra,

sive per Syrtis iter aestuosas   5
sive facturus per inhospitalem
Caucasum, vel quae loca fabulosus
    lambit Hydaspes.

namque me silva lupus in Sabina,
dum meam canto Lalagen et ultra   10
terminum curis vagor expeditis,
    fugit inermem,

quale portentum neque militaris
Daunias latis alit aesculetis,
nec Iubae tellus generat, leonum   15
    arida nutrix.

pone me, pigris ubi nulla campis
arbor aestiva recreatur aura,
quod latus mundi nebulae malusque
    Iuppiter urget,   20

pone sub curru nimium propinqui
solis in terra domibus negata:
dulce ridentem Lalagen amabo,
    dulce loquentem.

Ode 1.23

Vitas inuleo me similis, Chloe,
quaerenti pavidam montibus aviis
    matrem non sine vano
        aurarum et siluae metu.

nam seu mobilibus veris inhorruit   5
adventus foliis, seu virides rubum
    dimovere lacertae,
        et corde et genibus tremit.

atqui non ego te tigris ut aspera
Gaetulusve leo frangere persequor: 10
    tandem desine matrem
        tempestiva sequi viro.

Ode 1.24

Quis desiderio sit pudor aut modus
tam cari capitis? praecipe lugubris
cantus, Melpomene, cui liquidam pater
    vocem cum cithara dedit.

ergo Quintilium perpetuus sopor   5
urget? cui Pudor et Iustitiae soror,
incorrupta Fides nudaque Veritas
    quando ullum inveniet parem?

multis ille bonis flebilis occidit,
nulli flebilior, quam tibi, Vergili.   10
tu, frustra pius, heu, non ita creditum
    poscis Quintilium deos.

quid, si Threicio blandius Orpheo
auditam moderere arboribus fidem,
num vanae redeat sanguis imagini,   15
    quam virga semel horrida

non lenis precibus fata recludere
nigro compulerit Mercurius gregi?
durum, sed levius fit patientia,
    quicquid corrigere est nefas.   20

Ode 1.25

Parcius iunctas quatiunt fenestras
iactibus crebris iuvenes protervi,
nec tibi somnos adimunt, amatque
    ianua limen,

quae prius multum facilis movebat   5
cardines. audis minus et minus iam:
'me tuo longas pereunte noctes,
    Lydia, dormis?'

invicem moechos anus adrogantis
flebis in solo levis angiportu,   10
Thracio bacchante magis sub inter-
    lunia vento,

cum tibi flagrans amor et libido,
quae solet matres furiare equorum,
saeviet circa iecur ulcerosum,   15
    non sine questu,

laeta quod pubes hedera virenti
gaudeat pulla magis atque myrto,
aridas frondes hiemis sodali
    dedicet Hebro.   20

Ode 1.37

Nunc est bibendum, nunc pede libero
pulsanda tellus, nunc Saliaribus
   ornare pulvinar deorum
      tempus erat dapibus, sodales.

antehac nefas depromere Caecubum   5
cellis avitis, dum Capitolio
   regina dementis ruinas
      funus et imperio parabat

contaminato cum grege turpium
morbo virorum, quidlibet inpotens   10
   sperare fortunaque dulci
      ebria; sed minuit furorem

vix una sospes navis ab ignibus,
mentemque lymphatam Mareotico
   redegit in veros timores   15
      Caesar ab Italia volantem

remis adurgens, accipiter velut
mollis columbas aut leporem citus
   venator in campis nivalis
      Haemoniae, daret ut catenis   20

fatale monstrum, quae generosius
perire quaerens nec muliebriter
   expavit ensem, nec latentis
      classe cita reparavit oras,

ausa et iacentem visere regiam   25
voltu sereno, fortis et asperas
   tractare serpentes, ut atrum
      corpore combiberet venenum,

deliberata morte ferocior:
saevis Liburnis scilicet invidens   30
   privata deduci superbo
      non humilis mulier triumpho.

Ode 1.38

Persicos odi, puer, apparatus,
displicent nexae philyra coronae;
mitte sectari, rosa quo locorum
    sera moretur.

simplici myrto nihil adlabores   5
sedulus, curo: neque te ministrum
dedecet myrtus, neque me sub arta
    vite bibentem.

Ode 2.3

Aequam memento rebus in arduis
servare mentem, non secus in bonis
    ab insolenti temperatam
        laetitia, moriture Delli,

seu maestus omni tempore vixeris,   5
seu te in remoto gramine per dies
    festos reclinatum bearis
        interiore nota Falerni.

quo pinus ingens albaque populus
umbram hospitalem consociare amant   10
    ramis? quid obliquo laborat
        lympha fugax trepidare rivo?

huc vina et unguenta et nimium brevis
flores amoenae ferre iube rosae,
    dum res et aetas et sororum   15
        fila trium patiuntur atra.

cedes coemptis saltibus et domo
villaque, flavos quam Tiberis lavit,
    cedes, et exstructis in altum
        divitiis potietur heres.   20

divesne prisco natus ab Inacho,
nil interest, an pauper et infima
    de gente sub divo moreris,
        victima nil miserantis Orci:

omnes eodem cogimur, omnium   25
versatur urna serius ocius
    sors exitura et nos in aeternum
        exilium inpositura cumbae.

Ode 2.7

O saepe mecum tempus in ultimum
deducte Bruto militiae duce,
    quis te redonavit Quiritem
        dis patriis Italoque caelo,

Pompei, meorum prime sodalium,   5
cum quo morantem saepe diem mero
    fregi coronatus nitentis
        malobathro Syrio capillos?

tecum Philippos et celerem fugam
sensi relicta non bene parmula,   10
    cum fracta virtus et minaces
        turpe solum tetigere mento.

sed me per hostis Mercurius celer
denso paventem sustulit aere,
    te rursus in bellum resorbens   15
        unda fretis tulit aestuosis.

ergo obligatam redde Iovi dapem,
longaque fessum militia latus
    depone sub lauru mea, nec
        parce cadis tibi destinatis.   20

oblivioso levia Massico
ciboria exple, funde capacibus
    unguenta de conchis. quis udo
        deproperare apio coronas

curatve myrto? quem Venus arbitrum   25
dicet bibendi? non ego sanius
    bacchabor Edonis: recepto
        dulce mihi furere est amico.

Ode 2.10

Rectius vives, Licini, neque altum
semper urgendo, neque – dum procellas
cautus horrescis – nimium premendo
 litus iniquum.

auream quisquis mediocritatem   5
diligit, tutus caret obsoleti
sordibus tecti, caret invidenda
 sobrius aula.

saepius ventis agitatur ingens
pinus et celsae graviore casu   10
decidunt turres feriuntque summos
 fulgura montis.

sperat infestis, metuit secundis
alteram sortem bene praeparatum
pectus. informis hiemes reducit   15
 Iuppiter, idem

submovet. non, si male nunc, et olim
sic erit: quondam cithara tacentem
suscitat Musam, neque semper arcum
 tendit Apollo.   20

rebus angustis animosus atque
fortis appare: sapienter idem
contrahes vento nimium secundo
 turgida vela.

Ode 2.14

Eheu fugaces, Postume, Postume,
labuntur anni, nec pietas moram
   rugis et instanti senectae
      adferet indomitaeque morti,

non, si trecenis, quotquot eunt dies,   5
amice, places inlacrimabilem
   Plutona tauris, qui ter amplum
      Geryonen Tityonque tristi

conpescit unda, scilicet omnibus,
quicumque terrae munere vescimur,   10
   enaviganda, sive reges,
      sive inopes erimus coloni.

frustra cruento Marte carebimus
fractisque rauci fluctibus Hadriae,
   frustra per autumnos nocentem   15
      corporibus metuemus Austrum:

visendus ater flumine languido
Cocytos errans et Danai genus
   infame damnatusque longi
      Sisyphus Aeolides laboris.   20

linquenda tellus et domus et placens
uxor, neque harum, quas colis, arborum
   te praeter invisas cupressos
      ulla brevem dominum sequetur,

absumet heres Caecuba dignior   25
servata centum clavibus et mero
   tinguet pavimentum superbo,
      pontificum potiore cenis.

Ode 3.1

Odi profanum volgus et arceo.
favete linguis: carmina non prius
   audita Musarum sacerdos
      virginibus puerisque canto.

regum timendorum in proprios greges,   5
reges in ipsos imperium est Iovis,
   clari Giganteo triumpho,
      cuncta supercilio moventis.

est, ut viro vir latius ordinet
arbusta sulcis, hic generosior   10
   descendat in campum petitor,
      moribus hic meliorque fama

contendat, illi turba clientium
sit maior: aequa lege Necessitas
   sortitur insignis et imos,   15
      omne capax movet urna nomen.

destrictus ensis cui super impia
cervice pendet, non Siculae dapes
   dulcem elaborabunt saporem,
      non avium citharaeque cantus   20

somnum reducent: somnus agrestium
lenis virorum non humilis domos
   fastidit umbrosamque ripam,
      non Zephyris agitata Tempe.

desiderantem quod satis est neque   25
tumultuosum sollicitat mare,
   nec saevus Arcturi cadentis
      impetus aut orientis Haedi,

non verberatae grandine vineae
fundusque mendax, arbore nunc aquas   30
   culpante, nunc torrentia agros
      sidera, nunc hiemes iniquas.

contracta pisces aequora sentiunt
iactis in altum molibus: huc frequens
    caementa demittit redemptor   35
        cum famulis dominusque terrae

fastidiosus, sed Timor et Minae
scandunt eodem, quo dominus, neque
    decedit aerata triremi et
        post equitem sedet atra Cura.   40

quodsi dolentem nec Phrygius lapis,
nec purpurarum sidere clarior
    delenit usus, nec Falerna
        vitis Achaemeniumque costum,

cur invidendis postibus et novo   45
sublime ritu moliar atrium?
    cur valle permutem Sabina
        divitias operosiores?

Ode 3.9

Donec gratus eram tibi,
    nec quisquam potior brachia candidae
cervici iuvenis dabat,
    Persarum vigui rege beatior.

'donec non alia magis   5
    arsisti, neque erat Lydia post Chloen,
multi Lydia nominis
    Romana vigui clarior Ilia.'

me nunc Thressa Chloe regit,
    dulcis docta modos et citharae sciens,   10
pro qua non metuam mori,
    si parcent animae fata superstiti.

'me torret face mutua
    Thurini Calais filius Ornyti,
pro quo bis patiar mori,   15
    si parcent puero fata superstiti.'

quid si prisca redit Venus
    diductosque iugo cogit aeneo,
si flava excutitur Chloe,
    reiectaeque patet ianua Lydiae?   20

'quamquam sidere pulchrior
    ille est, tu levior cortice et inprobo
iracundior Hadria,
    tecum vivere amem, tecum obeam libens.'

Ode 3.13

O fons Bandusiae splendidior vitro,
dulci digne mero non sine floribus,
    cras donaberis haedo,
        cui frons turgida cornibus

primis et Venerem et proelia destinat,   5
frustra: nam gelidos inficiet tibi
    rubro sanguine rivos
        lascivi suboles gregis.

te flagrantis atrox hora Caniculae
nescit tangere, tu frigus amabile   10
    fessis vomere tauris
        praebes et pecori vago.

fies nobilium tu quoque fontium
me dicente cavis inpositam ilicem
    saxis, unde loquaces   15
        lymphae desiliunt tuae.

Ode 3.30

Exegi monumentum aere perennius
regalique situ pyramidum altius,

quod non imber edax, non Aquilo inpotens
possit diruere aut innumerabilis

annorum series et fuga temporum.   5
non omnis moriar, multaque pars mei

vitabit Libitinam: usque ego postera
crescam laude recens, dum Capitolium

scandet cum tacita virgine pontifex.
dicar, qua violens obstrepit Aufidus   10

et qua pauper aquae Daunus agrestium
regnavit populorum, ex humili potens

princeps Aeolium carmen ad Italos
deduxisse modos. sume superbiam

quaesitam meritis et mihi Delphica   15
lauro cinge volens, Melpomene, comam.

Ode 4.7

Diffugere nives, redeunt iam gramina campis
    arboribusque comae,
mutat terra vices et decrescentia ripas
    flumina praetereunt,

Gratia cum Nymphis geminisque sororibus audet   5
    ducere nuda choros.
inmortalia ne speres, monet annus et almum
    quae rapit hora diem.

frigora mitescunt Zephyris, ver proterit aestas
    interitura, simul   10
pomifer autumnus fruges effuderit, et mox
    bruma recurrit iners.

damna tamen celeres reparant caelestia lunae:
    nos ubi decidimus,
quo pater Aeneas, quo Tullus dives et Ancus,   15
    pulvis et umbra sumus.

quis scit, an adiciant hodiernae crastina summae
    tempora di superi?
cuncta manus avidas fugient heredis, amico
    quae dederis animo.   20

cum semel occideris, et de te splendida Minos
    fecerit arbitria,
non, Torquate, genus, non te facundia, non te
    restituet pietas:

infernis neque enim tenebris Diana pudicum   25
    liberat Hippolytum,
nec Lethaea valet Theseus abrumpere caro
    vincula Pirithoo.

VOCABULARY

In general, only long vowels in metrically indeterminate positions are marked. For example, the length of the "a" in "accipiter" need not be marked as long or short because the syllable in which it is contained must be long, regardless of the length of the vowel, because the vowel is followed by two consonants, "cc," (not a combination like "tr" which can create indeterminacy), while the "a" in "beātus" must be marked long because it occurs in a position where metrical rules cannot determine the length of the syllable in which it occurs.

A

ā/ab, prep. with abl., *from, by*

abeō, abīre, abiī, abitum, *go away, depart*

abrumpō, abrumpere, abrūpī, abruptum, *break, break apart*

absum, abesse, āfuī, āfutūrus, *be away, be absent*

absūmō, absūmere, absumpsī, absumptum, *spend, consume*

ac, conj., *and*

accendō, accendere, accendī, accensum, *kindle, arouse, ignite*

accipiter, accipitris, m., *hawk*

accurrō, accurrere, accurrī/accucurrī, accursum, *run or hurry up to*

Achaemenius, -a, -um, adj., *Persian, Parthian*

acūtus, -a, -um, adj., *sharp, severe*

ad, prep. with acc., *to, towards, near*

adferō, adferre, attulī, allātum, *bring, add*

adiciō, adicere, adiēcī, adiectum, *throw to, add*

adimō, adimere, adēmī, ademptum, *take away*

aditus, -ūs, m., *approach, access*

adiūtor, adiūtōris, m., *helper*

adlabōrō, adlabōrāre, *add to by taking trouble*

adolescō, adolescere, adolēvī, adultum, *grow up,* (of a season or time) *reach its peak*

adpōnō, adpōnere, adposuī, adpositum, *add; treat as, count as* (with **lucrum**)

adrogans, adrogantis, adj., *arrogant, insolent*

adsector, adsectārī, adsectātus sum, *follow closely, attend, escort*

adsum, adesse, adfuī, *be present;* in technical sense, *be present in court as a friend or adviser*

adurgeō, adurgēre, *press hard upon, pursue closely*

adventus, -ūs, m., *arrival, approach*

adversārius, adversāriī, m., *adversary, opponent*

Aenēās, Aenēae, m., *Aeneas,* son of Venus and Anchises, Trojan leader who brought his followers to Italy after the Trojan War and founded what would become the Roman state; hero of Vergil's *Aeneid*

aēneus, -a, -um, adj., *of bronze*

Aeolidēs, Aeolidae, m., *a son or more remote descendant of Aeolus*

Aeolius, -a, -um, adj., *Aeolian, Aeolic;* referring to Aeolia, the Greek area of Asia Minor, including the island of Lesbos where the Greek poets Sappho and Alcaeus lived, as well as to the dialect of Greek in which they wrote

aequor, aequoris, n., *a flat level surface, the flat surface of the sea,* (often used in pl.)

aequus, -a, -um, adj., *equal, even, impartial, fair*

āēr, āeris, m., *air, weather, mist*

aerātus, -a, -um, adj., *made of or fitted with bronze or brass*

aes, aeris, n., *copper, bronze, money*

aesculētum, -ī, n., *oak forest*

aestās, aestātis, f., *summer*

aestīvus, -a, -um, adj., *summer*

aestuōsus, -a, -um, adj., *very hot, agitated*

aetās, aetātis, f., *time, age*

aeternus, -a, -um, adj., *eternal, everlasting*

Āfricus, -a, -um, *African*

ager, agrī, m., *field, territory*

agitō, agitāre, agitāvī, agitātum, *stir, drive, agitate, excite*

agō, agere, ēgī, actum, *do, drive*

agrestis, -e, adj., *of the country, rustic, rural*

āiō, defective verb, *say yes, say*

albus, -a, -um, adj., *white, bright*

aliās, adv., *at another time*

aliēnus, -a, -um, adj., *of another, alien, strange* (with abl. or dat.)

alius, alia, aliud, adj., *other, another*

almus, -a, -um, adj., *providing nurture, kindly, gracious*

alō, alere, aluī, altum, *nourish*

alter, altera, alterum, adj., *another, one of two, the one, the other*

altum, -ī, n., *high place or position, heaven, sea, the deep*

altus, -a, -um, adj., *high, deep, tall*

amābilis, -e, adj., *lovable, delightful*

amīcus, -ī, m., *friend*

amō, amāre, amāvī, amātum, *love*

amoenus, -a, -um, adj., *charming, pleasing*

amor, amōris, m., *love*

amplius, adv., *more*

amplus, -a, -um, adj., *large, spacious*

an, conj., *whether, or*

Ancus, -ī, m., *Ancus Martius,* fourth king of Rome

angiportus, -ūs, m., *alley*

angulus, -ī, m., *angle, corner*

angustus, -a, -um, adj., *narrow, limited, difficult* (of circumstances)

anima, -ae, f., *breath, life, darling*

animōsus, -a, -um, adj., *spirited, bold*

animus, -ī, m., *mind; mind, as standing for the whole person*

annus, -ī, m., *year*

antehāc, adv., *previously*

antestor, antestārī, antestātus sum, *call as a witness*

antrum, -ī, n., *cave, hollow space*

anus, -ūs, f., *old woman*

aper, aprī, m., *wild boar*

apium, apiī, n., *parsley, celery*

Apollō, Apollinis, m., *Apollo,* son of Jupiter and Latona, brother of Diana, god of archery, music, poetry, etc.

apparātus, -ūs, m., *preparation, show, sumptuousness, paraphernalia*

appāreō, appārēre, appāruī, appāritum, *appear*

aqua, -ae, f., *water, body of water*

Aquilō, Aquilōnis, m., *the north wind*

arbiter, arbitrī, m., *judge, overseer*

arbitrium, arbitriī, n., *decision, judgement*

arbor, arboris, f., *tree*

arbustum, -ī, n., *wood, plantation,* (pl.) *trees*

arbutus, -ī, f., *the wild strawberry or arbutus tree*

arceō, arcēre, arcuī, *contain, keep away, spurn*

Arctūrus, -ī, m., *Arcturus,* the brightest star of the constellation Boōtes

arcus, -ūs, m., *bow*

ardeō, ardēre, arsī, *be on fire, burn, be in love* (with abl.)

arduus, -a, -um, adj., *steep, towering, lofty, high, difficult*

ārea, -ae, f., *open space, threshing floor*

arguō, arguere, arguī, argūtum, *prove, show*

āridus, -a, -um, adj., *dry*

Aristius, Aristiī, m., *Aristius Fuscus,* Horace's literary friend; cf. Satire 1.9 and Ode 1.22

arripiō, arripere, arripuī, arreptum, *seize, take hold of, arrest, bring before a court*

artus, -a, -um, adj., *close, thrifty, dense, economical*

asellus, -ī, m., *young ass, young donkey*

asper, aspera, asperum, adj., *fierce, rough*

at, conj., *but*

atavus, -ī, m., *a great-great-great grandfather, or remote ancestor*

āter, ātra, ātrum, adj., *black, dark, gloomy*

atque, conj., *and;* after comparatives, *than;* also, cf. **simul**

atquī, conj., *but, nevertheless*

ātrium, ātriī, n., *hall, first main room in a Roman-style house*

atrox, atrōcis, adj., *dreadful, fierce, cruel*

Attalicus, -a, -um, adj., *of King Attalus or his dynasty, rich, splendid*

audeō, audēre, ausus sum, *dare, wish*

audiō, audīre, audīvī, audītum, *hear, heed*

auferō, auferre, abstulī, ablātum, *take away, carry off, kill*

Aufidus, -ī, m., *Aufidus,* river in Apulia

aula, aulae, f., *noble residence, palace, hall*

aura, -ae, f., *breeze*

aureus, -a, -um, adj., *golden, splendid*

auricula, -ae, f., *ear*

auris, auris, f., *ear*

Auster, Austrī, m., *south wind*

aut, conj., *or;* **aut...aut,** *either...or*

autumnus, -ī, m., *autumn*

avidus, -a, -um, adj., *greedy, avaricious, eager*

avis, avis, f., *bird*

avītus, -a, -um, adj., *of a grandfather, ancestral*

āvius, -a, -um, adj., *pathless, remote*

B

Babylōnius, -a, -um, adj., *Babylonian*

bacchor, bacchārī, bacchātus sum, *celebrate the festival of Bacchus, rave, rage*

Bandusia, -ae, f., *Bandusia,* name of a spring, perhaps at Horace's Sabine farm or near Apulia, the area on which his hometown bordered

barbarē, adv., *roughly, cruelly*

barbitos, barbitī, m., *lyre*

beātus, -a, -um, adj., *happy, fortunate*

bellum, -ī, n., *war*

bene, adv., *well;* with adj. or adv., *quite*

benignē, adv., *lavishly, liberally*

beō, beāre, beāvī, beātum, *bless, make happy*

bibō, bibere, bibī, *drink*

bīlis, bīlis, f., *gall, bile, anger*

bis, adv., *twice*

blandus, -a, -um, adj., *charming, persuasive, seductive*

Bōlānus, -ī, m., *Bolanus,* Roman cognomen

bonus, -a, -um, adj., *good*

brāchium, brāchiī, n., *arm*

brevis, -e, adj., *short, brief*

brūma, -ae, f., *the shortest day, winter, wintry weather*

Brūtus, -ī, m., *Marcus Iunius Brutus,* one of the leaders, along with Cassius, of the conspiracy to kill Julius Caesar.

C

cadō, cadere, cecidī, cāsum, *fall, die, set* (of heavenly bodies)

cadus, -ī, m., *jar, flask* (especially for wine)

Caecubum, -ī, n., *choice wine from Caecubum,* a district in south Latium

caelestis, -e, adj., *of the sky, celestial, divine*

caelum, -ī, n., *sky, heavens, weather, world*

caementum, -ī, n., *small stones, rubble*

Caesar, Caesaris, m., *Caesar;* Octavian (later Augustus), in Ode 1.37; in Satire 1.9, Julius Caesar, (100–44 BCE), Roman general who defeated Pompey at the battle of Pharsalus in 48 BCE and was made dictator for life in 44 BCE, shortly before his assassination in the conspiracy led by Brutus and Cassius.

Calais, Calais, m., *Calais,* man's name

campus, -ī, m., *plain, level surface; plain, field;* often refers specifically to the Campus Martius in Rome

candidus, -a, -um, adj., *bright, radiant, white*

canīcula, -ae, f., *the Dog Star, Sirius,* in the constellation Canis Major, brightest star in the sky, thought to bring hot weather

cānitiēs, cānitiēī, f., *white or grey coloring, grey or white hair*

canō, canere, cecinī, cantum, *sing, sing about, recite, prophesy, foretell*

cantō, cantāre, cantāvī, cantātum, *sing, sing about, recite*

cantus, -ūs, m., *singing, song, poetry*

capax, capācis, adj., *spacious, capable*

Capitōlium, Capitōliī, n., *Capitolium,* the Capitoline hill in Rome on which the Capitoline gods, Jupiter, Juno, and Minerva, were worshipped

caput, capitis, n., *head, top, source, person, person's life*

cardō, cardinis, m., *hinge*

careō, carēre, caruī, caritum, *lack, be without* (with abl.)

carmen, carminis, n., *solemn or ritual utterance, song, poem, lyric poetry*

carpō, carpere, carpsī, carptum, *pluck, seize*

cārus, -a, -um, adj., *dear, beloved*

castra, castrōrum, n. pl., *military camp*

cāsus, -ūs, m., *fall, event, misfortune, chance*

catēna, -ae, f., *chain*

catulus, -ī, m., *a young animal,* especially *a young dog*

Caucasus, -ī, m., *Caucasus mountains*

cautus, -a, -um, adj., *on one's guard, wary, cautious, prudent*

cavus, -a, -um, adj., *hollow, concave*

cēdō, cēdere, cessī, cessum, *go, yield, withdraw*

celer, celeris, celere, adj., *swift, quick*

cella, -ae, f., *storeroom, wine cellar*

celsus, -a, -um, adj., *high, lofty, proud*

cēna, -ae, f., *dinner*

centum, indecl.adj., *a hundred*

cerebrum, -ī, n., *brain, seat of intelligence, seat of anger, anger*

cēreus, -a, -um, adj., *waxen, supple*

certō, certāre, certāvī, certātum, *contend, strive*

certus, -a, -um, adj., *certain, definite*

cerva, -ae, f., *deer, female deer*

cervix, cervīcis, f., *neck*

cēterus, -a, -um, adj., *the rest,* usually found in plural

Chloē, Chloēs, f., *Chloe,* Greek woman's name

chorēa, -ae, f., *dance*

chorus, -ī, m., *choral dance, people singing and dancing, crowd, troop*

cibōrium, cibōriī, n., *a kind of drinking cup*

cingō, cingere, cinxī, cinctum, *surround, encircle*

circā, prep. with acc., *around*

circumagō, circumagere, circumēgī, circumactum, *drive or lead around, lead around in circles*

cithara, -ae, f., *lyre*

citius, adv., *quicker, sooner*

citus, -a, -um, adj., *swift, quick*

cīvīlis, -e, adj., *civil*

clāmor, clāmōris, m., *shout, shouting, clamor*

clārus, -a, -um, adj., *clear, bright, famous*

classis, classis, f., *fleet, political class*

clāvis, clāvis, f., *key*

cliens, clientis, m., *client;* one who attaches himself to a person of greater influence or political power (**patrōnus**) for protection

Cōcȳtos, Cōcȳtī, m., *Cocytus,* one of the rivers of the underworld

coemō, coemere, coēmī, coemptum, *buy up*

coepī, coepisse, coeptum (typically appears in perfect system), *begin*

cognātus, -a, -um, adj., *related*

cōgō, cōgere, coēgī, coactum, *drive together, force*

cohibeō, cohibēre, cohibuī, cohibitum, *hold together, hold back, confine*

colligō, colligere, collēgī, collectum, *to gather or bring together, collect*

colō, colere, coluī, cultum, *cultivate, cherish*

colōnus, -ī, m., *farmer, settler*

color, colōris, m., *color*

columba, -ae, f., *dove, pigeon*

coma, -ae, f., *hair*

combibō, combibere, combibī, *drink up, drink completely*

compellō, compellere, compulī, compulsum, *bring together, drive together, round up*

compescō, compescere, compescuī, *confine, restrain, check*

compōnō, compōnere, composuī, compositum, *put together, arrange, compose, calm, bury*

concha, -ae, f., *shell fish, sea shell, perfume dish*

concursus, -ūs, m., *running to and fro*

condiciō, condiciōnis, f., *condition, term, agreement*

condō, condere, condidī, conditum, *found, establish, store up*

cōnficiō, cōnficere, cōnfēcī, cōnfectum, *complete, destroy, finish off, kill*

coniunx, coniugis, c., *spouse, wife, husband*

cōnsistō, cōnsistere, cōnstitī, *stop, pause, stand still, take a position*

cōnsociō, cōnsociāre, cōnsociāvī, cōnsociātum, *unite, connect, share*

cōnstō, cōnstāre, cōnstitī, *stand together, stand still*

cōnsūmō, cōnsūmere, cōnsumpsī, cōnsumptum, *consume, destroy, kill*

contāminātus, -a, -um, adj., *morally foul, impure*

contendō, contendere, contendī, contentum, *stretch, hasten, compete, contend*

contrahō, contrahere, contraxī, contractum, *draw together, narrow*

cōpula, -ae, f., *bond, link*

cor, cordis, n., *heart*

cornū, -ūs, n., *horn, anything horn-shaped*

corōna, -ae, f., *crown, garland*

corōnō, corōnāre, corōnāvī, corōnātum, *put a garland on, crown*

corpus, corporis, n., *body*

corrigō, corrigere, correxī, correctum, *make straight, correct, remedy*

corrumpō, corrumpere, corrūpī, corruptum, *damage, spoil, bribe, seduce*

cortex, corticis, m., *bark, rind, cork*

costum, -ī, n., *an aromatic plant*

crās, adv., *tomorrow*

crastinus, -a, -um, adj., *of tomorrow*

crēber, crēbra, crēbrum, adj., *crowded together, frequent*

crēdibilis, -e, adj., *believable*

crēdō, crēdere, crēdidī, crēditum, *trust, believe, entrust*

crēdulus, -a, -um, adj., *credulous, trustful*

crescō, crescere, crēvī, crētum, *arise, multiply, expand, increase*

cruentus, -a, -um, adj., *bloody, gory, cruel*

cubō, cubāre, cubuī, cubitum, *lie down or be lying down, recline, be in bed or on one's couch, be confined to bed by illness, recline at table*

culpō, culpāre, culpāvī, culpātum, *blame*

culter, cultrī, m., *knife*

cum, prep. with abl., *with;* conj. *when, since, although*

cumba, -ae, f., *small boat,* especially that in which Charon ferries the dead across the river Styx

cunctus, -a, -um, adj., *the whole of, all*

cupiō, cupere, cupīvī, cupītum, *wish, desire, long for*

cupressus, -ī, f., *cypress*

cūr, adv., *why*

cūra, -ae, f., *care, concern, worry, a person or thing constituting an object of care*

cūrō, cūrāre, cūrāvī, cūrātum, *care about, take care of, attend to*

curriculum, -ī, n., *a running, course, race, racing chariot*

currus, -ūs, m., *chariot*

curtus, -a, -um, adj., *having a part missing, mutilated, circumcized*

Cyprius, -a, -um, adj., *Cyprian, of the island of Cyprus*

D

damnō, damnāre, damnāvī, damnātum, *condemn, sentence*

damnum, -ī, n., *loss*

Danaus, -ī, m., *Danaus;* all but one of his fifty daughters, the Danaids, on instructions from their father, killed their husbands on their wedding night; they are punished in the underworld by having continuously to fill up leaky jars

daps, dapis, f., *feast, banquet*

Daunias, Dauniadis, f., *Apulia,* region of southeastern Italy

Daunus, -ī, m., *Daunus,* legendary king of Apulia

dē, prep. with abl., *about, concerning, down from, from*

dēbeō, dēbēre, dēbuī, dēbitum, *owe, ought, should, must*

dēbilitō, dēbilitāre, dēbilitāvī, dēbilitātum, *weaken*

dēcēdō, dēcēdere, dēcessī, dēcessum, *go away, depart, withdraw* (with abl.)

dēcidō, dēcidere, dēcidī, *fall down, die*

dēcrescō, dēcrescere, dēcrēvī, dēcrētum, *decrease, grow smaller, shrink*

decus, decoris, n., *that which adorns or beautifies, honor, glory*

dēdecet, dēdecēre, dēdecuit, used in third person, *be unsuitable for, be unbecoming to*

dēdicō, dēdicāre, dēdicāvī, dēdicātum, *dedicate*

dēdūcō, dēdūcere, dēduxi, dēductum, *lead away, lead down, escort, bring a person or army back with one to Rome, bring home in procession as a bride, spin, compose, adapt*

dēlēniō, dēlēnīre, dēlēnīvī, dēlēnītum, *soothe*

dēlīberō, dēlīberāre, dēlīberāvī, dēlīberātum, *consider carefully, deliberate, decide*

Dellius, Delliī, m., *Quintus Dellius, who first joined Dolabella, then Cassius, then Antony, and finally Octavian, right before Actium*

Delphicus, -a, -um, adj., *Delphic, of Delphi* (the site of the oracle of Apollo, god of poetry and the arts, among other things)

dēmens, dēmentis, adj., *out of one's senses, mad, insane*

dēmittō, dēmittere, dēmīsī, dēmissum, *let down, let fall, lower, sink*

dēmō, dēmere, dempsī, demptum, *take away, subtract*

dēmoveō, dēmovēre, dēmōvī, dēmōtum, *remove, drive out*

dens, dentis, m., *tooth*

densus, -a, -um, adj., *thick, dense*

dēpōnō, dēpōnere, dēposuī, dēpositum, *lay down*

dēproelior, dēproeliārī, *fight fiercely, struggle violently*

dēprōmō, dēprōmere, dēprompsī, dēpromptum, *bring out, produce*

dēproperō, dēproperāre, *hurry to complete*

dēripiō, dēripere, dēripuī, dēreptum, *tear down, snatch away*

descendō, descendere, descendī, descensum, *come or go down, descend*

dēsīderium, desideriī, n., *desire, longing* (for something or someone lost or absent)

dēsīderō, dēsīderāre, dēsīderāvī, dēsīderātum, *desire, want, long for*

dēsiliō, dēsilīre, dēsiluī, *leap or jump down*

dēsinō, dēsinere, dēsiī, dēsitum, *stop, cease*

dēsistō, dēsistere, destitī, *cease, desist*

destinō, destināre, destināvī, destinātum, *fix, determine, intend, destine, earmark*

destringō, destringere, destrinxī, destrictum, *strip off, scrape lightly, draw or unsheathe* (a weapon)

dēsum, dēesse, dēfuī, *be missing, fail* (with dat. of person)

dētestor, dētestārī, dētestātus sum, *pray against, curse*

deus, -ī, m., *god;* dī, alternate form of deī, nom. pl., dīs, alternate form of deīs, dat. and abl. pl.

dexter, dextra, dextrum, adj., *right, skillful*

Diāna, -ae, f., *the goddess Diana, daughter of Jupiter and Latona*

dīcō, dīcere, dixī, dictum, *say, tell, call*

dīdūcō, dīdūcere, dīduxī, dīductum, *separate, split*

diēs, diēī, m., (f.) *day*

difficilis, -e, adj., *difficult, troublesome, hard to manage*

diffugiō, diffugere, diffūgī, *flee in several directions, disperse, scatter*

digitus, -ī, m., *finger*

dignus, -a, -um, adj., *worthy, worthy of, deserving* (with abl.)

dīligō, dīligere, dīlexī, dīlectum, *love, esteem, hold dear, have special regard for*

dīmoveō, dīmovēre, dīmōvī, dīmōtum, *move apart, separate*

diōta, -ae, f., *two-handled wine jar*

dīruō, dīruere, dīruī, dīrutum, *cause to fall in ruin, demolish*

dīrus, -a, -um, adj., *terrible, awful, dire*

dīs, dītis, adj., *rich, wealthy*

discēdō, discēdere, discessi, discessum, *go away, depart*

dispereō, disperīre, disperiī, *perish,
be destroyed* (frequently hyperbolic)

**displiceō, displicēre, displicuī,
displicitum,** *displease*

**dissimulō, dissimulāre, dissimulāvī,
dissimulātum,** *pretend that
something is not what it is, pretend
not to notice, ignore*

**dissolvō, dissolvere, dissolvī,
dissolūtum,** *dissolve, free*

**distorqueō, distorquēre, distorsī,
distortum,** *twist this way and that,
distort, torment*

dīvellō, dīvellere, dīvellī, dīvolsum,
tear apart

dīves, dīvitis, adj., *rich, wealthy*

dīvīnus, -a, -um, adj., *divine*

dīvitiae, dīvitiārum, f. pl., *wealth,
riches*

dīvum, -ī, n., *sky*

dīvus, -a, -um, adj., *divine*

dīvus, -ī, m., *god*

dō, dare, dedī, datum, *give*

doctus, -a, -um, *learned, taught*

doleō, dolēre, doluī, dolitum, *suffer
mental or physical pain, be in pain,
grieve*

dolor, dolōris, m., *pain, anguish, grief*

dominus, -ī, m., *master, lord, ruler*

domus, -ūs/-ī, f., *house, home*

dōnec, conj., *as long as, while*

dōnō, dōnāre, dōnāvī, dōnātum,
present, endow, reward (with), with
abl. of thing given

**dormiō, dormīre, dormīvī,
dormītum,** *sleep*

dorsum, -ī, n., *back*

dubius, -a, -um, adj., *uncertain,
indecisive*

dūcō, dūcere, duxī, ductum, *lead, take,
consider*

dudum, adv., *some time ago, previously,
just now; for a long time* (with **iam**)

dulce, adv., *sweetly*

dulcis, -e, adj., *sweet,* (of persons) *dear,
beloved*

dum, conj., *while, as long as, provided
that, if only, until*

dūrus, -a, -um, adj., *hard, harsh*

dux, ducis, m., *leader, general,
commander*

E

ē/ex, prep. with abl., *out of, from*

ēbrius, -a, -um, adj., *drunk*

ecce, interj., *look, behold*

edax, edācis, adj., *greedy, devouring,
destructive*

ēditus, -a, -um, adj. (from **ēdo**),
descended from

ēdō, ēdere, ēdidī, ēditum, *put forth,
give out, give birth to*

Ēdōnus, -a, -um, adj., *Thracian;* the
Ēdōnī were a tribe celebrated for
their orgiastic worship of Bacchus

effundō, effundere, effūdī, effūsum,
pour out, pour forth

egeō, egēre, eguī, *need, want* (with
abl.)

ego, meī, mihi/mī, mē, mē, pron., *I,
me*

ēheu, interj. (expressing grief or pain),
alas

**ēlabōrō, ēlabōrāre, ēlabōrāvī,
ēlabōrātum,** *strive, work out,
develop, perfect*

ēmīror, ēmīrārī, *wonder at exceedingly,
be astonished at*

**ēnāvigō, ēnāvigāre, ēnāvigāvī,
ēnāvigātum,** *sail across, sail forth*

enim, conj., *for, truly*

ensis, ensis, m., *sword*

eō, adv., abl. of **is,** *therefore*

eō, īre, īvī/iī, itum, *go*

eōdem, adv., *to the same place*

eques, equitis, m., *horseman, rider,
member of the cavalry, member of the
equestrian order*

equus, -ī, m., *horse*

ergō, particle, *then, consequently, therefore*

ēripiō, ēripere, ēripuī, ēreptum, *snatch away, rescue*

errō, errāre, errāvī, errātum, *wander, make a mistake*

et, conj., *and, even;* et...et, *both...and*

Euterpē, Euterpēs, f., *Euterpe,* one of the Muses.

ēvehō, ēvehere, ēvexī, ēvectum, *carry out, lift up, raise*

ēvītō, ēvītāre, ēvītāvī, ēvītātum, *avoid*

exclūdō, exclūdere, exclūsī, exclūsum, *shut out, exclude*

excutiō, excutere, excussī, excussum, *shake out, drive out, banish*

exeō, exīre, exiī, exitum, *go out, come out, emerge*

exigō, exigere, exēgī, exactum, *drive out, complete, execute*

exilium, exiliī, n., *exile*

expavescō, expavescere, expāvī, *become frightened of, dread*

expediō, expedīre, expedīvī, expedītum, *free, extricate, release*

expleō, explēre, explēvī, explētum, *fill up*

expugnō, expugnāre, expugnāvī, expugnātum, *storm, conquer, overcome*

exstruō, exstruere, exstruxī, exstructum, *heap up, pile up, construct*

F

fābulōsus, -a, -um, adj., *legendary, storied*

facilis, -e, adj., *easy, quick*

faciō, facere, fēcī, factum, *make, do, regard*

fācundia, -ae, f., *eloquence*

Falernum, -ī, n., *Falernian wine,* wine from a district in northern Campania famous for its wine

Falernus, -a, -um, adj., *Falernian,* of a district in northern Campania famous for its wine

fallax, fallācis, adj., *deceitful, deceptive*

fāma, -ae, f., *fame, reputation*

famulus, -ī, m., *servant, attendant, slave*

fastīdiō, fastīdīre, fastīdīvī, fastīdītum, *show aversion to, scorn*

fastīdiōsus, -a, -um, adj., *critical, exacting, disdainful*

fātālis, -e, adj., *deadly, fatal*

fātum, -ī, n., *fate,* pl., *the Fates*

faveō, favēre, fāvī, fautum, *favor;* with linguīs (abl.), *avoid words of ill omen, be silent*

fax, facis, f., *torch, torch used at funerals and marriages, marriage, death*

fēlix, fēlīcis, adj., *happy, fortunate*

fenestra, -ae, f., *window*

feriō, ferīre, *strike, hit*

ferō, ferre, tulī, lātum, *bear, bring, carry, play* (a part, role)

ferox, ferōcis, adj., *bold*

fervens, ferventis, adj., *boiling, seething*

fervidus, -a, -um, adj., *boiling, burning, hot, impetuous*

fessus, -a, -um, adj., *tired, weary*

festus, -a, -um, adj., *festal, on holiday, festive*

fidēlis, -e, adj., *faithful*

fidēs, fideī, f., *trust, belief, faith, honesty, honor*

fidēs, fidis, f., *lyre*

filius, filiī, m., *son*

fīlum, -ī, n., *thread*

findō, findere, fidī, fissum, *split, separate, divide*

fīnis, fīnis, m., *boundary, limit, end*

fīō, fīerī, factus sum, *be made, become*

flagrans, flagrantis, adj., *hot, blazing, passionate*

flāvus, -a, -um, adj., *yellow, golden, blonde, auburn*

flēbilis, -e, adj., *worthy of tears, lamentable*

fleō, flēre, flēvī, flētum, *weep for, lament*

flōs, flōris, m., *flower*

fluctus, -ūs, m., *a flowing, wave, disturbance*

flūmen, flūminis, n., *river, waters of a river*

focus, -ī, m., *hearth, fireplace*

folium, foliī, n., *leaf*

fons, fontis, m., *spring, source*

fors, fortis, f., *chance, luck*

forte, adv., *by chance, as luck would have it, as it so happened*

fortis, -e, adj., *brave*

fortūna, -ae, f., *fortune, chance, luck*

frangō, frangere, frēgī, fractum, *break, crush*

frequens, frequentis, adj., *crowded, assiduous, constant, regular*

fretum, -ī, n., *strait, sea, violence*

frīgidus, -a, -um, *cold*

frīgus, frigoris, n., *cold*

frons, frondis, f., *leaf*

frons, frontis, f., *forehead, brow, front*

fruor, fruī, fructus sum, *enjoy* (with abl.)

frustrā, adv., *in vain, to no purpose*

frux, frūgis, f., usually in pl., *fruit, crops*

fuga, -ae, f., *flight, rout*

fugax, fugācis, adj., *swift, fugitive, elusive*

fugiō, fugere, fūgī, fugitum, *flee, flee from, avoid*

fulgur, fulguris, n., *a flash of lightning, flash of light*

fundō, fundere, fūdī, fūsum, *pour, spread, scatter, defeat*

fundus, -ī, m., *bottom, farm, estate*

fūnus, fūneris, n., *funeral, death, destruction*

furens, furentis, adj., *mad, wild*

furiō, furiāre, furiāvī, furiātum, *madden*

furō, furere, *behave wildly, be crazy*

furor, furōris, m., *madness, frenzy, fury*

furtim, adv., *secretly*

Fuscus, -ī, m., *Aristius Fuscus,* Horace's literary friend; cf. Satire 1.9 and Ode 1.22

G

Gaetūlus, -a, -um, adj., *Gaetulian, of Gaetulia,* region of northwest Africa known for its lions

garriō, garrīre, garrīvī, *talk rapidly, chatter,* (do this in writing)

garrulus, -a, -um, adj., *talkative, loquacious*

gaudeō, gaudēre, gāvīsus sum, *rejoice, delight in* (with abl.)

gelidus, -a, -um, adj., *cold, icy*

gelū, -ūs, n., *frost, cold, chill*

geminus, -a, -um, adj., *twin, double*

gena, -ae, f., *cheek*

generō, generāre, generāvī, generātum, *produce, create*

generōsē, adv., *nobly, with dignity*

generōsus, -a, -um, adj., *of noble birth, noble*

gens, gentis, f., *clan, tribe, family*

genū, -ūs, n., *knee*

genus, generis, n., *birth, race, kind, offspring*

Gēryōn, Gēryonis, m., *Geryon;* triple-headed or triple-bodied king whom Hercules killed when carrying off his cattle

Gigantēus, -a, -um, adj., *of the Giants,* a mythical race, who fought and were defeated by the Olympian gods

gracilis, -e, adj., *slender, thin*

grāmen, grāminis, n., *grass*

grandō, grandinis, f., *hail*

grātia, -ae, f., *goodwill, kindness, charm, attraction,* pl. personified, *the Graces,* goddesses (usually three in number) embodying charm and beauty

grātus, -a, -um, adj., *pleasing*

gravidus, -a, -um, adj., *laden, weighed down*

gravis, -e, adj., *heavy, weighty, serious*

grex, gregis, m., *flock, herd, company, crowd*

H

habeō, habēre, habuī, habitum, *have, hold, consider, keep*

Hadria, -ae, m., *Adriatic Sea*

haedus, -ī, m., *young goat, kid;* two stars in the constellation Auriga

Haemonia, -ae, f., *Thessaly*

haud, adv., *not*

Hebrus, -ī, m., *Hebrus,* river in Thrace

hedera, -ae, f., *ivy*

hērēs, hērēdis, c., *heir*

Hermogenēs, Hermogenis, m., *Hermogenes;* in Satire 1.10.80 Horace places a Hermogenes Tegellius in a group of people whose opinions do not matter to him as opposed to those of his literary friends.

heu, interj., expressing grief or pain, *oh, alas*

hīc, adv., *here, at this point*

hic, haec, hoc, demonstr. pron. and adj., *this, the latter*

hiems, hiemis, f., *winter, storm*

hinc, adv., *from here, here*

Hippolytus, -ī, m., *Hippolytus,* son of Theseus, whose rejection of the sexual advances of his stepmother, Phaedra, resulted in his death.

hodiē, adv., *today*

hodiernus, -a, -um, adj., *of today*

homō, hominis, m., *person, human being*

honor (honōs), honōris, m., *honor, office*

hōra, -ae, f., *hour, time, season*

horrescō, horrescere, horruī, *shudder at, tremble at*

horreum, -ī, n., *storehouse, granary*

horridus, -a, -um, adj., *rough, harsh, dreadful*

hortus, -ī, m., *garden;* usually in pl., *pleasure grounds or gardens*

hospitālis, -e, adj., *hospitable, belonging to a host or guest*

hosticus, -a, -um, adj., *belonging to an enemy*

hostis, hostis, c., *enemy*

hūc, adv., *to here, here*

humilis, -e, adj., *humble, low;* neuter as noun, *low position*

Hydaspēs, Hydaspis, m., *Hydaspes,* tributary of river Indus, the Jhelum

I

iaceō, iacēre, iacuī, *lie, be in ruins*

iaciō, iacere, iēcī, iactum, *throw, lay foundations*

iactus, -ūs, m., *throwing, hurling*

iaculum, -ī, n., *javelin*

iam, adv., *already, now*

iānua, -ae, f., *door*

Īcarius, -a, -um, adj., *of Icarus, Icarian*

īdem, eadem, idem, pron. and adj., *the same, too, likewise*

iecur, iecoris, n., *liver, the seat of the feelings*

ignis, ignis, m., *fire*

ignoscō, ignoscere, ignōvī, ignōtum, *forgive, pardon*

īlex, īlicis, f., *holm oak, ilex*

Īlia, -ae, f., *Ilia or Rhea Silvia,* mother of Romulus and Remus

ille, illa, illud, demonstr. pron. and adj., *that, the former*

illīc, adv., *there*

imāgō, imāginis, f., *image, likeness, shape*

imber, imbris, m., *rain, rain shower, water*

imbuō, imbuere, imbuī, imbūtum, *wet, fill, inspire*

imperium, imperiī, n., *power, command, government*

impetus, -ūs, m., *attack, onset, rapid motion*

impius, -a, -um, adj., *impious, undutiful, disloyal*

īmus, -a, -um, adj., *lowest, bottom of*

īn(n)uleus, -ī, m., *fawn*

in, prep. with abl., *in, on;* prep. with acc., *into, onto, against, over*

Īnachus, -ī, m., *Inachus,* first king of Argos

incipiō, incipere, incēpī, inceptum, *begin*

inclāmō, inclāmāre, inclāmāvī, inclāmātum, *call out, cry out*

incorruptus, -a, -um, adj., *uncorrupted, upright*

indicō, indicāre, indicāvī, indicātum, *point out, show, declare*

indocilis, -e, adj., *untrained, hard to instruct*

indomitus, -a, -um, adj., *unconquered, unconquerable*

inermis, -e, adj., *unarmed*

iners, inertis, adj., *lacking skill, inactive, lazy, impotent*

infāmis, -e, adj., *infamous, disreputable*

infernus, -a, -um, adj., *lower, of the lower world, infernal*

infestus, -a, -um, adj., *dangerous, hostile, insecure*

inficiō, inficere, infēcī, infectum, *dye, imbue, taint, stain*

infimus, -a, -um, adj., *lowest, most humble*

infirmus, -a, -um, adj., *weak, lacking strength of purpose, not resolute*

informis, -e, adj., *shapeless, deformed, ugly*

ingens, ingentis, adj., *huge*

inhorrescō, inhorrescere, inhorruī, *begin to tremble, bristle, become stiffly erect*

inhospitālis, -e, adj., *inhospitable*

inīquus, -a, -um, adj., *uneven, unfavorable, treacherous, discontented*

inlacrimābilis, -e, adj., *pitiless*

inmemor, inmemoris, adj., *forgetful, unmindful*

inmodicus, -a, -um, adj., *immoderate*

inmortālis, -e, adj., *immortal*

innumerābilis, -e, adj., *countless, numberless*

inops, inopis, adj., *lacking wealth, poor*

inpōnō, inpōnere, inposuī, inpositum, *place on or over, build on*

inpotens, inpotentis, adj., *powerless, weak, wild, violent*

inprimō, inprimere, inpressī, inpressum, *press upon*

inprobus, -a, -um, adj., *unprincipled, immoderate, unruly, relentless, shameless*

inquam, inquit, defective verb, only a few forms occur, most often used parenthetically or before or after a quotation, *say*

inruptus, -a, -um, *broken into, interrupted; unbroken*

inserō, inserere, inseruī, insertum, *introduce, insert, put in or among*

insignis, -e, adj., *distinguished*

insolens, insolentis, adj., *unaccustomed, excessive*

instans, instantis, adj., *pressing, urgent*

instō, instāre, institī, *be pressing, loom, threaten*

integer, integra, integrum, adj., *whole, untouched, upright*

intemptātus, -a, -um, adj., *untried, unattempted*

interdum, adv., *at times*

intereō, interīre, interiī, interitum, *perish, die*

interior, interius, adj., *inner, interior, private*

interlūnium, interlūniī, n., *the period between the old moon and the new*

interpellō, interpellāre, interpellāvī, interpellātum, *interrupt, break in on, impede*

intersum, interesse, interfuī, when used impersonally, *it makes a difference, it matters, it is of importance*

intumus, -a, -um, adj., *innermost, most secret*

inveniō, invenīre, invēnī, inventum, *find*

invicem, adv., *in turn*

invideō, invidēre, invīdī, invīsum, *envy, begrudge, refuse*

invidus, -a, -um, adj., *envious, jealous*

invīsus, -a, -um, adj., *hateful, odious*

ipse, ipsa, ipsum, pron., adj., *himself, herself, itself, oneself* etc.

īrācundus, -a, -um, adj., *angry, hot-tempered, prone to anger*

is, ea, id, pron. and adj., *he, she, it, this, that*

iste, ista, istud, pron. and adj., *that of yours, this, that* (often with derogatory sense)

ita, adv., *thus, so*

Italia, -ae, f., *Italy*

Italus, -a, -um, adj., *Italian*

iter, itineris, n., *journey*

Iuba, -ae, m., *Juba;* Juba I, Numidian king who supported Pompey in the civil war; Juba II, son of Juba I, fought for Octavian (Augustus) at the battle of Actium, made king of Mauretania by Augustus, known for his learning

iubeō, iubēre, iussī, iussum, *order, command, bid*

Iūdaeus, -ī, m., *Jew*

iugum, -ī, n., *yoke, bond*

iungō, iungere, iunxī, iunctum, *join, yoke, mate*

Iuppiter, Iovis, m., *Jupiter,* supreme god of the Romans, god of sky and weather

iūs, iūris, n., *law, right, court*

iustitia, -ae, f., *justice*

iuvenis, iuvenis, m., (f.), *young man, young woman*

iuvō, iuvāre, iūvī, iūtum, *please, delight, help*

L

lābor, lābī, lapsus sum, *glide, slip, pass*

labor, labōris, m., *work, effort, task*

labōrō, labōrāre, labōrāvī, labōrātum, *work, suffer, labor*

labrum, -ī, n., *lip*

lacerta, -ae, f., *lizard*

lacertus, -ī, m., *upper arm*

laedō, laedere, laesī, laesum, *harm, strike*

laetitia, -ae, f., *happiness, joy*

laetus, -a, -um, adj., *happy, glad, fertile*

Lalagē, Lalagēs, f., *Lalage,* woman's name; Greek for "chatterer"

lambō, lambere, lambī, *lick, wash*

languidus, -a, -um, adj., *languid, sluggish, slow*

lapis, lapidis, m., *stone*

largē, adv., *generously, plentifully*

lascīvus, -a, -um, adj., *playful, frisky, wanton*

lateō, latēre, latuī, *lie hidden*

lātus, -a, -um, adj., *wide*

latus, lateris, n., *side, extreme part or region, flank, lungs, body*

laudō, laudāre, laudāvī, laudātum, *praise*

laurus, -ī/-ūs, f., *laurel tree*

laus, laudis, f., *praise*

lavō, lavāre/lavere, lāvī, lavātum/ lautum/lōtum, *wash*

lēnis, -e, adj., *smooth, gentle, mild, soft*

lentus, -a, -um, adj., *slow, lingering, unresponsive*

leō, leōnis, m., *lion*

lepus, leporis, m., *hare, rabbit*

Lesbōus, -a, -um, adj., *Lesbian, of the Greek island of Lesbos*

Lēthaeus, -a, -um, adj., *relating to Lethe or the underworld;* Lethe is a place or river in the underworld whose waters, if drunk, were supposed to induce sleepiness or forgetfulness.

Leuconoē, Leuconoēs, f., *Leuconoe,* woman's name

levis, -e, adj., *light, swift, gentle, unimportant, fickle*

lēvis, -e, adj., *smooth, smooth* (from polishing)

lex, lēgis, f., *law, rule, particular condition or term*

libens, libentis, adj., *willing*

līber, lībera, līberum, adj., *free*

līberō, līberāre, līberāvī, līberātum, *free*

libīdō, libīdinis, f., *desire, lust*

Libitīna, -ae, f., *Libitina,* the goddess of funerals, *funeral couch*

Liburna, -ae, f., *light, fast sailing warship, galley;* name taken from the Liburnians, a people of Illyricum

Libycus, -a, -um, adj., *Libyan,* sometimes *African,* in general

licet, licēre, licuit/licitum est, impersonal verb, *it is permitted*

Licinius, Liciniī, m., *Licinius;* maybe Lucius Licinius Murena, brother-in- law of Maecenas, who was executed when trying to escape after his alleged participation in a conspiracy against Augustus.

lignum, -ī, n., *wood* (often in pl.)

līmen, līminis, n., *threshold*

lingua, -ae, f., *tongue, language*

linquō, linquere, līquī, *go away from, abandon, leave behind*

liquidus, -a, -um, adj., *flowing, clear, melodious, liquid*

liquō, liquāre, liquāvī, liquātum, *melt, strain*

līs, lītis, f., *quarrel, lawsuit*

lītus, lītoris, n., *shore, coast, beach*

lituus, lituī, m., *curved cavalry trumpet*

locus, -ī, m., *place, occasion;* m. pl., **-i;** n. pl., **-a**

longē, adv., *far, far off, far away in time*

longus, -a, -um, adj., *long*

loquax, loquācis, adj., *talkative, loquacious, talking*

loquor, loquī, locūtus sum, *speak*

lucrum, -ī, n., *profit, gain*

luctor, luctārī, luctātus sum, *wrestle, struggle, contend*

lūgubris, -e, adj., *mournful*

lūna, -ae, f., *moon*

lupus, -ī, m., *wolf*

Lȳdia, -ae, f., *Lydia,* woman's name

lympha, -ae, f., *water*

lymphātus, -a, -um, adj., *frenzied, distracted, frantic*

lyricus, -a, -um, adj., *of the lyre, lyric*

M

mācerō, mācerāre, mācerāvī, mācerātum, *soften, make weak, torment*

Maecēnās, Maecēnātis, m., *Gaius Cilnius Maecenas,* friend and supporter of Horace and of other contemporary poets, including Vergil

maestus, -a, -um, adj., *sad, sorrowful, dejected, gloomy*

magis, adv., *more*

magnus, -a, -um, adj., *large, big, great*

maior, maius, adj., *greater, larger*

male, adv., *badly, insufficiently, wickedly, scarcely*

mālobathrum, -ī, n., *the tree Cinnamomum tamala or its oil*

malus, -a, -um, adj., *bad, nasty, hostile, unfavorable*

maneō, manēre, mansī, mansum, *remain, stay, endure*

mānō, mānāre, mānāvī, mānātum, *flow, spread*

manus, -ūs, f., *hand, band*

mare, maris, n., *sea*

Mareōticum, -ī, n., *wine from Mareotis,* area around Alexandria in Egypt

Mars, Martis, m., *Mars,* god of war

Marsus, -a, -um, adj., *Marsian, of the* **Marsī,** a people of central Italy

Massicum, -ī, n., *Massic wine, wine from the area of* **Massicus,** a mountain in Campania

Massicus, -a, -um, adj., *Massic*

māter, mātris, f., *mother*

Maurus, -a, -um, adj., *Moorish, African*

mēcum = cum mē

mediocritās, mediocritātis, f., *mean, moderation, keeping of a middle course*

meditor, meditārī, meditātus sum, *think over, contemplate, practice*

melior, melius, adj., *better*

Melpomenē, Melpomenēs, f., *Melpomene,* one of the Muses

membrum, -ī, n., *limb or member of the body, limb, member, part of anything*

meminī, meminisse (perf. with pres. meaning), *remember, recollect*

memor, memoris, adj., *mindful, remembering*

mendax, mendācis, adj., *lying, false*

mens, mentis, f., *mind*

mentum, -ī, n., *chin*

mercātor, mercātōris, m., *merchant*

Mercurius, Mercuriī, m., *Mercury,* son of Jupiter and Maia

meritum, -ī, n., *that which one deserves, due reward, service, meritorious action*

merus, -a, -um, adj., *pure, unmixed;* with **vīnum** or with **vīnum** understood, *wine not mixed with water*

mēta, -ae, f., *turning point, end*

metuō, metuere, metuī, metūtum, *fear, be afraid of, be afraid*

metus, -ūs, m., *fear*

meus, -a, -um, adj., *my*

mī = mihi

mīlitāris, -e, adj., *military*

mīlitia, -ae, f., *military service, war, army*

minae, -ārum, f. pl., *threats, warning signs*

minax, minācis, adj., *threatening, projecting*

minimus, -a, -um, adj., *smallest, least*

minister, ministrī, m., *servant, assistant*

Mīnōs, Mīnōis/Minōnis, m., *Minos,* king of Crete, and later a judge in the underworld

minuō, minuere, minuī, minūtum, *make smaller, reduce, weaken*

minus, adv., *less*

misceō, miscēre, miscuī, mixtum, *mix, mingle*

miser, misera, miserum, adj., *unhappy, pitiful*

miserē, adv., *pitifully, desperately*

miseror, miserārī, miserātus sum, *pity, lament*

mītescō, mītescere, *become mild, soft, or ripe*

mittō, mittere, mīsī, missum, *release, let go, abandon, send*

mōbilis, -e, adj., *moveable, changeable, inconstant, pliant*

moderor, moderārī, moderātus sum, *handle, control, play*

modo, adv., *only, just now*

modus, -ī, m., *limit, way, rhythmic pattern;* in pl., *poetry*

moechus, -ī, m., *adulterer*

mōlēs, mōlis, f., *mass, bulk, massive structure*

mōlior, mōlīrī, mōlītus sum, *labor at, build*

mollis, -e, adj., *soft, gentle, flexible, voluptuous*

moneō, monēre, monuī, monitum, *bring to the notice of, remind, tell* (of), *warn*

mons, montis, m., *mountain*

monstrum, -ī, n., *portent, marvel, monster*

monumentum, -ī, n., *monument, memorial*

mora, -ae, f., *delay, hindrance*

morbus, -ī, m., *sickness, disease*

morior, morī, mortuus sum, *die*

moror, morārī, morātus sum, *delay, linger, be late in appearing*

mōrōsus, -a, -um, adj., *difficult*

mors, mortis, f., *death*

mortālis, -e, adj., *mortal*

mōs, mōris, m., *custom, tradition;* (pl.) *character, habits*

moveō, movēre, mōvī, mōtum, *move*

mox, adv., *soon*

muliebriter, adv., *like a woman*

mulier, mulieris, f., *woman, wife*

multum, adv., *much*

multus, -a, -um, *much, many, large* (with sing. noun)

munditia, -ae, f., *neatness, elegance*

mundus, -ī, m., *world*

mūnus, mūneris, n., *service, duty, gift, entertainment*

Mūsa, -ae, f., *muse;* one of the nine Muses, goddesses who were daughters of Zeus and Mnemosyne and presided over the arts

mūtō, mūtāre, mūtāvī, mūtātum, *change*

mūtuus, -a, -um, adj., *mutual, reciprocal*

Myrtōus, -a, -um, adj., *Myrtoan*

myrtus, -ī, f., *myrtle*

N

nam, conj., *for, because*

namque, conj., *for, because*

narrō, narrāre, narrāvī, narrātum, *tell*

nascor, nascī, nātus sum, *be born*

nauta, -ae, m., *sailor*

nāvis, nāvis, f., *ship*

nē, negative adv. and conj., *not, that not, so that not, lest;* used in negative purpose clauses and prohibitions, among other constructions

-ne, interr. particle, in direct questions; in indirect questions with alternatives, often used with **an,** *whether...or;* affirmative particle often used with infinitive in exclamations, *indeed*

nebula, -ae, f., *mist, fog*

nec, conj., *and not;* **nec...nec,** *neither... nor*

nectar, nectaris, n., *nectar,* drink of the gods

nectō, nectere, nexī, nexum, *tie, weave, bind, compose*

nefās, n., indecl., *crime, offense against divine law, sacrilege*

negō, negāre, negāvī, negātum, *say no, deny, refuse*

nēmō, nēminis, m., pron., *no one, nobody*

nemus, nemoris, n., *grove, forest*

neque, conj., *and not;* **neque...neque,** *neither...nor*

nesciō, nescīre, nescīvī, nescītum, *not know, be ignorant of, not to know how to, not to be able to*

nescius, -a, -um, adj., *ignorant, unaware*

niger, nigra, nigrum, adj., *black, dark, gloomy, black as a color of ill omen, evil*

nihil, n., indecl., *nothing*

nīl = nihil

nimium, adv., *too, too much, very*

nisi, conj., *if not, unless*

niteō, nitēre, nituī, *shine, be radiant with beauty*

nivālis, -e, adj., *snowy*

nix, nivis, f., *snow*

nōbilis, -e, adj., *noble*

noceō, nocēre, nocuī, nocitum, *harm* (with dat.)

nōmen, nōminis, n., *name*

nōn, adv., *not*

nōs, nostrī/nostrum, nōbīs, nōs, nōbīs, pron., *we, us*

noscō, noscere, nōvī, nōtum, *get to know learn; know* (in perfect tense)

nota, -ae, f., *mark, sign, wine of a specified quality or vintage*

nōtus, -a, -um, adj., *known, familiar*

novus, -a, -um, adj., *new, strange*

nox, noctis, f., *night*

nūdus, -a, -um, adj., *naked, bare, plain*

nūgae, -ārum, f. pl., *trifles, nonsense, things of no importance*

nullus, -a, -um, adj., *no, not any*

num, interr. particle, *certainly not*

numerus, -ī, m., *number*

numquam, adv., *never*

numquid, interr. particle, introduces question where a negative answer is expected, *surely...not; you don't, do you?*

nunc, adv., *now*

nūtō, nūtāre, nūtāvī, nūtātum, *nod with the head, nod, hesitate*

nūtrix, nūtrīcis, f., *nurse, especially a wet-nurse*

nympha, -ae, f., *nymph, semi-divine female spirit of nature*

O

ō, interj., *O* (with voc.)

obeō, obīre, obiī, obitum, *go to, meet, die*

obligō, obligāre, obligāvī, obligātum, *tie up, pledge, dedicate*

oblīquus, -a, -um, adj., *slanting, zigzag*

oblīviōsus, -a, -um, adj., *producing forgetfulness, forgetful*

obsolētus, -a, -um, adj., *worn out, shabby, ordinary*

obstrepō, obstrepere, obstrepuī, obstrepitum, *make a loud, noise, roar, drown by louder noise*

obvius, -a, -um, adj. (with dat.), *in the way, placed so as to meet, situated so as to confront*

occidō, occidere, occidī, occāsum, *fall, die*

occupō, occupāre, occupāvī, occupātum, *seize, forestall, take the lead over*

occurrō, occurrere, occurrī/occucurrī, occursum, *meet, hurry to meet, arrive, turn up*

ōcius, adv., *sooner, quicker*

oculus, -ī, m., *eye*

ōdī, ōdisse, ōsum (perfect with present sense), *have an aversion to, hate*

odor, odōris, m., *smell, odor, perfume*

officiō, officere, offēcī, offectum, *impede, interfere with* (with dat.)

ōlim, adv., *formerly, once, on an occasion, at some future date*

Olympicus, -a, -um, adj., *Olympic, Olympian*

omnis, -e, adj., *all, every*

onus, oneris, n., *burden*

operōsus, -a, -um, adj., *toilsome, laborious, painstaking, industrious*

oppēdō, oppēdere, *fart in the face of* (with dat.)

oppidum, -ī, n., *town*

oppōnō, oppōnere, opposuī, oppositum, *place against, place in front, especially put before someone for acceptance, proffer*

oppositus, -a, -um, *placed against, hostile*

opus, operis, n., *work, business, task, genre;* with **esse,** *be necessary, be needed* (with abl. of thing needed and dat. of person with the need)

ōra, -ae, f., *shore*

Orcus, Orcī, m., *Orcus, the god of the lower world, the lower world, death*

ordinō, ordināre, ordināvī, ordinātum, *set in order, arrange*

orior, orīrī, ortus sum, *rise, be born*

ornō, ornāre, ornāvī, ornātum, *prepare, decorate, adorn, honor* (with abl.)

ornus, -ī, f., *flowering ash tree*

Ornytus, -ī, m., *Ornytus,* man's name

Orpheus, -ī, m., *Orpheus;* he was able to charm animals and nature with his music

osculum, -ī, n., *kiss, mouth, lips* (as used in kissing)

ōtium, ōtiī, n., *free time, leisure, peace*

P

palma, -ae, f., *palm tree, palm branch, palm wreath, token of victory*

pār, paris, adj., *equal*

parcē, adv., *sparingly*

parcō, parcere, pepercī, parsum, *spare* (with dat.)

pariēs, parietis, m., *wall*

parmula, -ae, f., *little shield*

parō, parāre, parāvī, parātum, *prepare*

pars, partis, f., *part, party; stage role* (usually in pl.)

pateō, patēre, patuī, *be open*

pater, patris, m., *father*

patientia, -ae, f., *patience*

patior, patī, passus sum, *suffer, undergo, experience, endure, allow*

patrius, -a, -um, adj., *of a father, ancestral, native, inherited, belonging to one's country*

paucus, -a, -um, adj., in pl., *few*

paulum, adv., *for a short while*

paulum, -ī, n., *a little*

pauper, pauperis, adj., *poor* (with gen.)

pauperiēs, pauperiēī, f., *poverty*

paveō, pavēre, *be frightened, be terrified*

pavidus, -a, -um, adj., *frightened, terrified, trembling, fearful*

pavīmentum, -ī, n., *pavement, floor*

pectus, pectoris, n., *breast, chest*

pecus, pecoris, n., *farm animal;* sing. as collective, *farm animals, livestock, especially sheep and cattle*

pendeō, pendēre, pependī, *hang, hover, hang down, be suspended*

penitus, adv., *deeply*

per, prep. with acc., *through*

perdō, perdere, perdidī, perditum, *destroy, lose*

perennis, -e, adj., *lasting throughout the year, lasting for many years, enduring*

pereō, perīre, periī, peritum, *perish, die*

perfundō, perfundere, perfūdī, perfūsum, *pour over, fill with*

permisceō, permiscēre, permiscuī, permixtum, *mix together, confuse*

permittō, permittere, permīsī, permissum, *let go, allow, entrust*

permūtō, permūtāre, permūtāvī, permūtātum, *exchange, receive in exchange for* (with acc. of thing received and abl. of thing given up)

perpetuus, -a, -um, adj., *continuing, permanent, connected*

Persae, Persārum, m. pl., *Persians*

persequor, persequī, persecūtus sum, *pursue, chase*

Persicus, -a, -um, adj., *Persian*

pertinax, pertinācis, adj., *very tenacious, holding fast, persisting* pēs, pedis, m., *foot, metrical foot*

petītor, petītōris, m., *seeker, candidate*

pharetra, -ae, f., *quiver*

Philippī, -ōrum, m. pl., *Philippi,* town in eastern Macedonia where Brutus and Cassius were defeated

philyra, -ae, f., *fibrous membrane under the bark of the linden or lime tree, bast;* used to bind together elaborate garlands of flowers

Phrygius, -a, -um, adj., *Phrygian*

pietās, pietātis, f., *duty, devotion*

piger, pigra, pigrum, adj., *inactive, lazy*

pignus, pigneris/pignoris, n., *pledge, token, symbol*

pīnus, -ūs, f., *pine*

Pīrithous, -ī, m., *Pirithous,* a king of the Lapiths who fights with the Centaurs; son by Dia of Zeus or Ixion

piscis, piscis, m., *fish*

pius, -a, -um, adj., *dutiful, devoted*

placeō, placēre, placuī, placitum, *please*

plācō, plācāre, plācāvī, plācātum, *appease, calm*

plaga, -ae, f., *hunting net, trap*

plūs, plūris, n., *more;* plūrēs, plūra, pl. adj., *more*

Plūtō, Plūtōnis, m., *Pluto,* king of the underworld

pōculum, -ī, n., *cup, drink*

podagra, -ae, f., *gout*

Polyhymnia, -ae, f., *Polyhymnia,* one of the Muses

pōmifer, pōmifera, pōmiferum, adj., *fruit-bearing, fruitful*

Pompēius, Pompēiī, m., *Pompeius;* identity unknown

pōnō, pōnere, posuī, positum, *put, place*

pontifex, pontificis, m., *high priest, pontiff*

pōpulus, -ī, f., *poplar tree*

populus, -ī, m., *people, public, multitude*

portentum, -ī, n., *portent, abnormal phenomenon*

poscō, poscere, poposcī, *demand*

possum, posse, potuī, *be able, can*

post, prep. with acc., *behind, after*

posterus, -a, -um, adj., *next, following, future, later*

postis, postis, m., *door-post, door*

Postumus, -ī, m., *Postumus;* this name was often given to boys who were born after the death of their fathers

potens, potentis, adj., *able, powerful, potent*

potior, potīrī, potītus sum, *get possession of, obtain, possess*

potior, potius, adj., *more able, more powerful, preferable*

praebeō, praebēre, praebuī, praebitum, *give, supply, provide*

praecēdō, praecēdere, praecessī, praecessum, *go in front, go on ahead*

praecipiō, praecipere, praecēpī, praeceptum, *take beforehand, teach*

praemium, praemiī, n., *prize, reward*

praeparō, praeparāre, praeparāvī, praeparātum, *prepare*

praesidium, praesidiī, n., *protection, defense*

praeter, prep. with acc., *except, beyond*

praetereō, praeterīre, praeteriī, praeteritum, *go by, go past, pass by, go beyond, omit*

premō, premere, pressī, pressum, *press, follow closely*

pressō, pressāre, pressāvī, pressātum, *press*

prex, precis, f., *prayer*

prīmus, -a, -um, adj., *first*

princeps, principis, adj., *first in time, leading, first*

priscus, -a, -um, adj., *ancient, former*

prius, adv., *previously, before*

prīvātus, -a, -um, adj., *private, not in public life*

prō, prep. with abl., *for, on behalf of, in front of*

procella, -ae, f., *storm, trouble*

prōditor, prōditōris, m., *betrayer, traitor*

proelium, proeliī, n., *battle*

profānus, -a, -um, adj., *profane, secular, impious, uninitiated*

prope, prep. with acc., *near*

properō, properāre, properāvī, properātum, *hurry, hasten*

propinquus, -a, -um, adj., *near, neighboring*

proprius, -a, -um, adj., *one's own, personal*

prōterō, prōterere, prōtrīvī, prōtrītum, *trample down, crush*

protervus, -am, -um, adj., *bold, violent*

proxumus, -a, -um, adj., *nearest, next*

pūbēs, pūbis, f., *adult population, age of puberty, the pubic region*

pudīcus, -a, -um, adj., *having a sense of modesty or shame, modest, honorable, chaste*

pudor, pudōris, m., *restraint, feeling of shame*

puella, -ae, f., *girl, young woman, girlfriend*

puer, puerī, m., *boy, non-adult male, male beloved,* (young) *male slave*

pulcher, pulchra, pulchrum, adj., *beautiful*

pullus, -a, -um, adj., *gray, somber*

pulsō, pulsāre, pulsāvī, pulsātum, *beat, strike repeatedly*

pulvīnar, pulvīnāris, n., *sacred couch on which the image of a god was placed*

pulvis, pulveris, m., *dust*

pūmex, pūmicis, m., *pumice-stone*

purpura, -ae, f., *shellfish yielding a purple dye, the purple dye from the shellfish, purple-dyed cloth, purple*

pūrus, -a, -um, adj., *pure, innocent*

pȳramis, pȳramidis, f., *pyramid*

Pyrrha, -ae, f., *Pyrrha, woman's name*

Q

quā, adv., *where*

quadrīmus, -a, -um, adj., *four-year-old*

quaerō, quaerere, quaesīvī, quaesītum, *look for, seek, ask, acquire, earn*

quālis, -e, rel. adj., *of which sort*

quam, interr. and rel. adv., *how;* with the superlative, *as...as possible;* after a comparative, *than*

quamquam, conj., *although*

quandō, interr. adv., *when*

quandōcumque, adv., *at some time or other*

quārē, interr. and rel. adv., *in what way, how, why, because, therefore*

quartus, -a, -um, adj., *fourth*

quatiō, quatere, quassum, *shake, beat upon*

-que, enclitic conj., *and*

querimōnia, -ae, f., *complaint*

questus, -ūs, m., *complaint, lament*

quī, quae, quod, rel. pron., *who, which, that;* interr. adj. *what, which*

quia, conj., *because*

quīcumque, quaecumque, quodcumque, indef. pron., *whoever, whichever, whatever*

quid, adv., *why*

quīdam, quaedam, quiddam, pron., *a certain person, a certain thing*

quīlibet, quaelibet, quidlibet, pron., *anyone or anything whatever, whoever or whatever you please*

Quintilius, -Quintiliī, m., *Quintilius Varus,* friend of Horace and Vergil

quintus, -a, -um, adj., *fifth*

Quirīs, Quirītis, m., *Roman citizen*

quis, quid, interr. pron., *who, what;* indef. pron., *anyone, anything*

quisquam, quicquam, pron., *anyone, anything*

quisque, quaeque, quidque, pron., *each one*

quisquis, quidquid (or **quicquid**), pron. and adj., *whoever, whatever*

quō, adv., *where, for what purpose*

quod, conj., *because*

quodsī, conj., *but if*

quōmodo, interr., rel. adv., *how, in the manner in which*

quondam, adv., *once, formerly, sometimes, in the future*

quoque, adv., *also, too*

quotiens, adv., *how often*

quotquot, indecl. adj., *however many*

R

rāmus, -ī, m., *branch*

rapiō, rapere, rapuī, raptum, *seize, snatch away*

ratis, ratis, f., *raft, boat, ship*

raucus, -a, -um, adj., *hoarse, noisy, raucous*

recens, recentis, adj., *fresh, recent, modern*

recipiō, recipere, recēpī, receptum, *take back, accept, regain*

reclīnō, reclīnāre, reclīnāvī, reclīnātum, *cause to lean back*

reclūdō, reclūdere, reclūsī, reclūsum, *open up, undo*

recreō, recreāre, recreāvī, recreātum, *recreate, restore, revive*

rectus, -a, -um, adj., *straight, right, correct, proper*

recurrō, recurrere, recurrī, recursum, *run back, return*

reddō, reddere, reddidī, redditum, *give back, deliver*

redemptor, redemptōris, m., *contractor*

redeō, redīre, rediī, reditum, *go back, come back, return*

redigō, redigere, redēgī, redactum, *drive back, reduce*

redōnō, redōnāre, redōnāvī, redōnātum, *give back*

redūcō, redūcere, reduxī, reductum, *bring back*

reficiō, reficere, refēcī, refectum, *make again, repair*

refugiō, refugere, refūgī, *run away, avoid*

rēgālis, -e, adj., *royal, regal*

rēgia, -ae, f., *palace*

rēgīna, -ae, f., *queen*

regnō, regnāre, regnāvī, regnātum, *rule, rule over*

regō, regere, rexī, rectum, *guide, direct, rule*

rēiciō, rēicere, rēiēcī, rēiectum, *throw back, drive back, reject*

religiō, religiōnis, f., *religious awe or conscience, religious practice, particular set of religious observances, cult, religious feeling, superstition*

religō, religāre, religāvī, religātum, *tie, fasten behind; untie (occasionally)*

relinquō, relinquere, relīquī, relictum, *leave, leave behind, abandon*

removeō, removēre, remōvī, remōtum, *move back*

rēmus, -ī, m., *oar*

reor, rērī, ratus sum, *think*

reparō, reparāre, reparāvī, reparātum, *obtain in exchange for, recover*

repetō, repetere, repetīvī, repetītum, *seek again, recall, resume*

repōnō, repōnere, reposuī, repositum, *put down, place*

rēs, reī, f., *wealth, thing, circumstance, affair, legal matter*

resecō, resecāre, resecuī, resectum, *cut back, prune, restrain*

resorbeō, resorbēre, *suck back, swallow again*

respondeō, respondēre, respondī, responsum, *answer, reply;* technical sense, *appear in court*

restituō, restituere, restituī, restitūtum, *restore, revive*

restō, restāre, restitī, *remain, remain to be dealt with*

rex, rēgis, m., *king*

rīdeō, rīdēre, rīsī, rīsum, *laugh*

rīpa, -ae, f., *bank of a river, shore*

rīsus, -ūs, m., *laughter*

rītus, -ūs, m., *ritual, custom, manner, style*

rīvus, -ī, m., *stream*

rixa, -ae, f., *fight*

rogō, rogāre, rogāvī, rogātum, *ask, ask for*

Rōmānus, -a, -um, adj., *Roman*

rosa, -ae, f., *rose*

roseus, -a, -um, adj., *rosy*

rota, -ae, f., *wheel*

ruber, rubra, rubrum, adj., *red*

rubus, -ī, m., *bramble, prickly bush*

rūga, -ae, f., *wrinkle*

ruīna, -ae, f., *collapse, ruin*

rumpō, rumpere, rūpī, ruptum, *break, shatter, destroy*

rursus, adv., *back, again*

rūs, rūris, n., *the country* (as opposed to the town), *farm, estate*

S

sabbata, sabbatōrum, n. pl., *the Jewish sabbath*

Sabellus, -a, -um, adj., *Sabine;* the Sabines were a people of central Italy.

Sabīnus, -a, -um, adj., *Sabine;* the Sabines were a people of central Italy.

sacer, sacra, sacrum, adj., *sacred, holy*

sacerdōs, sacerdōtis, c., *priest or priestess*

saepe, adv., *often*

saeviō, saevīre, saeviī, saevītum, *rage, rave*

saevus, -a, -um, adj., *cruel, savage*

sagitta, -ae, f., *arrow*

Saliāris, -e, adj., *of the Salii,* who were a group of priests (at Rome usually associated with Mars), who performed ritual dances on certain occasions.

salsus, -a, -um, adj., *salted, witty, funny*

saltus, -ūs, m., *forest or mountain pasture, forest or mountain pass*

salvus, -a, -um, adj., *safe, alive, well*

sanguis, sanguinis, m., *blood*

sānus, -a, -um, adj., *healthy, sane*

sapienter, adv., *wisely*

sapiō, sapere, sapīvī, *have taste, be wise*

sapor, sapōris, m., *taste, flavor*

sarculum, -ī, n., *hoe*

satis, adv., *enough, sufficiently;* indecl. noun, *enough*

Satyrus, -ī, m., *satyr;* demi-god of wild places, especially forests, having the form of a man with some animal characteristics

saxum, -ī, n., *rock*

scandō, scandere, *climb, ascend, mount*

scelus, sceleris, n., *wrongdoing, crime, affliction*

scīlicet, adv., *evidently, of course, surely*

sciō, scīre, scīvī, scītum, *know*

scrībō, scrībere, scripsī, scriptum, *write*

sēcernō, sēcernere, sēcrēvī, sēcrētum, *separate, distinguish*

secō, secāre, secuī, sectum, *cut, divide, traverse*

sēcrētō, adv., *secretly*

sector, sectārī, sectātus sum, *pursue, chase*

secundus, -a, -um, adj., *following, second, favorable*

secus, adv., *otherwise, not so*

sed, conj., *but*

sedeō, sedēre, sēdī, sessum, *sit*

sēdēs, sēdis, f., *seat, site, home*

sēdulus, -a, -um, adj., *attentive, diligent*

semel, adv., *once, once and for all*

semper, adv., *always*

senecta, -ae, f., *old age*

sentiō, sentīre, sensī, sensum, *feel, sense, perceive, think, understand*

sequor, sequī, secūtus sum, *follow*

serēnus, -a, -um, adj., *calm*

seriēs (-ēī), f., *series, sequence, succession*

sērius, adv., *later*

serpens, serpentis, m., f., *snake, serpent*

sērus, -a, -um, adj., *late, blossoming after the normal time*

servō, servāre, servāvī, servātum, *keep, protect, save*

servus, -ī, m., *slave*

seu, conj., *or if,* seu...seu, *whether...or*

sī, conj., *if*

sīc, adv., *so, thus, in this way*

Siculus, -a, -um, adj., *Sicilian*

sīcut, adv., *just as, as*

sīdus, sīderis, n., *star; sky* (pl.)

silva, -ae, f., *forest*

similis, -e, adj., *similar, like*

simplex, simplicis, adj., *simple, artless, plain*

simul, conj., *as soon as* (also with atque); adv., *at the same time, together*

sine, prep. with abl., *without*

Sīsyphus, -ī, m., *Sisyphus;* son of Aeolus, committed various crimes and is punished in the underworld by forever having to roll a rock up a steep hill only to have it roll down again

situs, -ūs, m., *site*

situs, -ūs, m., *deterioration, neglect*

sīve, conj., *or if,* sīve...sīve, *whether...or*

sōbrius, -a, -um, adj., *sober, moderate, sensible*

sodālis, sodālis, m., *companion*

sōl, sōlis, m., *sun, a day* (as determined by the rising of the sun)

soleō, solēre, solitus sum, *be accustomed*

solidus, -a, -um, adj., *solid, complete, entire*

sollicitō, sollicitāre, sollicitāvī, sollicitātum, *rouse, excite, shake up, disturb with repeated attacks*

solum, -ī, n., *ground, floor, land*

sōlus, -a, -um, adj., *alone, lonely, deserted*

solvō, solvere, solvī, solūtum, *loosen, break up*

somnus, -ī, m., *sleep*

sonitus, -ūs, m., *sound*

sopor, sopōris, m., *sleep*

Sōracte, Sōractis, n., *Soracte,* mountain in the south of Etruria

sordēs, sordis, f., often used in pl., *dirt, squalor, baseness*

soror, sorōris, f., *sister*

sors, sortis, f., *lot, share*

sortior, sortīrī, sortītus sum, *cast lots over, choose*

sospes, sospitis, adj., *safe and sound, unhurt*

spatium, spatiī, n., *space, period of time*

spernō, spernere, sprēvī, sprētum, *remove, reject, scorn*

spērō, spērāre, spērāvī, spērātum, *hope, hope for, expect*

spēs, speī, f., *hope*

splendidus, -a, -um, adj., *bright, brilliant, glittering, illustrious*

sternō, sternere, strāvī, strātum, *stretch out, spread out, level, overthrow*

stō, stāre, stetī, statum, *stand*

suāviter, adv., *pleasantly, delightfully, nicely*

sub, prep. with acc. or abl., *under, below*

subeō, subīre, subiī, subitum, *go under, undergo*

sublīmis, -e, adj., *high, raised, elevated, sublime, lofty*

submoveō, submovēre, submōvī, submōtum, *move away, remove, ward off, banish*

subolēs, subolis, f., *offspring*

sūdor, sūdōris, m., *sweat*

sulcus, -ī, m., *a furrow, trench, track*

sum, esse, fuī, futūrus, *be*

summa, -ae, f., *sum, the whole*

summoveō = submoveō

summus, -a, -um, adj., *highest, topmost*

sūmō, sūmere, sumpsī, sumptum, *take, take on*

super, prep. with abl., *above*

superbia, -ae, f., *pride, arrogance*

superbus, -a, -um, adj., *proud, arrogant*

supercilium, superciliī, n., *eyebrow, nod*

superstes, superstitis, adj., *standing over, surviving*

superus, -a, -um, adj., *upper, higher*

suprēmus, -a, -um, adj., *last, final*

surgō, surgere, surrexī, surrectum, *get up, rise* (of heavenly bodies)

suscitō, suscitāre, suscitāvī, suscitātum, *rouse, awaken*

suspendō, suspendere, suspendī, suspensum, *hang up*

sustineō, sustinēre, sustinuī, sustentum, *hold up, support, withstand*

susurrus, -ī, m., *whispering*

suus, -a, -um, third person reflex. adj., *his, her, its, their* (own)

Syrius, -a, -um, adj., *Syrian*

Syrtis, Syrtis, f., *Syrtis* (especially pl.), name of two areas of sandy flats on the coast between Carthage and Cyrene; whole desert region next to this coast.

T

tabula, -ae, f., *board, plank, writing tablet,* (votive) *tablet*

taceō, tacēre, tacuī, tacitum, *be silent*

tacitus, -a, -um, adj., *silent*

tālus, -ī, m., *ankle bone, ankle, knuckle bone used in games*

tam, adv., *so*

tamen, adv., *nevertheless*

tandem, *at last, finally*

tangō, tangere, tetigī, tactum, *touch*

tantum, adv., *so much, only*

tantummodo, adv., *only*

tardus, -a, -um, adj., *slow, late, moving slowly, dull*

taurus, -ī, m., *bull*

tectum, -ī, n., *roof, house*

tēcum = cum tē

Tēlephus, -ī, m., *Telephus,* man's name

tellūs, tellūris, f., *land, earth, country, ground*

Tempē, n. pl. *Tempe,* valley of the Peneus river between Ossa and Olympus in Thessaly noted for its beauty; *any beautiful valley*

temperō, temperāre, temperāvī, temperātum, *moderate, hold back*

tempestīvus, -a, -um, adj., *timely, seasonable, ripe*

temptō, temptāre, temptāvī, temptātum, *try, attempt*

tempus, temporis, n., *time, occasion, proper time, an age or particular period in history, danger*

tendō, tendere, tetendī, tentum/ tensum, *stretch out, extend, proceed, direct one's course*

tenebrae, -ārum, f. pl., *darkness*

teneō, tenēre, tenuī, tentum, *hold, persist*

tener, tenera, tenerum, adj., *tender, delicate, soft, young*

ter, adv., *three times*

teres, teretis, adj., *rounded, smooth, polished*

tergeminus, -a, -um, adj., *triple*

terminus, -ī, m., *boundary line, limit*

terra, -ae, f., *land, ground, country*

Thaliarchus, -ī, m., *Thaliarchus,* Greek man's name

Thēseus, Thēseī/Thēseos, m., *Theseus,* son of Aegeus or Poseidon; national hero of Athens

Thrācius, -a, -um, adj., *Thracian*

Thrēicius, -a, -um, adj., *Thracian*

Thressa, -ae, f., *a Thracian woman;* as fem. adj., *Thracian*

Thūrīnus, -a, -um, adj., *pertaining to the town of Thurii in southern Italy*

Tiberis, Tiberis, m., *the river Tiber*

tībia, -ae, f., *shin bone, tibia, pipe, flute*

tigris, tigris/tigridis, f., *tiger*

timeō, timēre, timuī, *fear, be afraid, be afraid of*

timor, timōris, m., *fear*

tinguō, tinguere, tinxī, tinctum, *wet, stain*

Tityos, -ī, m., *Tityus;* giant primarily known for attempting to rape Latona, mother of Apollo and Diana; punished in the underworld by being stretched over nine acres while two vultures or snakes ate his heart or liver

tollō, tollere, sustulī, sublātum, *lift, raise, extol, take away, destroy*

Torquātus, -ī, m., *Torquatus;* identity uncertain; a Torqutus, an orator, also appears as addressee of Horace Epistle 1.5; an orator; may be a son of Lucius Manlius Torquatus, consul in 65 BCE, the year in which Horace was born

torreō, torrēre, torruī, tostum, *burn, parch*

tōtus, -a, -um, adj., *the whole of, all*

trabs, trabis, f., *beam of wood, trunk of tree, ship*

tractō, tractāre, tractāvī, tractātum, *handle*

trādō, trādere, trādidī, trāditum, *hand over, deliver, introduce*

trans, prep. with acc., *across*

trecēnī, trecēnae, trecēna, pl. adj., *three hundred each, three hundred at a time*

tremō, tremere, tremuī, *tremble, quiver*

trepidō, trepidāre, trepidāvī, trepidātum, *be agitated, hurry*

trēs, tria, adj., *three*

tribuō, tribuere, tribuī, tribūtum, *allot, assign*

trīcēsimus, -a, -um, adj., *thirtieth*

trirēmis, trirēmis, f., *ship having three banks of oars; trireme*

tristis, -e, adj., *sad*

triumphus, -ī, m., *triumph, triumphal procession*

trivium, triviī, n., *meeting place of three roads, crossroads*

tū, tuī, tibi, tē, tē, pron., *you* (sing.)

tuba, -ae, f., *straight war trumpet*

Tullus, -ī, m., *Tullus Hostilius,* third king of Rome

tum, adv., *then*

tumeō, tumēre, tumuī, *swell*

tumultuōsus, -a, -um, adj., *full of commotion, turbulent*

tunc, adv., *then*

turba, -ae, f., *crowd*

turgidus, -a, -um, adj., *swollen, turgid*

turpis, -e, adj., *ugly, shameful, disgraceful*

turpō, turpāre, turpāvī, turpātum, *make ugly*

turris, -is, f., *tower*

tussis, tussis, f., *cough*

tūtus, -a, -um, adj., *safe, secure*

tuus, -a, -um, adj., *your* (sing.)

Tyrrhēnus, -a, -um, adj., *Tyrrhenian, Etruscan*

U

ubi, rel. adv., *where, when;* interr. adv., *where*

ūdus, -a, -um, adj., *wet, pliant*

ulcerōsus, -a, -um, adj., *full of ulcers or sores*

ullus, -a, -um, adj., *any*

ultimus, -a, -um, adj., *last, farthest, extreme*

ultrā, prep. with acc., *beyond*

umbra, -ae, f., *shade, shadow, ghost*

umbrōsus, -a, -um, adj., *shady*

umerus, -ī, m., *shoulder*

ūmor, ūmōris, m., *moisture, liquid*

unda, -ae, f., *wave, water*

unde, interr. and rel. adv., *from where, from whom, from which*

undique, adv., *on all sides, everywhere*

unguentum, -ī, n., *ointment, perfume*

ūnus, -a, -um, adj., *one, sole*

urbs, urbis, f., *city; the city of Rome*

urgeō, urgēre, ursī, *push, press upon*

urna, -ae, f., *urn*

ūrō, ūrere, ussī, ustum, *burn;* in pass., *be on fire*

usque, adv., *continuously, continually, all the way*

ūsus, -ūs, m., *use, enjoyment*

ut, conj. with indic., *as, like, when, considering how;* with subj., *so that, that, to;* interr. adv., *how*

ūtor, ūtī, ūsus sum (with abl.), *use, enjoy*

utrimque, adv., *on both sides*

ūvidus, -a, -um, *wet*

uxor, uxōris, f., *wife*

V

vacuus, -a, -um, adj., *empty, free, available*

vador, vadārī, vadātus sum, (of a plaintiff) *to accept a guarantee from the other party that the party will appear or reappear in court at an appointed date*

vae, interj., *alas, woe*

vagor, vagārī, vagātus sum, *wander*

vagus, -a, -um, adj., *roaming, wandering*

valeō, valēre, valuī, valitum, *be powerful, be strong enough to, be well*

vallēs, vallis, f., *valley*

vānus, -a, -um, adj., *empty, groundless, imaginary*

Varius, Variī, m., *L.Varius Rufus,* writer of epic and tragedy, important literary friend of Horace

vātēs, vātis, c., *prophet, singer, poet*

-ve, conj., *or*

vel, conj., *or*

vellō, vellere, vellī, vulsum, *pull, tug at*

vēlum, -ī, n., *sail*

velut, adv., *as, just as*

vēnātor, vēnātōris, m., *hunter*

venēnātus, -a, -um, adj., *poisonous*

venēnum, -ī, n., *poison, magical or medicinal potion*

veniō, venīre, vēnī, ventum, *come*

ventus, -ī, m., *wind*

venus, veneris, f., *Venus,* Roman goddess of love; *love, charm, sexual activity; best throw at dice*

vēr, vēris, n., *spring*

verberō, verberāre, verberāvī, verberātum, *beat, lash*

Vergilius, Vergiliī, m., *Publius Vergilius Maro* (70–19 BCE)

vēritās, vēritātis, f., *truth*

vērō, adv., *in fact, indeed, certainly, truly*

verrō, verrere, versum, *sweep together, collect*

versō, versāre, versāvī, versātum, *keep turning, stir*

versus, -ūs, m., *line of verse*

vertex, verticis, m., *head, summit*

vērus, -a, -um, adj., *true, real*

vescor, vescī, *enjoy, feed on, eat* (with abl.)

Vesta, -ae, f., *Vesta,* Roman goddess of the domestic hearth; *temple or shrine of Vesta*

vestīmentum, -ī, n., *clothes, garments*

vetus, veteris, adj., *old*

via, -ae, f., *road, street, way*

vicis (gen.), f., *turn, succession, alternation*

victima, -ae, f., *victim, sacrifice*

victor, victōris, m., *victor, winner, conqueror*

vīcus, -ī, m., *group of dwellings, village; block of houses, street, group of streets,* often forming a social or administrative unit (used of specific districts in Rome)

videō, vidēre, vīdī, vīsum, *see*

vigeō, vigēre, viguī, *flourish, thrive*

villa, -ae, f., *country-house, estate, farm*

vincō, vincere, vīcī, victum, *conquer, defeat*

vinculum, -ī, n., *chain, bond*

vīnea, -ae, f., *vineyard*

vīnum, -ī, n., *wine*

violens, violentis, adj., *violent, vehement*

vir, -ī, m., *man, husband*

vireō, virēre, viruī, *be green, youthful, fresh*

virga, -ae, f., *staff, wand*

virgō, virginis, f., *girl of marriageable age, young woman, virgin*

viridis, -e, adj., *green, fresh, young*

virtūs, virtūtis, f., *manhood, courage, valor, virtue*

Viscus, -ī, m., *Viscus;* there were two brothers with this name; both were literary figures and friends of Horace and Maecenas

vīsō, vīsere, vīsī, *look at, go and see*

vīta, -ae, f., *life*

vītis, vītis, f., *vine*

vītō, vītāre, vītāvī, vītātum, *avoid, shun*

vitrum, -ī, n., *glass*

vīvō, vīvere, vixī, victum, *live*

vix, adv., *hardly, scarcely*

volens, volentis, adj., *willing*

volgus, -ī, n., *the common people, the general public, crowd*

volō, velle, voluī, *wish, want, be willing*

volō, volāre, volāvī, volātum, *fly, speed*

voltus, -ūs, m., *face, expression*

vōmer, vōmeris, m., *plowshare;* by metonymy, *the plow*

vōtīva, -a, -um, *votive, relating to a vow*

vox, vōcis, f., *voice*

Z

zephyrus, -ī, m., *west wind, zephyr*

ADVANCED PLACEMENT* TEXTS

WRITING PASSION: A Catullus Reader
Ronnie Ancona
Student: xxxv + 261 pp. (2004) Paperback, ISBN 978-0-86516-482-6
Teacher: vi + 122 pp. (2004) Paperback, ISBN 9780-86516-483-3

CICERO'S PRO CAELIO, 3rd edition
Stephen Ciraolo
xxxi + 239 pp. (1997, 3rd edition 2003)
6" x 9" Paperback, ISBN 978-0-86516-559-5

HORACE SATIRE I.9: The Boor
Margaret A. Brucia and Madeleine M. Henry
Student Text: Illus., 45 pp., (1998, Reprint 2000)
Paperback, ISBN 978-0-86516-413-0

Teacher's Guide: 20 pp., (1998)
Paperback, ISBN 978-0-86516-429-1

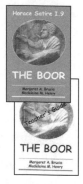

OVID: Amores Metamorphoses Selections
2nd Edition
Charbra Adams Jestin and Phyllis B. Katz
Student: xx + 195 pp. (1999, Revised Reprint, 2000)
Paperback, ISBN 978-0-86516-431-4
Teacher: viii + 72 pp. (1999, Revised Reprint, 2000)
Hardbound, ISBN 978-0-86516-496-3

VERGIL'S AENEID
Selections from Books 1, 2, 4, 6, 10, and 12
2nd Edition
Barbara Weiden Boyd
Student: (2nd Editon, 2004)
Paperback, ISBN 978-0-86516-584-7
Hardbound, ISBN 0-86516-583-0
Teacher: (2002)
Paperback, ISBN 978-0-86516-481-9

VERGIL'S AENEID, 10 & 12
Pallas & Turnus
Barbara Weiden Boyd
Student Text: xii + 44 pp. (1998)
Paperback, ISBN 978-0-86516-415-4
Teacher's Guide: vi + 13 pp. (1998)
Paperback, ISBN 978-0-86516-428-4

VERGIL'S AENEID: Books I–VI
Clyde Pharr
Illus., xvii + 518 pp. + fold-out (1964, Reprint 1998)
Paperback, ISBN 978-0-86516-421-5
Hardbound, ISBN 978-0-86516-433-8

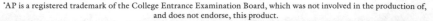

 BOLCHAZY-CARDUCCI PUBLISHERS, INC.
WWW.BOLCHAZY.COM

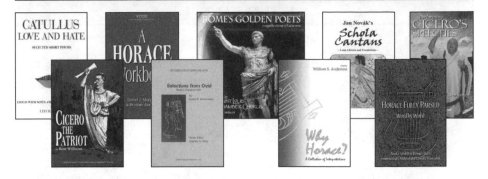